PATIENTS' RIGHTS

ETHICAL AND LEGAL ISSUES IN HEALTH CARE AND NURSING

J. STORCH

PATIENTS' RIGHTS

ETHICAL AND LEGAL
ISSUES IN HEALTH
CARE AND NURSING

JANET STORCH
University of Alberta

McGRAW-HILL RYERSON LIMITED
Toronto   Montréal   New York   St. Louis   San Francisco
Auckland   Bogotá   Guatemala   Hamburg   Johannesburg
Lisbon London Madrid Mexico New Delhi Panama Paris
San Juan São Paulo Singapore Sydney Tokyo

ISBN 0-07-548477-3

1 2 3 4 5 6 7 8 9 0 HR 1 0 9 8 7 6 5 4 3 2

Printed and bound in Canada

Canadian Cataloguing in Publication Data

Storch, Janet L.
  Patient's rights : ethical and legal issues in health care and nursing

Bibliography: p.
Includes index.
ISBN 0-07-548477-3

1. Medical care—Canada—Moral and ethical aspects.
2. Nurse and patient—Canada—Moral and ethical aspects.
3. Sick—Legal status, laws, etc.—Canada.   4. Hospital patients—Legal status, laws, etc.—Canada.   I. Title.

RT85.S76   610.73'06'99   C82-095060-2

Contents

For Don,
Whose presence in my life
has made many things
possible.

Preface

During the course of the past four years, I have been invited to address numerous seminars, workshops, in-service sessions, hospital trustee institutes, annual meetings and conferences on issues of patients' rights. The impetus for these requests arose as a result of my Master's thesis work on "Consumer Rights and Nursing." The experience on the speaker's circuit and the related classroom teaching in ethics and law have given me opportunities to test out my hypotheses, clarify my thinking, and to gain new insights and understandings into the significance of patients' rights issues, and the tremendous potential the patients' rights movement provides to teach about ethics and about law in health care.

I believe that this movement represents a significant challenge to health professionals, calling them to re-evaluate their roles in society, and to re-examine the nature of the relationship they share with patients. That is why an analysis of patients' rights concerns can be so useful to health professionals: it enables them to understand how and where and why problems have arisen in that special relationship. The analysis can also help health professionals to gain greater insights into the changes necessary in re-defining the relationship.

In this book, I use Patients' Rights as a means to examine and re-define health professional-patient relationships. The focus is, in large part, on the nurse-patient relationship, but the applications to other health professions and occupations are similar. In Chapter One, the substance of patients' rights is conveyed through a series of vignettes, and some of the origins of patients' rights concerns are reviewed. In Chapter Two, the context of patients' rights is described, as grounded in two disciplines which focus on social relationships-ethics and law.

Chapters Three through Seven then deal with an examination of specific issues in patients' rights based on the four principles of the Consumers Association of Canada Statement on Consumer Rights in Health Care: the right to be informed, the right to be respected, the right to participate and the right to equal access to care. A number of special rights concerns are addressed in Chapter Seven: concerns faced by specific groups in society by reason of age, illness, or cultural background. These concerns are common to the issues discussed in Chapters Three through Six, but take on added significance because some of these groups of consumers are more vulnerable in health care.

Chapter Eight diverges slightly from the discussion of ethical and legal issues in the previous chapters by focusing on the social, structural, and behavioral constraints which health professionals, particularly nurses, must deal with in re-defining relationships. Further, some preliminary discussion is aimed at identifying strategies to effect humanized relationships.

The diagram on the opposite page provides a schematic presentation of the text.

I am aware that this book is only a beginning. Its purpose is to alert health professionals to ethical and legal issues in patient care; sensitize them to the need for changed and changing relationships with patients; and encourage them to pursue further study in ethics and law so that they might gain skills in evaluating these issues.

The book has been a joy to write because not only have I sensed my own need to put this material together in a logical manner, but I have also sensed a need in the health care field to have a readily available source to begin a study of these issues.

As with any effort of this nature, there are many people to thank for input, encouragement, challenge and support. My first round of thanks goes to former patients who taught me so much about what it is to be sick and to be their own person in sickness. My second round of thanks must go to all those organizations, associations, and groups who asked me to be a speaker at their educational events—laboratory technicians, health service executives, nurses, patients, hospital trustees, medical record technicians, physicians, x-ray technologists, and others. I have learned much in preparing for these sessions, but learned even more from the participants at these events. So many have raised basic questions and issues discussed in this book and have challenged me to re-assess my position and enlarge my thinking.

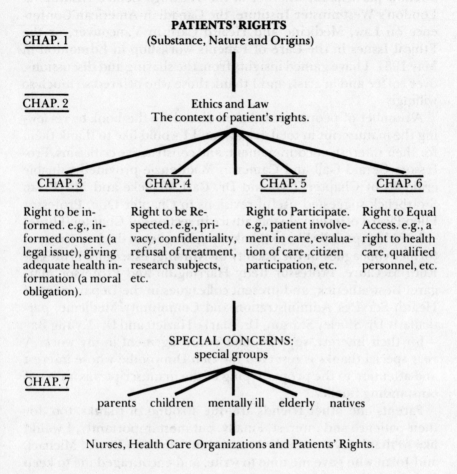

PATIENTS' RIGHTS
(Substance, Nature and Origins)

CHAP. 1

CHAP. 2

Ethics and Law
The context of patient's rights.

CHAP. 3

Right to be in-
formed. e.g., in-
formed consent (a
legal issue), giving
adequate health in-
formation (a moral
obligation).

CHAP. 4

Right to be Re-
spected. e.g., pri-
vacy, confidentiality,
refusal of treatment,
research subjects,
etc.

CHAP. 5

Right to Participate.
e.g., patient involve-
ment in care, evalua-
tion of care, citizen
participation, etc.

CHAP. 6

Right to Equal
Access. e.g., a
right to health
care, qualified
personnel, etc.

SPECIAL CONCERNS:
special groups

CHAP. 7

parents   children   mentally ill   elderly   natives

Nurses, Health Care Organizations and Patients' Rights.

CHAP. 8

A. Organizational: Structural, Social and
   Behavioral Constraints.

B. Strategies for Humanized Care
   Strategies within Organizations
   System Wide Strategies.

I would also like to thank participants in conferences where I was a fellow participant, whether at the Hastings Centre Institute at London's Westminster Institute, the Canadian-American Conference on Law, Medicine and Health Care in Vancouver, or the Ethical Issues in the Care of Patients workshop in Edmonton in May 1981. I have gained insights from the sharing and discussions, over coffee and in class, and I thank those who offered so much so willingly.

A number of people contributed directly to this book by reviewing the manuscript in total or part, and I would like to thank them for their interest, encouragement, and constructive criticisms. Professors Gerald Gall and Cameron MacKenzie provided valuable critiques of Chapter Two and Dr. Carl Meilicke and Mr. Brian Swarbruck suggested useful revisions to Chapter One. Professor Ellen Picard offered valuable advice in sections of Chapter Three.

I would especially like to thank my colleagues at the University—former colleagues in the Faculty of Nursing, especially Professor Ruth McClure, Professor Betty Harrington and Professor Margaret Beswetherick; and present colleagues in the Department of Health Services Administration and Community Medicine, particularly Dr. Shirley Stinson, Dr. Clarke Hazlett and Dr. Kyung Bay—for their interest, support, and encouragement in my work. A very special thanks is reserved for Gen Dinwoodie whose interest and attention to the proper typing of the manuscript was an act of outstanding fidelity.

Parents and other friends are due a round of thanks, too, for their patience and interest. Finally, but most importantly, I would like to thank my husband, Don, and my children David, Michael, and Jolan who gave me time to write, and encouraged me to keep with it when the going was grim. Their love and support has seen this work through to its completion.

Janet L. Storch
University of Alberta

Foreword

What you have before you is a unique and important book. Unique because the author has managed to combine and clarify both ethical and legal issues in health care and nursing; bring a Canadian law, ethics and health care system focus to bear; and provide an outstanding annotated bibliography for each chapter, along with a unique compendium of codes of ethics and other documents of special relevance to patients' rights.

It is an important book because it is written from the standpoint of one who is concerned about practical, day-to-day problems in identifying what are "patients' rights" and outlining approaches; yet it is written, too, with the first-hand knowledge that good intentions are not enough.

Specifically, there is a pervasive theme that ethical and legal problems and solutions require sound knowledge of the moral and legal principles that underlie and govern the special relationship between the health care professional and the client.

Because it constitutes the most comprehensive, authoritative book on the subject of ethical and legal issues related to patients' rights in health care and nursing, this book is of special significance to a wide range of individuals and organizations: health professionals of all types, and in all health care sectors, learners, practitioners, teachers, administrators and researchers; consumer groups; individual patients; inservice educators; workshop and seminar groups; government health policy makers and consultants; and professional organizations. It is a book that can make a real difference both to those who read it — and, hopefully, to those they encounter.

Shirley M. Stinson, R.N., Ed.D., LL.D.
Professor, Faculty of Nursing, and
Department of Health Services
Administration and Community Medicine   June 7, 1982

CHAPTER 1 Patients' Rights: Substance and Origins

This book is about patients' rights. It is directed not to patients but to health professionals, whose responsibility it is to see that patients' rights are respected and protected. Throughout the text, nursing examples are used to illustrate the discussion, as these are closest to the author's work experience.

In today's health-care system, violations of human rights are common; they are sometimes intentional, most often unintentional. These violations lead to the charges of dehumanized and depersonalized care so often levelled against health professionals and the health-care system in general.

It is the author's contention that a first step in correcting the difficulties encountered by patients in health care is that health professionals understand the issues involved in patients' rights. Awareness and understanding of these issues can assist in redefining the relationship between patient and professional, since this relationship is at the core of humanized care.

Patients' rights issues include both the common and day-to-day ethical and legal issues of patient care, such as patient privacy or confidentiality; and the more spectacular ethical-legal issues in health care, such as informed consent and euthanasia. Therefore, an examination of patients' rights becomes an easily understandable and useful means to explore these legal and ethical dimensions of patient care.

1

WHAT RIGHTS?

The substance of patients' rights concerns can be illustrated by four vignettes of patient encounters with the health-care system.

Vignette #1

In a very poignant account entitled "On the Death of a Baby," Robert and Peggy Stinson describe a six-month ordeal and the heroic efforts of an intensive-care unit to maintain the life of Andrew, their premature baby. The account is a history of lack of information for the parents; their lack of involvement in decision-making; and a tendency on the part of health professionals to fault the parents for their anxious, concerned behavior. Early on in the treatment, the parents objected to the prolongation of the infant's life by continued ventilation. They describe the doctor's response to their objection:

> *Dr Farrell accused us of wanting to "play God" and to "go back to the law of the jungle." Apparently not recognizing his responsibility to obtain our informed consent to Andrew's treatment, he reduced the issue to its most absurd level. "I would not presume," he told us, "to tell my auto mechanic how to fix my car."*[1]

Vignette #2

Martha Weinman Lear, in *Heartsounds*, offers a gripping analysis of her husband's struggle with repeated heart attacks and heart surgery. Throughout the book, Lear provides a sensitive account of a patient (her husband, a urologist) and his spouse who must cope with a long-term, debilitating illness. Numerous insightful examples might be drawn from her book. The one chosen here describes her feelings, as the patient's wife, about a somewhat callous and superficial patient-physician encounter.

> *[He] had been handed back his questions, unopened, and had been left feeling rejected, abandoned. Moses [the physician], I thought, feeling now a fury of my own, that was a bad thing to do. You do not do such a thing, Moses, to such a patient who comes to you at such a time, humbled by disease. You perhaps have never been deeply and chronically sick; you perhaps do not know from within how sickness humbles – how it clouds and corrodes and befouls the sense of self. I do not know why this is so, that physical disease plays such cruel vanishing tricks upon the ego, even the*

sturdiest ego, given time enough. But I have seen it happen here, to this fine strong man, and I have read a bit about such things and I know that this is classic in long chronic disease; this is what the failures of the body do unerringly to the soul. And if I know this much, Moses, surely you know it too. And you are neither an unkind nor an uncaring man. So why do you reject him now, when his ego is so fragile? Could it be that yours is not fragile enough? Too thick a hide, eh? Or that you are angry at this sick patient for remaining so intransigently sick? Or... that you can do nothing for him and so choose... to wash your hands?[2*]

Vignette #3

In "Notes of a Dying Professor," Archie Hanlan described his experience as a person generally well-informed, intelligent, and independent in his work role, now thrust into a system that recognized none of his capabilities:

I did not want to go to the particular hospital he mentioned; I preferred another. But he did not practise at that hospital. Suddenly I felt fear and panic, as though decisions were being made for me; that I didn't take any part in them. That process, of feeling myself reduced in making decisions about my own fate, became increasingly reinforced and was very destructive psychologically.[3]

Vignette #4

The first five years in the life of a neurologically damaged child, Sigrette, are recounted, demonstrating the parents' long and difficult search for adequate diagnosis, a treatment plan, and continuity of care.

Why did it take so long to help Sigrette? We faced her problems from the beginning. We live near a city with distinguished medical and educational facilities. We had professional contacts among our friends. We were able to pay, if necessary. Yet somehow Sigrette fell through the spaces and three precious years were lost. What was wrong? What should we have done differently? All we can decide is that something seems to be wrong with the whole system.[4]

These four vignettes vividly portray problems patients and their families experience in health care: a lack of information, a lack of respect, a lack of participation, and a lack of access to appropriate health services. These concerns have been translated into demands for patients' rights, as articulated in the Consumers Association of Canada's Statement on Consumer Rights in Health Care.[5]

Health professionals can interpret these patient (or consumer) rights statements and activities from two perspectives. If seen from a negative perspective, patients' rights talk contributes to an adversarial relationship between two persons or groups. If viewed from a positive perspective, where issues are seen as genuine expressions of patients' concerns, patients' rights issues can illuminate practices that interfere with a demonstration of respect for patients as persons and can identify avenues towards improvement.

To establish a broader perspective on patients' rights issues, the issues must be viewed within the context of a changed and changing society. Patients and health professionals are part of this broader society in which a general concern for human rights has arisen.

CHANGES IN SOCIETY AND IN HEALTH CARE

There is no lack of individuals and groups laying claim to rights in society today. One hears of rights of women, rights of the unborn, rights of native people, and, more recently, rights of patients.

> While there is some discomfort in philosophical circles about rights, and while it is probably true that rights talk does as much to exacerbate as to resolve complex social issues, it is nevertheless the case... [that] there is evidence that one of the dominant, reforming ideological currents of our time is essentially grounded in rights talk.[6]

As described above, rights are essentially claims to which an individual or a group feels entitled. That such statements of claim are necessary would appear to be symptomatic of deeper problems in Canadian society, problems that exist as a result of changes during the past thirty to forty years.

A number of changes are evident: urbanization, bureaucratization, specialization, a transfer of functions to government auspices, and a change in values.[7] Each of these significant changes has had a profound effect on the Canadian health-care system of the 1980s, the health professionals who work in it, and the patients served by it.

Urbanization

During the past three decades there has been a spectacular acceleration in the growth of cities and in the changing social structures and behavioral patterns associated with city living. Rural-to-urban migration in Canada has progressed at an alarming rate; some have predicted that, in the coming years, there will be a continued migration leading to several megalopolises in Canada, and an increasingly limited rural population.

While the maladies of city living are widely criticized, the virtues of urban life are not always extolled. Clustering of a population permits a range and variety of resource availability not generally possible in isolated settings. Community clinics, day-care centers, recreational facilities, centers for the performing arts, and super-markets rely on a certain population base to be effective and efficient. In health care, hospitals, particularly large teaching and referral hospitals, are dependent on a large population base. Visiting-home nursing care and support home-care services have generally been more prevalent and more service-inclusive in urban centers than in rural areas. Medical laboratories, radiological clinics, rehabilitation centers, and psychiatric clinics can exist only where high-volume utilization is a reality.

These benefits do not exist for all rural residents, and frequently those in inner-city areas cannot take advantage of urban benefits because of unequal distribution of personnel and of facilities. Physicians, nurses, and other health personnel tend to cluster (along with the majority of the people) in larger centers and higher-status areas, where they perceive better job opportunities and greater choice of extra work activities.

Another side effect of urbanization that has had a significant impact on the health-care system is the loss of social-support structures. The nuclear family must survive without an extended-family support system; frequently nuclear families or individuals who live alone in the city use the health-care system as a substitute for family support.

Bureaucratization

The growth of organizations is another societal change that has exerted a significant effect on health care. Organizations have grown from simple cottage-industry settings to massive industrial or service complexes.

Like urbanization, bureaucratization has had positive effects. By increasing the size of an organization, economies of scale that permit a range and variety of services to be offered by a single organization may often be achieved. Broad service availability is convenient for consumers.

But the benefits of bureaucracies are seriously offset by abuse of the very characteristics that make them rational solutions to the handling of complex problems. Alienation of employees, apathy, red tape, rigidity, lack of co-ordination, inefficiency, work-to-rule attitudes, and resistance to change are some common pathologies of large organizations.[8] People may do things in the name of an organization that they would not consider doing on their own.

The health-care system has not been immune from this growth in bureaucracies. In fact, the hospital, a key part of today's health system, represents one of the most complex bureaucracies in society today. Numerous services, professional and technical, are provided by the hospital in Canadian communities, and the benefits to consumers have been substantial. Nevertheless, as hospitals have become increasingly complex, there have been accusations that they have become impersonal and dehumanizing organizations. Staff have been accused of an over-reliance on rules and regulations, of buck-passing and of apathetic behavior. Patients sometimes feel caught in a massive organization in which they feel powerless to control or direct their own destiny. Because the number of patients in a hospital is so large, the possibility that one individual patient might receive personalized care can be remote.

While hospitals may be the largest and most visible bureaucracies in health care today, they certainly are not the only bureaucracies. Public-health units, home-care organizations, and nursing homes are also health-care bureaucracies. These organizations are frequently linked to parent organizations or governmental departments, and thus become complex bureaucracies. Again, certain beneficial effects can accrue by larger size and by external linkage. Expert consultation and a greater range of services are possible. But size and linkage factors can also interfere with the care and attention available to a single and unique individual, as attention is directed towards maintaining uniformity in the distribution of services.

Specialization

The division of labor is probably one of the most sensational changes in society at large, and in health care, during the past three decades. Due to technological advances, health-care workers have become specialized and sub-specialized, to the point where there are more than three hundred workers of various types involved in the provision of health services.[9] This specialization is partly the result of new technologies, and has had many good effects. Specialized treatment protocols have the potential to increase longevity and enhance the quality of life for many patients.

But specialization has had some negative side-effects. Fragmentation of patient care may occur because each specialist becomes preoccupied with his or her own special function and may be interested only in part of the patient: the kidneys, the heart, or the leg. Patients often experience the feeling that no one really cares about their total well-being.[10] Specialization and super-specialization have led to wide competence gaps between care-givers and consumers of care. Patients rarely possess the level of medical knowledge of the care-giver, and so are at a disadvantage in participating as equal partners in decisions that affect their well-being. In addition, the division of labor that allows specialization can create a social distance between provider and patient; that distance produces a tension in the relationship.[11] Professionalism may add to such distancing.

The trend towards professionalization of occupational groups in the health industry is an important aspect in specialization in health care. Medicine has traditionally been considered one of the oldest professions, and many groups have aspired towards the advantages that accrue to an occupation that gravitates towards professionalism. Based upon the traditional professions (medicine, law, and the clergy), the following attributes are associated with a profession: a skill-knowledge component, a service ideal, autonomy, and a code of ethics.[12] The service ideal and the code of ethics of a health profession can generally be regarded as positive influences towards ensuring patient rights; however, concerns about professional self-interest continue to be expressed. The division of labor and the specialization in health care appear to be significantly affected by the professional status of key health-occupation groups; these do not always function in the best interests of the patient.

Transfer of Functions to Government

There has been a substantial shift, in Canadian society, from privately owned to publicly owned services of many types. In the past, individuals were mainly responsible for obtaining many of their own goods and services, but governments have increasingly become involved in the management and provision of essential services. Nowhere is this shift more dramatic than in the fields of health and welfare. In Canada, federal and provincial governments have become involved in legislation and in payments for health services.

The transfer of functions to government has been beneficial to Canadians, perhaps more beneficial than many young Canadians can appreciate.

> *It is impossible for anyone under the age of forty today, protected as we now are with a full panoply of social insurance programs, to appreciate, or perhaps even to comprehend, the threats to individual and family independence and integrity that characterized the thirties and extended, to a declining degree, into the forties and fifties. But to millions the threats had been real and, for hundreds of thousands, had come to pass.*[13]

But concerns about the negative aspects of governmental health insurance are abundant. Among these concerns are possibilities of negation of individual responsibilities for health care, the potential abuse of "free" health care, the inevitable erosion of professional prerogative in health care, and inattention to quality patient care. Government involvement in health care is discussed further in Chapter Six.

Changes in Values

As basic patterns of production, distribution, and consumption of goods and services change, a culture also changes, as do the underlying principles on which people make their choices. These changes in values concur with, and allow, patterns of change in given directions. For example, the gradual acceptance of government involvement in an increasing number of fields has allowed the responsibility for health care to shift from the individual to the government. There is a sense that a government should do more for its people – that, in addition to medicare, denticare and pharmicare programs are essential. This is not to imply that consumers will not loudly decry the growing tax base required to support these programs; but many consumers believe that the government should be responsible for making available some of these costly services.

Perhaps the shifting responsibility can be seen most clearly in the care of the aged. Care of aged parents was generally a responsibility automatically assumed by children when the parents were no longer able to maintain themselves in their own homes. Over the past decades, there has been a shift away from family responsibility to public responsibility. Old-folks' homes, nursing homes and auxiliary hospitals have become the norm for those unable to manage their own households. Middle-aged children are not able (or see themselves as not able) to cope with an aging parent because of heavy demands on their time. Families face economic demands (two parents must work to earn a living); social demands (there are numerous clubs or associations that further their careers or their children's interests); and personal demands (there is limited time for nuclear family "togetherness").

Changes in other values have had a profound effect on health care as well. The growing devaluation of professional and institutional authority in society has been felt in the health care industry. National leaders – in neighboring countries and in Canada – have been known to deceive people from time to time; distrust of these leaders is growing. A general distrust has been fed by national and international scandals involving those in leadership positions; at the same time, general educational levels in the population have risen. Society has begun to question and to criticize general societal affairs, as well as health-care affairs. Potentially, such questioning can create a patient who is more active and involved in health care, as opposed to a patient who is a passive recipient of care subject to a paternalistic care-provider. However, many health professionals have not adapted to this role and find an active stance on the part of the patient not in keeping with their concept of professional-patient relations. Many health professionals feel that their professional authority has been, and continues to be, eroded by these consumer attitudes.

Finally, there has been a shift from a belief in charity to a belief in justice. The poor or disadvantaged no longer rely on the whims of the advantaged to provide services such as illness care or relief monies. Instead, society has generally begun to value a citizen's rights to certain basic services – rights that exist in the name of justice and equality. This shift is not a unanimous one and is subject to some controversial debates – the one surrounding social-security programs, for example. As a general rule, however, such rights have been accepted in Canada to a high but not maximum degree. Limitations in the application of these values can be seen in social welfare, where social allowances tend to provide sustenance-level income. Health care generally fares somewhat better for several reasons, not the least of which are the status of the medical profession, the infatuation with medical technologies, and the fact that spending money on health-care programs produces visible results.

The valuing of justice and equality in health care has led to a demand for equal access to health services and to the notion of a right to health care. Sometimes it is even suggested that good health is a right. As will be discussed in subsequent chapters, justice and equality in health care are linked to some basic human-rights concerns, and the development of these concerns parallels these dramatic changes in society.

GROWTH OF HUMAN-RIGHTS CONCERNS

In the period following World War I, the western world experienced a growing awareness of injustice, inequality, and the suppression of human liberty in Russia, Italy, and Germany. After the depression, and during World War II, the need to safeguard human rights became a mounting concern. Canadians gradually became aware of atrocities abroad (for example, Nazi and Fascist brutalities) and violations of individual liberties at home (for example, the treatment of the Japanese people in Canada).

At the instigation of western countries, a statement about human rights began to take shape; the attempt eventually culminated in the Universal Declaration of Human Rights. The Declaration, adopted in 1948, represented the first inter-governmental statement on human rights in history. It was formulated because of the need, in the post-war period, to define rights. The Declaration was adopted as a non-binding resolution of the United Nations General

Assembly; it was seen as an instrument that contained goals and aspirations, rather than as a legally binding commitment.[14] There have been many subsequent attempts, by countries, states, and provinces, to provide for the promotion of human rights, (similar to those rights embodied in the Universal Declaration of Rights) by the introduction of bills of rights.

Bills of Rights and Patients' Bills of Rights

Bills or statements of human rights have been adopted in various countries. Examples are the European Convention on Human Rights, the Nigerian Bill of Rights, and the Commonwealth Bill of Rights. Some countries have appended human-rights statements to their constitutions (for example France and India).[15] And the first ten amendments to its Constitution comprise the Bill of Rights for the United States.[16] In 1960, the Parliament of Canada passed an Act for the Recognition and Protection of Human Rights and Fundamental Freedoms, commonly known as the Canadian Bill of Rights. Because this Act is a non-entrenched piece of legislation, its potential to be legally significant has been minimal. The constitutional resolution, passed by the British Parliament and proclaimed in Canada in April of 1982, includes an entrenched Charter of Rights and Freedoms for Canadians (see Appendix D).

Generally, enforcement of these bills of rights or statements of rights, particularly non-entrenched bills, has been problematic. Attitudes of respect and concern are difficult to enforce. But attitudes are central to the assurance of rights, and therefore problems arise.

The same problem exists in the enforcement of patients' rights. The American Hospital Association (AHA) issued a Statement on a Patients Bill of Rights in November 1972; essentially, the document was a statement of goals and aspirations, and contained only a few legally binding commitments. The "bill" has been adopted by several state legislatures (in those states, the bill must be posted in hospitals) and by many US hospitals at their initiative. But problems of enforcement abound.

The AHA document contains twelve patient-rights statements. These can be summarized as follows:

1) the rights to considerate and respectful care;
2) the right to obtain from the physician information concerning one's own diagnosis, treatment, and progress;

3) the right to receive from the physician information necessary to give an informed consent to any procedures;

4) the right to refuse treatment to the extent permitted by law;

5) the right to privacy concerning one's own medical care;

6) the right to confidentiality in all communications and records relating to one's own care;

7) the right to reasonable responses to requests for service;

8) the right to information concerning other health-care and educational institutions related to one's own care;

9) the right to be advised if the hospital plans to perform human experimentation affecting one's own care and to refuse to participate in same;

10) the right to expect reasonable continuity of care;

11) the right to examine and receive explanation of one's hospital bill; and

12) the right to know what hospital rules and regulations apply to one's conduct as a patient.[17] (See Appendix A.)

In the early seventies, several Canadian groups evidenced a concern and interest in a patient's bill of rights.[18] Undoubtedly, the most significant document to emerge from this interest and activity was the resolution published by the Consumers' Association of Canada (CAC), which formulated a four-point charter. The resolution entitled "Consumer Rights in Health Care" states that the consumer has:

1) the right to be informed;

2) the right to be respected;

3) the right to participate in decision-making affecting his or her health;

4) the right to equal access to health care.[19] (See Appendix A.)

This four-point charter will constitute the framework for discussing patients' rights in this book. The four rights of the charter include moral and legal rights of patients. For example, respect for the dignity and autonomy of the patient is largely accomplished by ethical imperatives of the health professional's practice and through the moral commitment of the professional individual. Where these are insufficiently attended to, legal imperatives are often involved. Chapter Two, therefore, is an overview of ethics and law, which will establish the concepts and the context of patients' rights.

Before proceeding to that overview, a clarification of terms is necessary. The AHA Bill is entitled "A Statement on Patient's Rights," while the CAC Bill is called "Consumer Rights in Health Care." Are the terms "patient" and "consumer" interchangeable?

PATIENTS OR CONSUMERS?

By questioning the appropriate terminology for use in this discussion, that is, whether a person is a patient or a consumer, one is forced to examine the nature of the relationship between the health-care professional and the person who seeks health care. Each term has a particular set of meanings for that relationship.

The term "patient" generally denotes one who has entered the health-care system who is in a vulnerable position, at times very dependent upon care-givers. "Patients" are often anxious and uncertain, and they seek help from health professionals whom they perceive as having technical competence to deal with their problems. Because "patients" do not have the knowledge or the technical expertise to deal with their problems, they are in a position of dependency, and are very concerned for their self-interests.

The term "consumer" refers to a person who uses goods and services to satisfy his or her needs and who generally has a right to receive goods or services, or both, under a consumer transaction.[20] In health care, a "consumer" is one who is, or can be, actively involved and able to participate in health-care decisions. "Consumers" are knowledgeable, intelligent, thinking individiuals who have important ideas and insights to offer and who inevitably must be involved in their plan of care.

> *The mere use of the term "consumers" to replace [patients] or "clients" initiates a different perspective...the switching of labels tends to change the fabric of social relationships between practitioners in the health care delivery system and their clients. The process of social change evidenced by the evolution in relationships from client-practitioner to consumer-provider may be indicative of structural changes in this social relationship.*[21]

The term "consumer" emphasizes the independence and the self-determining nature of the person in health care.[22] Further, it includes all those persons who are not in the health-care system but who are potential patients, all patients affected by health-promotion efforts and the self-care movement, and all citizens who may be involved in planning and evaluating health services.

Although each of the concepts – "patient" and "consumer"* – offers some valuable insights towards understanding the nature of health-care relationships, many writers have cautioned against substituting the term "consumer" for "patient." Some argue that the use of the term "consumer" detracts from the human and healing aspects of the health-care system, and instead focuses on the technical.[23]

Throughout this book, the term "patient" will usually be employed. However, when the discussion focuses on potential patients, or when citizen participation is being discussed, "consumer" may be substituted for "patient."

---

*The term "client" has frequently been used in health care to emphasize many of the same characteristics of the professional-patient relationship.

REFERENCES FOR CHAPTER 1

[1]Robert Stinson and Peggy Stinson, "On the Death of a Baby," *The Atlantic* 244 (July 1979): 66.

[2]Martha Weinman Lear, *Heartsounds* (New York: Simon and Schuster, 1980), p. 232.

[3]Archie Hanlan, "Notes of a Dying Professor," *Nursing Digest* 4 (May 1974): 37. Reprinted with permission from the March, 1972, issue of *The Pennsylvania Gazette*, alumni magazine of the University of Pennsylvania. Copyright © 1972.

[4]Mary Olafsson, "Falling Through the Spaces," *The Exceptional Parent* (October 1978), p. S14.

[5]"Consumer Rights in Health Care," *Canadian Consumer* 4 (April 1974): 1.

[6]Laurence B. McCullaugh, "Rights, Health Care, and Public Policy," *The Journal of Medicine and Philosophy* 4 (June 1979): 204–215.

[7]Roland Warren identified seven major societal changes, five of which have been adapted here to describe the changes in society and in health care. See Roland L. Warren, *The Community in America* 2nd ed. (Chicago: Rand McNally and Co., 1972), p. 54. See also Janet L. Storch, "Consumer Rights and Nursing," unpublished Master's thesis, Division of Health Services Administration, University of Alberta, Edmonton, 1977, for further expansion of this discussion.

[8]Pradip N. Khandwalla, *The Design of Organizations* (New York: Harcourt, Brace Jovanovich Inc., 1977), p. 137.

[9]*New Directions in Education for Changing Health Care Systems* (Paris: Organization for Economic Cooperation and Development, 1975), p. 31.

[10]Robert Straus, "Hospital Organization from the Viewpoint of Patient-Centered Goals," in *Organization Research on Health Institutions*, ed. Basil S. Georgopoulos (Ann Arbor: University of Michigan, 1972), p. 217.

[11]Terence Johnson, *Professions and Power* (London: Macmillan Press, 1972), p. 41.

[12]Shirley M. Stinson, "Deprofessionalization in Nursing?" (Unpublished Ed.D. dissertation, Teacher's College, Columbia University, New York, 1969), pp. 29–31.

[13]Malcolm G. Taylor, *Health Insurance and Canadian Public Policy* (Montreal: McGill-Queen's University Press, 1978), p. 2.

[14]Robert E. Asher, *et al.*, *The United Nations and the Promotion of General Welfare* (Washington, D.C.: The Brookings Institute, 1957), p. 653.

[15]Walter Surma Tarnopolsky, *The Canadian Bill of Rights* 2nd revised edition (Toronto: McClelland and Stewart Ltd., 1975), pp. 87–88.

[16]Kenneth R. Wing, *The Law and the Public's Health* (St. Louis: C. V. Mosby, 1976), p. 19.

[17]"Statement on a Patient's Bill of Rights," *Hospitals*, *J.A.H.A.* 47 (February 16, 1973): 41.

[18]For examples, see "Bill of Rights for Patients to be Established in Nova Scotia," *Canadian Nurse* 69 (March 1973): 19–20; Edward A. Pickering, *Report of the Special Study Regarding the Medical Profession in Ontario* (Toronto: Ontario Medical Association, 1973), pp. 91–93; "Ottawa Hospital Adopts Patients' Bill of Rights," *Hospital Administration in Canada* 16 (December 1974): 45.

[19]"Consumer Rights in Health Care," *Canadian Consumer* 4 (April 1974): p. 1.

[20]See *Webster's New World Dictionary* (Toronto: Foster and Scott Ltd., 1960), p. 317; see also the Unfair Trade Practices Act, RSA 1975, c. 33.

[21]Leo G. Reeder, "Patient-Client as Consumer: Some Observations on the Changing Professional-Client Relationship," in *Humanizing Hospital Care*, eds. Gerald P. Turner and Joseph Mapa (Toronto: McGraw-Hill Ryerson, 1979), p. 139.

[22]Wim. J.A. Van De Heuval, "The Role of the Consumer in Health Care Policy," *Social Science and Medicine* 14A:5 (October 1980): 424.

[23]Aaron Antonovsky, *Health, Stress and Coping* (San Francisco: Jossey-Bass Publishers, 1979), pp. 209–210.

SUGGESTED REFERENCES FOR FURTHER STUDY, CHAPTER 1

Allentuck, A. *Who Speaks for the Patient?* Don Mills, Ontario: Burns and MacEachern Ltd., 1978.

In 105 provocative pages many of the problems and issues in Canadian health care are discussed. The author describes over-supply and misutilization of hospital beds; the need to reform the method of physician payment is reviewed; and the problems of unionization of paramedical workers are described. Several new technologies are discussed and the need to more carefully appraise costs and benefits of these technologies is stressed. Proliferation and misuse of drugs are reviewed, as are the process and costs of medical education. Finally, patient-rights issues and the dilemma of medical malpractice are examined. Discussion of any one issue tends to be brief but useful, and references allow the reader to pursue each topic in greater depth.

Annas, George J. *The Rights of Hospital Patients.* New York: Avon Books, 1975.

This pocketbook was developed as a handbook for the American Civil Liberties Union. In question-and-answer format, the book includes a brief commentary on the patient-rights movement, an introduction to hospital organization, and a topical approach to central issues in patients' rights. These include admission and discharge, consent to treatment, refusing treatment, experiments done on humans, hospital records, and other relevant issues.

Rozovsky, Lorne E. *The Canadian Patient's Book of Rights.* Toronto: Doubleday Canada Ltd., 1980.

Rozovsky provides the Canadian counterpart to Annas's book. This is a consumer's guide to Canadian health law. Rozovsky discusses the American Hospital Association's statement on patient rights, and outlines the Canadian hospital-insurance and medicare provisions as a prelude to a discussion of specific patients' issues – such as the right to a doctor of one's own choice, consent to treatment, standards of care and negligence, abortion, and death. He concludes with some practical suggestions regarding proper procedures in presenting patient complaints.

Storch, Janet L. *"Consumer Rights and Nursing."* M.H.S.A. thesis, University of Alberta, 1977. (available through the University of Alberta Bookstore)

This master's thesis provides material on major societal changes, on the nature of rights, and on the growth of human-rights concerns. A thorough analysis of some of these major societal changes as they affect health-care organization and practice is provided; there is also a preliminary discussion of consumer rights, and a review of the development of the ombudsman concept and its influence in health services. The thesis focuses on nursing, both changes in the profession, and how consumer rights affect the profession.

Tarnopolsky, Walter Surma. *The Canadian Bill of Rights* (2nd revised edition). Toronto: McClelland and Stewart Ltd., 1975.

Tarnopolsky provides a comprehensive description and analysis of civil liberties in Canada, and of the Canadian Bill of Rights. He discusses notions of rights, freedoms, and liberties; the distribution of legislative power in regard to civil liberties; and the entrenchment of the Canadian Bill of Rights. Political, economic, legal, and egalitarian civil liberties are then discussed, and a chapter on the War Measures Act is provided. Included as appendices are the Canadian and American Bills of Rights, a proposed Canadian Charter of Human Rights, and excerpts from the Canadian Constitutional Charter. This book is a thorough and comprehensive source book for investigating human rights in Canada.

Turner, G.P., and Mapa, J., eds. *Humanizing Hospital Care.* Toronto: McGraw-Hill Ryerson, 1979.

Problems created by the combinations of humanism and science, care and cure, are the focus of these readings, which are directed toward a re-emphasis of the subject of humanism in hospital care. An article written in 1927 establishes the philosophical approach of the book: it emphasizes that people are the principle components of the health-care process. The multiple factors that create dehumanizing tendencies in health care are discussed; there are selections devoted to sociological aspects of illness behavior and patient care. Strategies that would promote humanistic practices in health care, such as consumer evaluation of care and education of physicians towards greater sensitivity to patients, are presented; and environmental changes that impinge upon humanistic considerations in care conclude the volume. This is an excellent current resource on humanizing patient care.

CHAPTER 2 Ethics and the Law: The Context of Patients' Rights

To discuss the issue of rights without considering their foundation in law and in ethics is to merely identify and list patient-rights concerns. The very concept of a "right" is based in ethics and in law. Attention to the legal and ethical foundations of patients' rights affords rich opportunities to develop a greater understanding of the significance of law and ethics to the health-professional-patient relationship.

Both law and ethics are grounded in social history and are designed to protect different interests. Although they are not co-extensive there is a close, albeit uneasy, relationship between law and ethics "because legal decisions commonly appeal to moral principles and rules, or raise issues that must be handled by moral deliberations."[1] The two disciplines defy abbreviation of explanation; however, an attempt has been made in this chapter to explain ethics and law as they pertain to health care.*

*The author is indebted to Professor Gerald Gall, Faculty of Law, University of Alberta, and to Professor Cameron MacKenzie, Department of Philosophy, University of Alberta, for their critical comments and suggestions on early drafts of this chapter. Any remaining misinterpretation of the two disciplines is solely my own. Because the material is necessarily an overview, the reader is encouraged to consult the footnotes and the references, provided at the end of the chapter, for further study.

ETHICS AND HEALTH CARE

The variety and complexity of changes in society, and in that component of society known as the health-care system, have necessitated increased attention to ethical issues. In other eras, good character was assumed to be the basis of good judgment and morally correct action. But great conflicts and controversies have arisen in health care, and one can no longer take for granted that all personnel will agree on how to evaluate and respond to various dilemmas. Through the study of ethics, health professionals can act and judge with greater clarity and understanding.

A variety of terms highlights the renewed importance of ethics in health care, for example, "bioethics," "biomedical ethics," "medical ethics," and "ethics and health care." Few would dispute the need for a greater awareness of ethics in health care. But many of the newer terms suggest a new and independent field of study rather than an area of study that is intrinsically linked to philosophy.

Philosophy is defined as "the study of truth or principles underlying all knowledge."[2] Ethics is a branch of philosophy commonly called moral philosophy; it focuses on questions of moral judgments. The term "ethics" (moral philosophy) and the term "morals" are often used interchangeably. One author, Harmon Smith, from Duke University, provides a useful distinction when he suggests that the "moral question is a 'what' question...the ethical question is a 'why' question."[3] Smith states that ethics

> ...does not attempt to supply solutions for moral dilemmas, but it does undertake to provide a rational framework for comprehending the complexities of moral judgement....In other words, ethical questions attempt to reference action to an affirmative warrant, they ask whether there is a proper reason for making a particular choice, and whether there is coherence and congruency between what one believes and how one behaves.[4]

Smith's distinction is particularly helpful for health professionals who sometimes experience dissatisfaction and disillusionment when a study of ethics provides no clear and immediate answer to a particular dilemma. Understanding the complexities of a situation and determining "coherence and congruency" between beliefs and actions are essential prerequisites to moral conduct and decision-making.

History of Ethics in Nursing

Nurses and other health professionals have long been concerned about their conduct in relation to their patients and to other health professionals. Florence Nightingale was clear in her delineation of the nurse's duties to the patient and to the physician. In regard to patients, for example, Nightingale advocated a genuine respect for those who are sick or suffering, and a strict attention to keeping patient information confidential.[5] In regard to physicians, Nightingale stressed the importance of the physician as the person "in charge."

Codes of conduct began to emerge in the late nineteenth century, when the Johns Hopkins Training School Nurses Alumnae Association produced the "Florence Nightingale Pledge"[6] (See Appendix B). The pledge spells out a duty to patients and duties to physicians. Moral dilemmas in nursing were not generally discussed until the early twentieth century, and even then good character was envisioned as the primary basis of good moral conduct.[7]

After World War II, formal codes of ethics were adopted by national and international nursing associations; for example, there were the American Nurses Association Code in 1950 and the International Council of Nurses Code in 1953 (see Appendix B). These codes were in keeping with the Universal Declaration of Human Rights of 1948, which emphasized human worth and human dignity. The preamble to the code adopted by the Grand Council of the International Council of Nurses includes this statement:

Inherent in the Code is the fundamental concept that the nurse believes in the essential freedoms of mankind and in the preservation of human life.[8]

In 1980, two codes of ethics for nurses in Canada were developed: the CNA Code of Ethics and the Guidelines for Ethical Behavior in Nursing (College of Nurses of Ontario). The CNA code, based on the concept of caring, was presented to the Annual Convention of the Canadian Nurses' Association for acceptance. The guidelines, adopted by the College of Nurses in 1980, were linked to the College's mandate to develop standards of nursing practice.[9]

Most professional codes of ethics are "a mixture of creeds and commandments:"[10] they contain both statements of belief and statements of laws that regulate conduct. These regulations pre-

scribe minimum standards of acceptable ethical conduct and indicate some of the ethical concerns professionals must consider in
deciding conduct.

Codes are an essential characteristic of a profession, and are a
statement of the acceptance of the trust and responsibility the
public has placed in a profession. In addition, they serve as a major
educational tool in teaching standards of ethical conduct to beginning practitioners.

Although codes of ethics are important in the development of
beliefs, guidelines, and standards, their utility and their limitations
must be kept in mind.

First, since health-care codes are developed by professionals, for
the profession, and since they address issues of professional conduct, they may not include all issues of concern to the patient.
Patients' bills of rights can reflect these outstanding concerns
because they are addressed to patients in care. Secondly, codes are
limited because moral dilemmas in health care and nursing do not
generally occur as a series of problems and questions to be solved
with a series of guidelines. Rather, moral dilemmas are situations of
complexity and conflict.

If one imagines a hierarchy of ethical reasoning or justification,
the hierarchy will begin with individual judgments and actions,
then progress to rules, then principles, and finally to ethical theories.[11] Within such a hierarchy, codes of ethics can be viewed as a
second-level approach to ethics. Codes of ethics are like rules or
guidelines, and are insufficient in themselves to guide nurses in
moral or ethical dilemmas. This is not, however, to understate the
importance of such codes as guidelines and as a basis of legal
standards.

Beyond Codes of Ethics

Nurses are confronted daily with moral and ethical dilemmas.
These dilemmas are manifest in situations where the nurse's duties
are in conflict and where there is weighty evidence on each side of
an issue. In any given situation, there might be evidence to indicate
that one act is morally right, but evidence might also exist to
indicate that that act is morally wrong; on the face of it, the nurse
should and should not perform that act.

Such situations give rise to a renewed concern for a framework in
which to make decisions. Most nurses are aware that visceral and
affective (emotional) feelings and reactions are not sufficient for

morally appropriate practice. How might nurses become better equipped to deal with ethical dilemmas?

At least four conditions are necessary for ethical decision-making. First, one must have a commitment to do good, a desire to do what is right and good. Without such a commitment, the nurse faces no real dilemma, although a severe dilemma may be experienced by the patient. Second, one must have knowledge of the relevant facts of the situation. Third, there must be clarity of thought in dealing with these facts. Factual knowledge and clarity of thought can pre-empt emotionalism, and can overcome a tendency to inflict one's own sense of values on another person. Fourth, some basic ethical principles or theory are needed as a guide to thinking through a dilemma, retrospectively and prospectively.

For purposes of this discussion, the first prerequisite, a commitment to do good, will be assumed. An ability to discern the relevant facts of a situation is a problem-solving skill that will not be discussed here, except to stress the importance of obtaining as much information about the situation as is possible. This information must then be carefully evaluated, to determine its accuracy and its authenticity. Further, emotions and assumptions must be carefully separated from facts. But there are times when information is not available; it is often hard to get the facts. How does one act with integrity in relative ignorance?

Clarity of thought is essential to ethical decision-making. Although this, too, is substance for a separate learning exercise, it should be noted that many nurses and other persons in the helping professions have used values-clarification strategies to examine their own values or frame of reference and to determine whether their actions are consistent with their values.

Values clarification offers a process for sorting through the issues we face and can help us close the gap between what we say and what we do.[12]

Clarity of thought and understanding can assist nurses in examining how their values may influence their actions; as well, values-clarification strategies can teach a sensitivity to what patients value.

Concepts and Principles of Ethics
A number of concepts and principles of ethics are central to understanding ethical issues in health care, and to enabling the decision-maker to assess whether a particular decision will advance

or contravene ethical principles. Some of these concepts and principles are briefly described. The reader should keep in mind that (a) the discussion does not fully represent all perspectives on a particular concept or principle (therefore the reader is encouraged to use the references in this section for further study), and (b) any one principle may override all other principles (for example, autonomy is often discussed as "an overriding principle").

Personhood. The concept of personhood is central to ethics in patient care. What is it to be a person? Does being a member of the species *homo sapiens* make one a person?

Some have suggested that personhood is conferred according to rights: for example, a person's right to life, the right to information, and so on.[13] Others suggest that personhood is defined in terms of autonomy, another ethical concept.

Joseph Fletcher, a well-respected theologian, developed a series of "indicators of humanhood," or personhood, which included the following qualities: minimal intelligence, self-awareness, self-control, sense of future, sense of past, capacity to relate to others, communication, and curiosity.[14] Numerous writers have modified or redefined Fletcher's indicators, but one basic quality is self-awareness. Self-awareness includes not only an awareness of the past and an awareness of existence over time, but also the qualities of experiencing, communicating, and relating.

The notion that human personal life (personhood) and human biological life (being a member of the human species) are separate concepts[15] appears to be a significant trend; it relates to the issues of abortion, fetal research, and withdrawal of life-support systems to terminally ill patients.

Autonomy. Autonomy is another key concept in moral philosophy. It includes several related qualities: independence, authenticity, effective deliberation, and moral reflection. Independence implies that one acts freely; that is, one engages in purely voluntary and intentional acts. Authenticity implies that one acts in a manner consistent with one's own values, one's own life plan.[16] Awareness of alternatives and the consequences of those alternatives in choosing a course of action is implied in the capacity for effective deliberation. Moral reflection is a final trait associated with autonomy: one must have the freedom and capacity to evaluate a situation from a moral perspective.

The idea is one of being one's own man, and from that position entering into relations of friendship, love, generosity and service. In the relation of medical care this means that both patient and doctor fully define their relation to each other, neither being imposed on as a resource at the command of the other.[17]

For some philosophers, autonomy is seen as the most important moral value, the value one should attempt to preserve even at the cost of other values. Under what circumstances is a violation of autonomy permissible? For example, if individuals exhibit self-destructive behavior, do they forfeit their right to autonomy? **Paternalism.** This concept involves the placing of restrictions on a person's liberty where the justification for restraint is the attempt to do good to the person being restrained. The concept is based upon the relationship of a loving and caring father (*pater*) towards an immature child. To decide whether an act is a paternalistic one, a number of criteria have been suggested:

1) the actor believes his or her action is for the person's good;
2) the actor is qualified to act on behalf of the person;
3) the actor's action violates the person's moral freedom in some way – for example, the person's right to autonomy;
4) the actor believes he or she is justified in acting independent of the person's consent; and
5) the person believes that he or she (the person) knows what is for his or her own good.[18]

Physicians and other health professionals frequently find themselves in a paternalistic role for a number of reasons: uncertainties surrounding patient diagnosis, the questionable condition of many patients, the gap in medical knowledge between patients and health professionals, and the patient's inability or unwillingness to make difficult decisions. In such circumstances, health professionals feel justified in acting on the patient's behalf, sometimes without the patient's consent.[19]

The limits and justifications of paternalism are important considerations for all health professionals.

The central thesis of John Stuart Mill and other individualists about paternalism is that the full voluntary choice or consent of a mature and rational human being concerning matters that affect only his own interests is such a precious thing that no one else (and certainly not the state) has a right to interfere with it simply for the person's "own good."[20]

But there are instances in health care when paternalism can be justified. A practitioner's intervention is not always a negative event: however, the practitioner must carefully weigh the effects of intervening paternalistically in any situation.

An example of morally proper intervention is provided by the late Dr. Franz Ingelfinger. After years of treating patients with gastroesophageal problems, the doctor found himself a victim of glandular cancer astride the gastroesophageal junction. He received numerous and conflicting opinions regarding proposed treatment. He began to wish for someone who would dominate; who would, in a paternalistic manner, assume some responsibility for his care.[21]

Coercion. Under what circumstances is coercion justified? At least one writer in ethics suggests that the harm coercion causes a coerced person will outweigh any good it might produce.[22] However, others suggest that persons who are "not in a position to act in a sufficiently autonomous manner" may require some degree of coercive action for their own good.[23]

Coercive actions are taken with considerable justification by those who care for infants and irrationally suicidal patients. However, when one deals with mentally ill persons, aged persons, or older children, defense of coercion is often more difficult. These particular groups, and other vulnerable groups, demand careful and individualized assessments by health professionals.

Justice. The concept of justice is based on the notion of allotment to persons. Generally, two ideas of justice prevail: first, the idea that justice has been accorded when a person gets what he or she deserves; second, the idea of distributive justice, which refers to the "proper distribution of social benefits and burdens."[24] These benefits and burdens may include opportunities, penalties, privileges, roles, duties, goods, offices, or other costs and benefits.[25]

The notion of justice as desert, as a measure of fairness, has been significant in health care, but recent attention has been directed toward the idea of distributive justice. Distributive justice implies some competition for scarce economic benefit: there are no problems in which distributive justice may apply, and no principles of distributive justice are needed, unless there exists some measure of scarcity.[26]

At least four principles of distributive justice have been advocated and are evident in society:

1) to each according to his or her individual need;
2) to each according to his or her worth;

3) to each according to his or her individual effort; and
4) to each according to his or her merit.[27]

Theories of distributive justice are developed by an elaboration of one or more of these and other principles. For example, Marxist theories emphasize individual needs and society's efforts to meet those needs; egalitarian theories emphasize individual human worth (the intrinsic value of individual human beings) as the basis for equal access to goods and services; utilitarian theories attempt to maximize public and private utility; and libertarian theories emphasize individual effort, merit, and the operation of a free market.[28]

How to allot health and welfare services to the Canadian people has been a subject of debate amongst politicians, health professionals, and the public. An egalitarian approach has been a principle of the Canadian health-care system since at least the late 1960s, but the political debate still rages.

Egalitarian approaches are not without problems. Unjust distribution might arise if there is a failure to distinguish between groups or classes of people who are actually different, for example, the poor or the handicapped. It has been argued that many groups of people should receive a greater share of free resources than do their healthy or wealthy counterparts.

Other Concepts Pertinent to Health Care. There are numerous other moral concepts and principles relevant to ethics in health care; these are identified and discussed briefly.

The concept of **beneficence** is based on the notion of duty, as distinct from kindness or charity. At least two principles are central to beneficence: that benefits are provided and that there is a balancing of benefits and harms. The duty to provide care with minimal risk is based on an implicit contract between the provider and the recipient; that contract establishes a special social and moral relationship between provider and recipient.[29]

The concept of **non-maleficence** is best described by the dictum "Do no harm," and embodies both intentional harm and the risk of harm. Principles surrounding non-maleficence become particularly significant where "due care" becomes a central criterion in establishing medical negligence. Another significant area of decision-making is the matter of permitting or causing death.[30]

Fidelity is generally described as faithfulness of one person to another. Duties of fidelity are those based on social contract, but fidelity implies a faithfulness to another human being above and beyond a formal or implied contract. **Veracity** implies the duty "to tell the truth and not to lie or deceive others." It is an essential aspect of faithfulness, and is necessary for establishing a relationship of trust. As with other duties or principles, the duty to tell the truth is not absolute. "Non-disclosure, deception, and even lying can sometimes be justified when veracity conflicts with other duties."[31] For example, to force information on a patient who has indicated a desire not to receive such information may be to act paternalistically and to violate autonomy.[32]

Rights and **responsibilities** are concepts of central importance to ethics. Rights are those justified claims that persons or groups can make upon others or upon society. Individuals who make such claims are answerable or accountable–responsible–for their behavior.

The centrality accorded to the principle of rights in this book does not argue the importance of this ethical (or legal) principle over all others. Instead, the intent is to use rights as a common framework for a discussion that spans the disciplines of law and ethics, and to provide practical applications of these disciplines to situations of conflict in health care.

Ethical Theories
Two major philosophic perspectives embody the approaches important to morality. These are the theories of John Stuart Mill and the theories of Immanuel Kant. Together, they "represent the most significant theories developed by persons trying to face the problems of living morally."[33] The two perspectives or theoretical approaches–the teleological approach of John Stuart Mill and the deontological approach of Immanuel Kant–will be described briefly.

A Theory of Consequences. One perspective, the teleological approach, gauges the worth of an action by its ends or consequences.[34] The most prominent version of the theory was developed by John Stuart Mill, who advocated that decisions be based on the principle of utility (thus the label "utilitarianism").

The basic principle of Mill's utilitarianism is that the goal sought or the consequence desired must be the greatest happiness of the greatest number, and that this consequence should provide the rationale for all our moral judgments. Mill sees the concept of personal happiness as an intrinsic goal (a good in itself).[35]

To adhere to this theoretical position, we may have to sacrifice the happiness (and sometimes the life) of one individual or small group for the sake of a larger group. For example, we may decide to allow a mongoloid child with atresia to die in order to spare the child's parents and society the burden of care for the child.

The utility principle can be applied in at least two different ways: *act* utilitarianism and *rule* utilitarianism. In act utilitarianism, each act is gauged directly by the greatest-happiness-of-the-greatest-number principle. In rule utilitarianism, the concept of utility applies only to general moral rules, which are interposed between the act and the utilitarian principle. In rule utilitarianism the question is, "Which rule has the greatest utility?"[36]

A Theory of Duty. The second ethical theory suggests that "features of some acts other than their consequences make them right or wrong."[37] This theoretical perspective is known as the *deontological approach* (*"deon"* means *duty*). The many variations of the theory can generally be classified as monistic or pluralistic. Those who advocate a monistic approach suggest that one general principle or rule prevails, from which all other rules or principles can be derived. Pluralists suggest that there is more than one rule, that there are several basic moral principles.

Immanuel Kant advocated a monistic approach to deontological theory. Kant ascribed less significance to the consequences of actions, and emphasized the duty to treat people as ends, never as means to an end. He maintained that persons have absolute value, and that the principle that should guide our actions is to be found in the ability to make an action universal. In other words: rational beings should always ask the question, "How would things stand if my maxim became a universal law?"[38] For example, suppose you decided not to tell a patient the truth. You would then have to ask, "How would things stand if all persons decided not to tell the truth?"

The pluralistic deontological approach recognizes the likely existence of several basic moral principles. Pluralists believe that the number and the substance of these principles begs the questions, "From where or whom are these principles derived? Who decides which principles and how many?" Some suggest the source is divine revelation, for example, the Ten Commandments. Others point to natural law, and yet others to intuition or common sense. Sets of principles or rules lead to rule deontology, and philosophical principles such as autonomy, justice, and personhood may form the substance of rule deontology.[39]

Other Ethical "Theories." Two other ethical approaches are commonly discussed in relation to health care, and the reader should be aware of these approaches and their limitations.

Situation ethics suggest that each moral dilemma must be decided on its own merits, with no universal guidelines. Some general rules of conduct are recognized, but they are regarded as summary rules or rules of thumb, and are considered expendable in decision-making.[40]

Moral relativism is closely related to situation ethics but goes further. Relativists believe that there are no moral rules: each culture creates its own meanings. "When we say that a certain type of behavior is 'morally right,' all we can possibly mean is that some society approves of it and positively sanctions it."[41]

Since neither situation ethics nor moral relativism offers discrete maxims or principles, each is limited as a guide to action in situations of moral conflict.

No one ethical theory can be fully satisfactory on all counts and theorists have recognized the conflicting demands imposed by many theories. Therefore, it would seem that an understanding of the basic theories is necessary; one must select and blend those that will best serve in situations of ethical dilemma.

Anne Davis has suggested the need for a theory of **ethical pluralism**, which would encompass both consequences and duty. She suggests that right conduct be governed by a combined teleological and deontological theory.[42] Other writers have suggested a similar blending, although one author labels such a blend as a mixed deontological theory that recognizes the principle of utility but insists on another principle: justice.[43]

Many forms of rule utilitarianism and rule deontology can lead to identical rules and actions, albeit for different reasons.[44] Perhaps, then, the actual selection of a theory is not as important as the process of investigating, valuing, and choosing an approach, through principles or theory, that best matches the individual's work situation and assists an understanding of the complexities of a dilemma.

*It remains true, nevertheless, that a man must in the moment of decision do
what he thinks is right. He cannot do otherwise. This does not mean that
what he does will be right or even that he will not be worthy of blame or
punishment. He simply has no choice, for he cannot at that moment see any
discrepancy between what is right and what he thinks is right. The life of
man, even if he would be moral, is not without its risks.* [45]

THE LAW AND HEALTH CARE

Law is essentially a statement of relationship. The laws that govern
a society are a statement of relationships between people; they spell
out existing legal rights and duties in the society. [46]

Early rules of conduct were essentially ethical principles, which
became law when they were written down. Therefore, the standards the law expects a citizen to meet often have, as their basis,
ethical standards. In some cases, the law demands more than
ethical standards would demand; in some cases the law differs
from ethical standards; and in some cases the law is silent with
respect to any ethical standards. [47]

There are many sources of law. Some laws were given by "great
law-givers" (for example, the Ten Commandments); some are
internal laws that govern professional practice. Law has been
derived from several related sources including:

1) formal sources, for example, a legal sovereign or the state;
2) historical sources, such as Roman law or mercantile custom;
3) literary sources, such as law reports or books of authority; or
4) legal sources, such as legislative or judicial law. [48]

This discussion will focus on legal sources of Canadian law.

Canadian Law [49]

Canadian law is derived from statutes enacted by Parliament or the
provincial legislatures; case law, enunciated by our courts in deciding cases; the Quebec Civil Code; constitutional sources of law; and
miscellaneous sources, which might include royal prerogatives,
custom and convention, juristic writings, and principles of morality.

Statute law includes all legislative enactments, at both the federal
and provincial levels of government. Statute law is developed by
civil servants (often with public input), is approved by the Cabinet,
and is debated in the House of Commons or provincial legislature.

Statutes must have three readings before passage in the House, and become law sometime after the passage. Examples of federal statute law are the Medical Care Act of 1967 and the Federal-Provincial Fiscal Arrangements and Established Programs Financing Act of 1977. Provincial statutes include the Mental Health Act, the Public Health Act, and the Registered Nurses' Act. There are ten Canadian provinces and two territories; each jurisdiction may have its own specific title for a statute, and the contents of each will vary.

Case law stems from the decisions courts reach when adjudicating cases. As decisions are reached, the judge often sets out the reasons for those decisions (*ratio decidendi*). If another court is later asked to decide a similar matter, it is bound to follow the first court's precedent. (Higher courts or courts in other jurisdictions are not bound by the first court's precedent.)

> *Decisions from American courts are rarely cited for authority in Canada. But while they are neither binding nor even persuasive to a Canadian court they are sometimes helpful when decisions are required on matters which have not yet come before our courts, but have been decided in the United States.*[50]

The body of case law is called "common law," and is based on British tradition. In feudal England, the king would hear complaints and resolve disputes based on local customs. In time, the mechanism for adjudicating disputes became more formalized; a court system evolved. But decisions were still based on common customs or common laws, and judges were obliged to abide by past decisions.

The British colonies in North America chose to adopt some basic features of English common law, although the system was accepted somewhat differently in each province. In accepting the common-law system, the country accepted the doctrines of precedent and *stare decisis* (meaning, literally, to stand by decisions and not to disturb settled matters).[51]

The province of Quebec, however, based its legal system on Roman and French traditions that emphasized the codification of law. The Quebec Civil Code, adopted in 1866, is an adaptation of the Napoleonic or French Civil Code. When law is "codified," judges need not abide by precedent. Instead, they can rely on their own interpretations of provisions in the Quebec Civil Code. Precedent is less important than in the common-law system, since all courts are free to return to the civil code to extract principles and to apply the principles to the facts of the case.

Another significant aspect of Canadian law is the doctrine of parliamentary sovereignty. Subject to the constitutional division of legislative powers, the parliament of Canada has the power to modify or repeal any principles that have been established by case law, or enacted by parliament in the past. Because the Canadian constitution is derived from several sources, the constitutional basis of legislative and judicial authority in Canada is complex.

A number of statutes of the parliament of Great Britain have provided the basic framework of the Canadian constitution. These statutes include the British North America Act of 1867, (the BNA Act), which forms the main element of our written constitution, and the Statute of Westminster of 1931.[52] However, the Constitution Act of 1982 is a dramatic addition to this constitutional package. Essentially, the Constitution Act incorporates all the existing provisions of the BNA Act, adds to the former BNA Act a Canadian Charter of Rights and Freedoms, and provides for a means by which Canadians can amend the Constitution in Canada without having to go to the Parliament of Great Britain.

The BNA Act (now the Constitution Act, 1867) is significant to health professionals. The BNA Act created the federation of Canadian provinces in 1867; that federation was based on the premise of a strong, central government. Basic distribution of federal and provincial powers is set out in sections 91 and 92 of the Act; matters of health and welfare are dealt with in these sections (see Appendix D).

The responsibilities of the federal government, as established in Section 91, included only two health-related matters: "The Census and Statistics" and "Quarantine and the Establishment and Maintenance of Marine Hospitals." Other functions assigned to the federal government, of consequence to the Canadian health-care system, were the taxing and spending powers given to the federal government, the responsibility for Indians, the responsibility for the quality of food and drugs, and the Criminal Law.[53]

Provincial legislatures were given, in section 92 of the BNA Act, responsibility for:

7. *The Establishment, Maintenance, and Management of Hospitals, Asylums, Charities, and Eleemosynary Institutions in and for the Province, other than Marine Hospitals.*

16. *Generally all Matters of a merely local or private Nature in the Province.*[54]

These responsibilities were thought, in 1867, to be matters of a minor nature and of purely local concern. "Given the state of health services in 1867, these provisions have been interpreted to give jurisdiction over health services in each province to the provincial government."[55]

The division of federal-provincial powers has meant that there are, in effect, ten different but related health systems in Canada.[56] Only through the federal government's placement of conditions on the disbursement of funds to the provinces – for example, through hospital insurance and Medicare – has any degree of uniformity been attained.[57]

Main Divisions of Law[58]

As can be discerned from the preceding discussion, there is no single, homogeneous entity we can call "the law," but rather a complex paradigm, with many divisions and subdivisions, that forms a complicated but integrated system.

The most important positive law ("positive law" is law set out in legal sources) is domestic law, that is, law within one nation. Domestic law can further be divided into procedural law (mechanisms by which law can be made operational) and substantive law. Substantive law is the substance of a country's law, and consists of both public law and private law. Public law includes constitutional law, administrative law, and criminal law; private law includes contracts, torts, and property. Figure 1 diagrams these essential divisions of law.

The BNA Act (the Constitution Act, 1867) specifies federal and provincial responsibilities in health care; it also makes the federal Parliament responsible for law governing criminal acts. Only the federal parliament can make laws governing criminal acts; therefore the Criminal Code of Canada applies to every province in Canada. It includes, for example, laws governing murder.[59] Certain sections of the Criminal Code have particular relevance to health professionals in respect to their legal duties to patients. Professional duties include the preservation of life; some duties might give rise to conditions of assault.[60]

Provincial statutes are part of public and private law at the provincial level. Many provincial statutes affect health care and nursing, and it is important that nurses become acquainted with the contents of acts such as The Hospitals Act, the Labor Relations

Act, the Good Samaritan Act, and others. Nurses should be familiar with relevant provincial laws (for example, community-health nurses should be familiar with the Public Health Act, nursing-home nurses with the Nursing Homes Act, and so on.) The laws contained in these acts apply to rights and duties, and the consequences for breach of such duty.[61]

Figure 2.1 **THE SOURCES OF LAW**

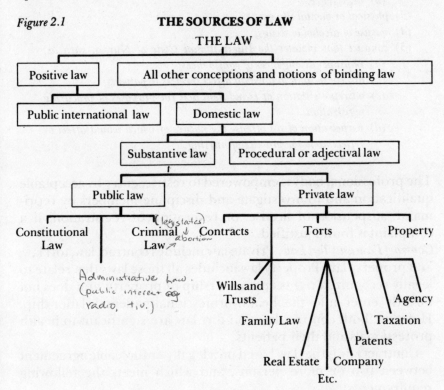

Source: Gerald L. Gall, *The Canadian Legal System* (Toronto: The Carswell Company Ltd., 1977), page 35.

One provincial statute of considerable import to all nurses is the Registered Nurses' Act (or its equivalent in each province). Under this legislation, a professional body is empowered to register and to discipline its members. Registration involves criteria for initial certification as well as for renewal of certification. Discipline is generally restricted to the processing of complaints against a member; such complaints are based on unbecoming conduct, incompetence, or incapacity. In one province, examples of "unbecoming conduct, incompetence, or incapacity" are specified in the Bylaws of the Act as:

(1) professional incompetence;
(2) unsafe practice due to:
    (a) limited or inadequate knowledge;
    (b) negligence;
(3) physical or mental illness;
(4) misuse of alcohol or drugs;
(5) conduct that violates the International Code of Nurses, such as:
    (a) improper divulgences of confidences;
    (b) discrimination that would affect services to patients;
    (c) misrepresentation of fraudulent acts for purposes of procuring registration;
    (d) perpetration of an offense the nature of which would affect or reflect upon the practice of nursing.[62]

The professional body is empowered to restrict entry by acceptable qualification and to investigate and discipline members by reprimand, suspension of license, or revocation of registration, if a complaint is found justified.

Contract Law and Tort Law. Private law includes contract law, tort law, and property law. Property law includes all those laws that relate to legally recognized rights and ownership of property, and does not directly enter into the health-professional-patient relationship. However, both contract law and tort law are significant to health professionals and their patients.

Contract law is that law based on a legally enforceable agreement between two or more persons, and which meets the following requirements:

1) there be an intention to create legal relations;
2) the parties be known and competent;
3) the terms be certain or ascertainable;
4) there be consideration.[63]

Contracts or legally enforceable agreements between parties may be written or implied. For example, a nurse employed by a hospital or other health agency may possess a written or formal contract, or may be working on an "implied" – or informal – contract.[64] With the trend towards unionization of nurses across Canada, most nurses are covered by a collective agreement or contract – a legally binding contract governed by laws of industrial relations in each province. Nurses should know the terms of their contracts.

Although the traditional doctor-patient relationship is clearly a contractual relationship,[65] the nurse-patient relationship is not as clear in relation to contract law. It is generally agreed that the relationship between a patient and a private-duty nurse meets the requirements of contract law. But nurses employed by hospitals and other agencies are not generally considered to be in a contractual arrangement with their patients. The hospital is involved in an implied contract with patients and has a direct responsibility for its own acts and for the acts of its "servants, employees and agents when they are acting in those capacities."[66] Thus the hospital is vicariously liable – the rule of vicarious liability – or, in other words, responsible for the acts of others. By virtue of this liability, the master (employer) is responsible for the conduct of the servant (employee). In legal terms, this is known as the doctrine of *respondent superior* ("Let the master answer"). The employer's responsibility does not extend, however, to employee actions that are "extraordinarily inappropriate" or that the employer could not reasonably foresee.[67]

If there is a problem in the physician-patient contract, a patient may sue for breach of contract. This is not a common occurence; however, nurses should understand the nature of contract law, particularly if they are contemplating a move towards independent practice.[68]

Tort law is concerned with "intentional violations of private rights of others, and the negligent abrogation of legally recognized duties of care owed to others."[69] "Tort" essentially means "wrong," and tort law includes four main types of wrongs of concern to nurses:

1) battery and assault;
2) false imprisonment;
3) negligence; and
4) defamation.

"Battery is committed by intentionally bringing about harmful or offensive contact with another.... An assault is an apprehension of a battery."[70] Normally these actions occur together, but they may be separate torts, and the validity of either rests on the absence of the person's consent. Thus, the principles surrounding patient consent (discussed in Chapter Three) are critical to the nurse's understanding of law governing battery and assault liability.

A tort of false imprisonment "developed from the desire to protect the liberty of a person to move at will and when he wishes to do so."[71]

> *If a person subjects another to a restraint of movement against his will and without his consent or legal justification, he will be liable in law for false imprisonment.*[72]

Although false imprisonment is not a common basis for legal suit, nurses should be cognizant of their responsibilities and rights, particularly in relation to restraining the elderly, the mentally ill, patients with communicable diseases, and delirious or temporarily confused patients.[73] Statutory enactments, such as provincial mental-health or public-health acts, frequently protect a nurse from liability in these areas. But such statutes may cloud the nurse's perceptions of patient rights, and must be both understood and carefully administered in the context of the nurse-patient relationship. Further, the patient's informed desire to leave the institution of treatment must be handled carefully, with attention to the institution's responsibility.

The tort of defamation involves any statement, oral or written, about another person that is untrue and that causes or is "designed to cause an injury to the person's good name."[74] Written defamation is called libel; spoken defamation is called slander.[75] Derogatory statements about patients or staff members have no place in health care, and often result in breaches of confidentiality. (Issues of confidentiality are addressed further in Chapter Four.)

Finally, there is the tort of negligence. "Negligence is one of the most common bases for a lawsuit against a doctor or hospital."[76] And, increasingly, the lawsuits are brought against nurses. Generally, negligence refers to unintentional harm or harm due to careless treatment.[77] There are four requisites to establishing nursing negligence:

    a) the nurse must owe a duty to the patient to exercise care;
    b) the nurse must have breached the standard of care established by law for nursing conduct;

   c) the patient must have sustained harm or loss as a result of the breach;

   d) the alleged breach of conduct must have been the immediate cause (or proximate cause) of the patient's loss or injury.[78]

"The nurse-patient relationship is a legal status created the moment a nurse actually provides nursing care to another person."[79] The relationship involves special duties and responsibilities. Once the relationship is established, the nurse legally owes a special duty of care.

Based on this duty of care, the nurse is expected to meet a certain standard of care in her care of the patient. The standard of care is the standard a "reasonably prudent nurse of like training and experience" would exercise.[80] In law, any failure to meet this standard, if that failure is the proximate cause of reasonably foreseeable injury to the patient, would be regarded as negligence. (This is a good example of how this law can fall short in protecting patients' rights. Morally, any failure to meet the standard of care is a negligent act, even if it produces no injury.)

To determine what constitutes a reasonable standard of care, judges may look to several sources. They may look to the professional act – for example, the Registered Nurses Act – for guidance; they may look to the Professional Association of Nurses, to determine if standards have been developed; they may refer to the Professional Code of Ethics of nurses, and use statements in the code as standards. In addition, judges might call expert witnesses (for example, other nurses) to clarify reasonably acceptable standards.

Several writers advise nurses to take precautions in order to avoid charges of negligence. First, it is important for nurses to continue their education, so that they may provide a reasonable standard of care. Second, accurate and punctual charting is essential in order to demonstrate that a reasonable standard of care has been provided.[81]

It is possible "for a nurse to practise at a level substandard to the nursing profession's requirements and yet escape involvement in legal action."[82] This might occur if the patient suffers no injury or harm. (The nurse may, however, be answerable to her professional disciplinary body for professional misconduct.) Because of the rule of vicarious liability, under which the hospital is responsible for the acts of its employees, nurses have been somewhat protected from a direct legal accountability to patients. However, this situation may well change. More and more nurses are working outside hospitals; as well, trends in recent court cases have been placing more responsibility on the nurses' shoulders.[83] Moreover, a patient may sue both the negligent nurse and the hospital, and obtain judgment against both.

These anomalies serve to emphasize the strengths and the limitations of the law in ensuring or protecting patient's rights. They also indicate the importance of understanding the whole scope of professional responsibility, both legal obligations and moral obligations. Such obligations are important, given the nurse's pivotal position in patient care.

SUMMARY AND CONCLUSIONS

In this overview of ethics and of law, an attempt has been made to focus on the context of the patient's moral and legal rights and to suggest approaches toward understanding and analyzing these rights. Codes of ethics are important and substantial components of ethics in nursing practice, but limited in their guidance for day-to-day decision-making. Concepts and principles of ethics are suggested as workable tools for ethical decision-making in health care, and a number of these have been identified. Two major philosophical perspectives are then offered as a tool for ethical decision-making, with the conclusion that no one theory or approach can provide a complete guide to right conduct; rather, some combination of theory and principles will likely be of greatest benefit.

The bases of formalized rights are reviewed, with specific attention to Canadian law and to the legal division of federal and provincial responsibilities in health care. The main divisions of the law in Canada are explained; statute law and tort law are described.

It should be apparent, from the foregoing discussion, that the boundaries between moral rights and legal rights are not as distinct as one might believe. Yet it is important that nurses have a sound general understanding of what the law imposes on them (what they must do) and what morality dictates (what they ought to do). Further, it should be emphasized that respect for patient's moral and legal rights is of increased importance in health care, since much depends on personal relationships.

Significance of the Nurse's Role in the Protection of Patients' Rights

The nurse has a major role to play in the protection of patients' rights. To some degree, patients' rights can be protected only to the extent that the nurse is a concerned person. The nurse's responsibility in the protection of rights is great: of all health professionals, nurses are generally closest to the most vulnerable group of persons – patients. Nurses have sustained contact with patients; they exist throughout the health-care system; and there are comparatively great numbers of nurses in relation to other health professionals.

> The significance of the nurse stems not only from her authority in interpreting, applying, and enforcing the orders of the physician but, in addition, from the fact that she can judge and react to the patient's behaviour more continuously than the physician. From the patient's point of view, he also depends on the nurse as intermediary in the provision of many other institutional services.[84]

Nurses, therefore, become a central communication link between patients and doctors, between patients and other health providers, and among all health-care providers through both verbal communication and written records. They may monitor standards because their presence at the bedside places them in a key position to observe good or poor practice. But the nurse's role, while pivotal, embodies its own set of contradictions and problems.

> What is special about nursing from a moral standpoint is the question of authority and power on the health care team. Special moral dilemmas for nursing may arise out of such power conflicts. Such conflicts frequently involve disagreements about moral principles and judgements ... when the nurse has to decide whether to continue to co-operate on a health care team, whether to follow doctors' instructions, etc. ....[85]

The centrality of the nurse's role in the assurance of patients' rights, and conflicting role dilemmas, will form the basis of the discussion of patients' rights in the next several chapters. A final chapter will address the conflicts of nurses within the health-care organization, conflicts that become apparent during the course of discussion of patients' rights. These conflicts lead to questions. To whom is the nurse accountable? To her employer? To the physician? To the patient? Or to the professional standard?[86]

References for Chapter 2

[1]Tom Beauchamp and James Childress, *Principles of Biomedical Ethics* (New York: Oxford University Press, 1979), p. viii.

[2]*The Gage Canadian Dictionary* (Gage Educational Publishing Ltd., 1973), p. 834.

[3]Harmon L. Smith, "Ethical Considerations in Research Involving Human Subjects," *Social Science and Medicine* 14A (1980): 453.

[4]*Ibid*, p. 453. Reprinted with permission from *Social Science and Medicine* 14A, Harmon L. Smith, "Ethical Considerations in Research Involving Human Subjects," copyright 1980, Pergamon Press, Ltd.

[5]Florence Nightingale, *Notes on Nursing* (New York: Dover Publications Inc., 1969), pp. 38–39, 125.

[6]*The Nurse's Dilemma: Ethical Considerations in Nursing Practice* (Geneva: International Council of Nurses, 1977), p. 72.

[7]Marianne Lamb, "Nursing Ethics in Canada: Two Decades," unpublished Masters of Nursing thesis (Edmonton: University of Alberta, 1981), p. 82.

[8]"International Code of Nursing Ethics," *Nursing Outlook* 53 (September 1973): p. 1070.

[9]M. Josephine Flaherty, "Two Canadian Nursing Codes," *Westminster Institute Review* 1:3(October 1981):11. For a more complete discussion of the CNA Code see "Reflections on a Code of Ethics for Nurses in Canada," a background paper prepared by M. Simone Roach. Ottawa: Canadian Nurses Association, 1980.

[10]Martin Benjamin and Joy Curtis. *Ethics in Nursing* (New York: Oxford University Press, 1981), p. 6.

[11]Beauchamp and Childress, p. 5.

[12]Dianne B. Uustall, "Values Clarification in Nursing: Application to Practice," *American Journal of Nursing* 78 (December 1978): 2060.

[13]Michael Tooley, "Abortion and Infanticide," *Philosophy and Public Affairs* 2:1 (1972): 37–65.

[14]Joseph Fletcher, "Indicators of Humanhood: A Tentative Profile of Man." *The Hastings Center Report* 2:5 (November 1972): 1–4.

[15]Edward W. Keyserlinck, *Sanctity of Life or Quality of Life* (Ottawa: Law Reform Commission, 1979), pp. 60–65.

[16]Gerald Dworkin, "Autonomy and Behaviour Control," in *Ethical Issues in Modern Medicine*, ed. Robert Hunt and John Arras (Palo Alto: Mayfield Publishing Co., 1977), p. 366.

[17]Charles Fried, *Medical Experimentation: Personal Integrity and Social Policy* (New York: American Elsevier Publishing Co., Inc., 1974), p. 102.

[18]Bernard Gert and Charles M. Culver, "Paternalistic Behaviour," *Philosophy and Public Affairs* 6:1 (Fall 1976): 44-50; and Gerald Dworkin, "Paternalism," in *Moral Problems in Medicine*, ed. Samuel Gorovitz *et al.* (Englewood Cliffs, N.J.: Prentice-Hall Inc., 1976), p. 185.

[19]Beauchamp and Childress, p. 162.

[20]Joel Feinberg, "Legal Paternalism," *Canadian Journal of Philosophy* 1 (September 1971): 111.

[21]Franz J. Ingelfinger, "Arrogance," *New England Journal of Medicine* 303 (December 25, 1980): 1507–1511.

[22]Feinberg, p. 120.

[23]Beauchamp and Childress, p. 60.

[24]*Ibid*, p. 169.

[25]William K. Frankena, "The Nature of Social Justice," in *Moral Problems in*

Medicine, eds. Samuel Gorovitz, Andrew L. Jameton, Ruth Macklin, John M. O' Connor, Eugene V. Perrin, Beverly Page St. Clair, and Susan Sherwin (Englewood Cliffs, N.J.: Prentice-Hall, Inc., 1976), p. 431.

[26]Tom L. Beauchamp and Norman E. Bowie, *Ethical Theory and Business* (Englewood Cliffs, N.J.: Prentice Hall, 1979), p. 30.

[27]Beauchamp and Bowie, p. 31; and Gregory Vlastos, "Justice and Equality," in *Ethical Issues in Business* eds. T. Donaldson and P. Werhane (Englewood Cliffs: Prentice-Hall, 1979), pp. 257-270.

[28]Beauchamp and Bowie, p. 31.

[29]For further discussion of the principle of beneficence see Beauchamp and Childress, Chapter 5.

[30]For further discussion of the principle of non-maleficence see Beauchamp and Childress, Chapter 4.

[31]Beauchamp and Childress, p. 204.

[32]Fidelity and veracity are discussed in Beauchamp and Childress, Chapter 7.

[33]John M. O'Conner, "Introduction" in *Moral Problems in Medicine*, eds. Gorovitz *et al*, p. 16.

[34]Beauchamp and Childress, pp. 20-21.

[35]Robert G. Olson, *Ethics: A Short Introduction* (New York: Random House, 1978), p. 4.

[36]William A. Frankena, *Ethics* (Englewood Cliffs, N.J.: Prentice-Hall Inc., 1963), p. 30.

[37]Beauchamp and Childress, p. 33.

[38]Immanuel Kant, "Fundamental Principles of the Metaphysics of Morals," in *Moral Problems in Medicine*, ed. Samuel Gorovitz *et al* (Englewood Cliffs, N.J.: Prentice-Hall Inc., 1976) p. 23.

[39]Beauchamp and Childress, pp. 33-35.

[40]*Ibid*, p. 43.

[41]Olson, p. 145.

[42]Anne Davis, *Ethical Dilemmas in Nursing Practice* (New York: Appleton-Century-Crofts, 1978), pp. 27-29.

[43]Frankena, William A., *Ethics*, p. 35.

[44]Beauchamp and Childress, p. 40.

[45]William K. Frakena, ETHICS, © 1973 2nd Ed., p. 60. Reprinted by permission of Prentice-Hall, Inc., Englewood Cliffs, New Jersey.

[46]Lorne E. Rozovsky, "Health Law Seminar," University of Alberta, November 1980.

[47]Discussion with E. Picard, Professor of Law, University of Alberta, April 1979.

[48]Gerald Gall, *The Canadian Legal System* (Toronto: The Carswell Co. Ltd., 1977), pp. 15-17.

[49]Unless otherwise indicated, the material in this section is drawn from G. Gall, *The Canadian Legal System* (Toronto: The Carswell Co. Ltd., 1977), pp. 23-30, 39-46.

[50]Ellen I. Picard, *Legal Liability of Doctors and Hospitals in Canada* (Toronto: The Carswell Company Ltd., 1978) p. 4.

[51]Gall, p. 180. The reader is encouraged to note pp. 193-195 as well for a discussion of the purposes and advantages of precedent and *stare decisis*.

[52]Gall, pp. 53-55.

[53]Richard J. Van Loon and Michael S. Whittington, *The Canadian Political System: Environment, Structure, and Process*, 2nd ed. (Toronto: McGraw-Hill Ryerson Ltd., 1976), pp. 480-482.

[54]*Ibid*, pp. 483-484. The BNA Act is now incorporated as part of the Constitution Act of 1982.

[55] Lee Soderstrom, *The Canadian Health System* (London: Croom Helm, 1978), p. 16.

[56] *Ibid*, p. 17.

[57] Picard, p. 2.

[58] Unless otherwise indicated, material in this section is drawn from G. Gall, pp. 30–36. Reprinted with the kind permission of the Publisher, The Carswell Co. Ltd., Agincourt, Ontario.

[59] Tevie H. Miller and Colin Taylor, "Criminal Law and the Nurse," in *Contemporary Issues in Canadian Law for Nurses*, eds. Shirley R. Good and Janet C. Kerr (Toronto: Holt, Rinehart and Winston of Canada Ltd., 1973), p. 20.

[60] The reader is referred to the chapter by Miller and Taylor for further detail about the Criminal Code.

[61] Copies of these statutes can be obtained from Queen's Printers' offices in each province for a nominal charge.

[62] Alberta Association of Registered Nurses, *Bylaws*, February 1980.

[63] Picard, p. 52.

[64] Jack M. Giles and A. Keith Mitchell, "Nurses and Contracts," in *Contemporary Issues in Canadian Law for Nurses*, ed. Shirley T. Good and Janet C. Kerr (Toronto: Holt, Rinehart and Winston of Canada, Ltd., 1973), pp. 40–47.

[65] Picard, pp. 52–54.

[66] Lorne E. Rozovsky, *Canadian Hospital Law*, 2nd ed. (Ottawa: Canadian Hospital Association, 1979), p. 17.

[67] Kathleen M. Fenner, *Ethics and Law in Nursing* (New York: Van Nostrand Reinhold Co., 1980), p. 91.

[68] For further clarification of contract law in relation to nursing, see Shirley T. Good and Janet C. Kerr, Chapter 5.

[69] Gall, p. 33.

[70] Picard, pp. 45–46.

[71] J.W. Rose, "Torts and Liability," in *Contemporary Issues in Canadian Law for Nurses*, ed. Shirley R. Good and Janet C. Kerr (Toronto: Holt, Rinehart and Winston of Canada, Ltd., 1973), p. 54.

[72] *Ibid*, p. 54.

[73] The reader is encouraged to read J.W. Rose, "Torts and Liability," for further clarification.

[74] Rose, p. 55.

[75] Corinne Sklar, "Unwarranted Disclosure," *Canadian Nurse* 74 (May 1978): 8.

[76] Picard, p. 49.

[77] Rose, p. 52.

[78] Picard, p. 49.

[79] Eli Bernzweig, *The Nurse's Liability for Malpractice* (New York: McGraw-Hill Book Co., 1975), p. 31.

[80] Corinne Sklar, "Error of Judgement: Is It Always Negligence?" *Canadian Nurse* 75 (March 1979): 14–16.

[81] See, for example, Corinne Sklar, "The Legal Significance of Charting," *Canadian Nurse* 74 (March 1978): 10–11; Peter E. Grady, "The Law and Nurses' Notes," in *Contemporary Issues in Canadian Law for Nurses*, ed. Shirley R. Good and Janet C. Kerr (Toronto: Holt, Rinehart and Winston of Canada Ltd., 1973), pp. 127–129. See also Corinne Sklar, "On Trial," *Canadian Nurse* 75 (February 1979): pp. 8–10.

[82] Sklar, "Error of Judgement: Is It Always Negligence?" p. 14.

[83] See Corinne Sklar, "The Extension of Hospital Liability: A Landmark Decision in the Making," *Canadian Nurse* 76 (February 1980): 8–11, 48. Also see

Corinne Sklar, "Sinners or Saints? The Legal Perspective," *Canadian Nurse* 75 (November 1979): 14-16, and "Sinners or Saints? The Legal Perspective, Part Two," *Canadian Nurse* 75 (December 1979): pp. 16-21. Because of the timeliness of legal cases, readers should consult current journals.

[84]Daisy L. Tagliacozzo and Hans O. Mauksch, "The Patient's View of the Patient's Role," in *Humanizing Hospital Care*, ed. Gerald P. Turner and Joseph Mapa (Toronto: McGraw-Hill Ryerson, 1979), p. 81.

[85]Beauchamp and Childress, pp. ix-x.

[86]Jane Greenlaw, "To Whom is the Nurse Accountable?" *Nursing Law and Ethics* 1:1 (January 1980): p. 3.

SUGGESTED REFERENCES FOR FURTHER STUDY, CHAPTER 2

Beauchamp, Tom L. and Childress, James F. *Principles of Biomedical Ethics*. New York: Oxford University Press, 1979.

This book focuses on the principles the authors have identified as most significant in biomedical ethics: autonomy, non-maleficence, beneficence, and justice. Introductory material is provided on morality and ethical theories as a prelude to the discussion of moral principles. Professional-patient relationships and the place of ideals, virtues, and integrity as shapers of morality are also discussed. A series of cases and a number of codes of ethics are included in the appendices.

Benjamin, Martin and Curtis, Joy. *Ethics in Nursing*. New York: Oxford University Press, 1981.

Benjamin and Curtis provide a useful introductory text in the identification and the analysis of ethical issues in health care and nursing, based on systematic philosophical enquiry. They discuss moral dilemmas in nursing and ethical principles and theories, and analyze nurse-client, nurse-physician, and nurse-nurse relationships in health care. They conclude with a brief discussion of personal responsibility for institutional and public policy, highlighting three issues in nursing: short-staffing, nursing strikes, and hospice care. The book, which includes thirty-one cases and a brief appendix, is a valuable resource for education in nursing ethics.

Curtin, Leah and Flaherty, M. Josephine. *Nursing Ethics: Theories and Pragmatics*. Bowie, Md: Robert J. Brady Co., 1982.

This American-Canadian author team has provided an excellent textbook in nursing ethics. True to its title, the book offers a combination of the theoretical and the practical. In the first two chapters, the nature of human rights is examined and health care as a right is discussed. The nature of ethical dilemmas and the guidance provided by ethical theory are then addressed, and a model for ethical decision-making is provided. In the final theoretical section, nurses' multiple relationships are explored—their contract with society, and their relationships to the patient, the profession, the family, and other nurses, physicians, and the institution. The final section of the book includes fifteen highly generative case studies that reflect a wide range of ethical issues in a diverstiy of practice settings. Each study includes an analysis, generally followed by a commentary that provides valuable insights into ethical decision-making in nursing practice.

Davis, A.J. and Aroskar, M.A. *Ethical Dilemmas and Nursing Practice*. New York: Appleton-Century-Crofts, 1978.

The first four chapters in this book contain introductory material on health-care ethics and ethical dilemmas, ethical approaches, professional ethics, and patients' rights. Six chapters are then devoted to specific issues: informed consent, abortion, dying and death, behavior control, mental retardation, and public policy and health-care delivery. In each of these chapters the historical, social and legal context of each issue is presented, followed by a discussion on ethical implications for nursing. A brief final chapter contains case studies with questions for study.

Fenner, Kathleen M. *Ethics and Law in Nursing.* New York: Van Nostrand Reinhold Co., 1980.

Fenner's book consists of five chapters, the first of which includes a rationale for the study of ethics, values, and law. In a second chapter, devoted to ethics, Fenner discusses the nature of ethics, moral development, and codes of ethics, comparing several professional codes. A short chapter is devoted to values clarification, followed by a chapter on law, which includes a brief discussion on origins of law, principles of law, and legal responsibilities of health providers. In a final chapter, Fenner touches on several controversial issues including abortion, collective bargaining, behavior control, death and dying, genetic engineering, the environmental crises, and the allocation of scarce medical resources. Suggestions for further reading with brief annotations, case studies, exercises, or games are provided for each chapter.

Gall, Gerald L. *The Canadian Legal System.* Toronto: The Carswell Co. Ltd., 1977.

In this 300-page book, Gall provides a description of the Canadian legal system. The book commences with a discussion on the nature of law which leads into a terse description of the sources of law. Gall presents background material on common-law and civil-law systems before a discussion of the constitutional basis of Canadian law. The role of the courts in Canada, the division of federal and provincial court responsibility, and the role of lawyers and judges (including a study on judicial attitudes and on the doctrines of precedent and *stare decisis*), rules and principles of statutory interpretaton, and justice in the administrative process are discussed. Gall concludes with a discussion of trends in law, in the legal profession, in continuing education, and in law reform.

Good, Shirley, R. and Kerr, Janet C. eds. *Contemporary Issues in Canadian Law for Nurses.* Toronto: Holt, Rinehart and Winston of Canada, Ltd., 1973.

In an attempt to meet the nurse's needs for a clear and concise explanation of Canadian law relevant to nursing, the authors have developed this book of readings. The book has been divided into three sections: the first deals with general aspects of Canadian law such as criminal law, nurses and contracts, and torts and liability. Section two focuses on law related to nursing practice: provincial variations in nursing functions, liability for negligence, legal aspects of mental disorder, and other topics. Law related to nursing education, research, and labor relations are discussed in section three. Because this book focuses on Canadian law, it is a relevant resource for all nurses.

Gorovitz, Samuel, Jametin, Andrew L., Macklin, Ruth, O'Connor, John H., Perrin, Eugene V., St. Clair, Beverly Page, and Sherwin, Susan, eds. *Moral Problems in Medicine.* Englewood Cliffs, N.J.: Prentice-Hall Inc., 1976.

This anthology is presented in four major sections. The first section deals with moral philosophy and includes a general introduction, plus excerpts from the writings of Mill, Kant, and Sartre. A second section is devoted to moral problems in the physician-patient relationship and includes articles on confidentiality, truth-telling, coercion and paternalism. Abortion, birth defects, and death and dignity are subjects of the series of articles in the section on moral problems concerning life and death. A final section focuses on issues of social justice, a right to health care, and allocation of scarce medical resources.

Picard, Ellen I. *Legal Liability of Doctors and Hospitals in Canada*. Toronto: The Carswell Company Limited, 1978.

Designed for use by both the legal profession and health-care professionals, this book is a resource and summary of Canadian law relevant to doctors and hospitals. Picard details the conduct of a civil action, describes the doctor-patient relationship, and outlines the substance of relevant civil actions before describing the nature of consent and the basis of negligence. Each discussion is replete with case examples and lengthy footnotes documenting the specific legal cases or relevant statutes. Defense in negligence, proof of negligence, and the roles of the physician in the court are discussed, and physician and hospital liability are described. An extensive appendix includes an index of legal cases and case digests, and serves as a valuable reference resource.

Sharpe, Gilbert and Sawyer, Glenn. *Doctors and the Law*. Toronto: Butterworth & Co. (Canada) Ltd., 1978.

This book is designed to deal with the most significant and practical problems of most physicians in regard to health-law topics. Included are some historical highlights in Canadian health care, and a brief introduction to relevant legal concepts and terms, followed by a discourse on consent to treatment, "Good-Samaritan" laws, hospital liability, medical-staff privileges, confidentiality, and medical records. The authors then discuss areas where the legal system and the medical-care system interface, for example, in medical-legal reports, malpractice suits, and licensing and regulation. Additional topics, such as the law and psychiatry and experimentation are discussed, as is the need for medico-legal education. The lengthy appendices include a summary of provincial legislation and a listing of Canadian health-law cases since 1900, referenced to chapter discussion.

The Nurse's Dilemma: Ethical Considerations in Nursing Practice. **Barbara L. Tate, Project Director**. Geneva: International Council of Nurses, 1977.

This booklet is an edited compilation of ethical problems based on real-life situations of nurses in many countries. Its purpose is to serve as a basis for discussion among nurses in regards to appropriate behaviors in complex ethical situations. The problem-situations are organized according to the components of the ICN Code and each problem is followed by a series of discussion questions. The appendices include a number of pledges, codes, statements, and guidelines.

CHAPTER 3 The Right To Be Informed

The patient's right to be informed encompasses both legal and moral rights. Legally, patients have a right to make decisions, based on adequate information, regarding the care and treatment of their persons: they have a right to be free of interference from other individuals, or the state, in relation to treatment without their consent. Morally, patients have a right to be treated as autonomous persons, and to be told the truth. The legal basis of the patient's right to informed consent to treatment is found in tort law; the moral basis of the patient's right to be informed is embodied in the ethical principles of autonomy, veracity, and beneficence.

There are several levels and types of information required in order that a consumer/patient might be informed. The consumer needs information about health promotion and health-prevention strategies, and information about the health system. When the consumer actually becomes a patient, by entering the system of care, he or she needs further information about expected social behavior in that system, about his or her own diagnosis, treatment plan, and prognosis.

This chapter will focus on the right to be informed, as it relates to the principles of autonomy, veracity, beneficence, and paternalism, before turning to the legal doctrine of informed consent. Autonomy (defined in the previous chapter) is liberty of action: autonomous individuals freely determine their own course of action,

47

based upon their personal choice of a plan of action.[1] Patients must have enough information to make an informed decision, and they must be allowed to decide. Veracity, the obligation to tell the truth and not to deceive others,[2] requires that the health professional act to ensure that accurate and necessary information is supplied to the patient. In addition, the health professional has a duty to provide information to consumers/patients, and an obligation not to restrict information. ✳

HOW TO STAY HEALTHY

Included in the consumer's right to be informed is the right to information about how to stay healthy. Until the 1960s, information relating to health promotion* and disease prevention was focused largely on prenatal, well-child, and school-health programs. Consumers who wanted to understand their health situation and to effect preventive strategies had access to very limited information.

In the 1940s, new medical technologies were being discovered rapidly. As these technologies were implemented, there was a concomitant increase in specialization of health personnel and a growth of health professions. Health professionals were caught up in a knowledge explosion that seemed to prove misleading at times, even to the professionals. Scientific medicine was envisioned as the answer to a multitude of health problems, and the knowledge gap between the health professional and the health consumer widened.

Technological advances added to the mystique of medicine. Consumers began to believe that the medical establishment had all the answers to health problems.

---

*Aaron Antonovsky, a leading medical sociologist, has provided a thought-provoking analysis of the problem of suitable health promotion. He suggests that the whole system has for too long been focused on the causes of disease rather than on those factors that maintain and promote health. (See A. Antonovsky, *Health Stress and Coping*, San Francisco, Jossey-Bass Publishers, Inc., 1979). Such preoccupation hinders the ability of health professionals to facilitate "health" promotion in its fullest sense. Given the present lack of knowledge in this regard, this discussion about the consumer's right to know how to stay healthy is largely limited to a disease-model of health promotion, that is, a model that focuses on those factors known to cause disease.

Man's instinctual self-care and self-regulating potential and resources became censored and silenced....As a result, health sciences and health technology became more and more advanced and complex, and in turn, more power and authority was vested in the medical profession and health institutions.[3]

The unrealistic expectations created by these developments have proven detrimental to health professionals and to consumers.

Health information has become more available to consumers since the 1960s. In the eighties, consumers are literally deluged with information about health promotion and illness prevention. In Canada, health promotion is a fundamental part of an articulated health policy.[4] Canadians have been urged to change their lifestyles to prevent disease, and to direct their energies toward health-promotion activities such as jogging, exercise, and better nutrition. Anti-smoking and anti-drinking campaigns have received considerable governmental encouragement and participation. All these promotional campaigns have been accompanied by information relevant to healthy living, relayed via television, radio, milk cartons, family-allowance mailing inserts, newspapers, and workshop presentations.

A plethora of printed material directed toward consumer health has flooded newsstands and public bookstores during the past decade, as well. The printed material contains a variety of information about basic health practices, about minor illness remedies, and about the health-care system. Most of the pamphlets and books are designed to equip the consumer, through information and understanding, with a greater ability to move towards sound health practices. Many consumers have trouble sorting through the available health information to assess its accuracy and relevancy to their situation. There would seem to be a need for health professionals to develop ways for consumers to receive more accurate and reliable information, and to help consumers become more adept at evaluating the competing claims of health guarantees and illness remedies.

Health professionals may experience moral conflicts in their health-promotion and health-education efforts because of the changing and uncertain state of medical knowledge regarding healthful practices. These moral conflicts are particularly apparent in dealing with young children, especially when a professional sponsors programs that attempt to modify personal health-practices of school pupils and their families, because evidence of the benefits of the prescribed health practices may be open to question.[5]

Health professionals have a duty to provide information. But at the same time, consumers have an obligation to become informed, to seek information necessary for good health, and to become involved in the care of their health. Two very prominent "movements" have developed: the self-help movement and the self-care movement. These phenomena demonstrate areas where consumers have taken responsibility for their health and their health care and have moved towards a different health-professional-patient relationship. Many health professionals view these "movements" as contentious; they are uneasy about consumers' attempts to redefine the scope of health-professional prerogative, power, and paternalism.

Self-Help and Self-Care

These two consumer movements are directed towards the regaining of a sense of control over one's health care. Several reasons have been suggested for the consumer's interest in health care, among them a "demystification" of medical care, an increase in consumerism, an increased level of public education, a lack of availability of convenient medical services, and an emphasis on cost containment.[6] In addition, the success of self-help groups in areas where medical intervention has proven only minimally successful – groups like Alcoholics Anonymous and Weight Watchers – has further stimulated interest in self-help and self-care strategies.

"Self-help" refers to a group phenomenon based on mutal concern. Self-help groups have existed for some time as support structures and as change mechanisms for individuals with common needs or concerns. There are four types of self-help groups:

1) those that focus on behavioral control, such as Weight Watchers or Alcoholics Anonymous;

2) those that focus on coping with a shared predicament, such as Parents Without Partners, ostomy assocations, mastectomy clubs, or "lost-chord" clubs;

3) those that are survival-oriented, which are comprised of people society has discriminated against, such as native brotherhood associations or feminist health collectives;

4) those that focus on personal growth, such as meditation groups and creative-thinking groups.[7]

Members of these groups function as both consumers of and providers of care. "Professionals may be assigned an absent, secondary, or collaborative role"[8] in these groups.

Whatever the assigned role of the health professional, at a minimum, health professionals must acknowledge the powerful impact such groups have had in modifying behavior and in enhancing the quality of life for many participants. It has been estimated that, in the United States, some five million people now belong to physical or mental self-help groups.[9] That so many people join self-help groups should encourage health professionals to see these groups as partners in health care, and as groups worthy of attention and support. Although there are some problems within some of the groups – for example, their stress on conformity and the focus on maintenance of the group at the expense of the needs of individual members – these concerns should not pre-empt a belief in the potential benefits of self-help groups. Rather, nurses and other health professionals need to become better informed about self-help groups in the community. Health-care workers should provide accurate information to consumers, and give permission for them to join such organizations.[10] While some have proposed that professionals should become more directly involved, and that universities should be equipping health professionals for such involvement, others recognize that too much interference with self-help groups could undermine a "value uniquely cherished by the self-help; the perceived ability to help itself."[11]

"Self-care" has been defined as "a process whereby a lay person functions on his/her own behalf in health promotion and prevention and in disease detection and treatment at the level of the primary health resource in the health care system."[12] Self-care generally refers to more individualistic behavior than that implied in the collective process of self-help, and is even more challenging to professional power.

Fairly prominent in the concept of self-care is the notion that "man has a natural capacity to care for himself but...the health care system distorts and destroys the growth and development of this capacity."[13] Ivan Illich and many other writers would concur with the idea that the health-care system often interferes with a person's self-care ability.[14]

In Canadian health-care rhetoric, much attention has been focused on the development of healthy lifestyles and greater responsibility for self-care. Self-care has been described as a strategy for both health restoration and health maintenance,[15] and considerable attention has been given to the potential benefits of self-care by countries in the western world. Victor Fuchs, a health economist, encapsulates the intent of recent political statements:

> By changing institutions and creating new programs we can make medical care more accessible and deliver it more efficiently, but the greatest potential for improving health lies in what we do and don't do for and to ourselves.[16]

Since the thrust for health-care initiatives rests with the consumer, and with the desire for autonomy and responsiblity, the self-care movement can be seen as a positive influence. However, as health planners, health providers, and politicians have become involved in promoting self-care, some fear that self-care might become a political strategy against more equitable care, or that the self-care approach could easily become one of "blaming the victim."[17]

As the pinch of cost containment in health services becomes more acute, excuses may be found to justify substituting self-care for properly trained manpower and well-developed health services,[18] particularly for the disadvantaged. Those who tout self-care as the solution for health problems might neglect to provide services for information and education for self-care. Because effective self-care requires valuing health, motivation, and follow-through, it has been suggested that the self-care movement is a white, middle-class movement unsuited to the disadvantaged.

Self-care might cause another problem: the persons most wronged by society may be blamed for their difficulties. But structural problems such as poverty, slum life, air pollution, or poor nutrition are generally beyond consumer control. Further, the short-sighted blaming approach neglects the fact that the locus of major improvements in the health status of North Americans during the last fifty years has been through changes in environmental conditions – such as sanitation and social status – and not medical care and self-care.[19]

Whatever the limitations, it would seem that the moves towards increased self-care and increased individual responsibility for care represent advantages for both consumers and providers. This is true only insofar as such moves do not compromise or distort good health-care delivery, or be seen as a substitute for needed social changes, by becoming a panacea for the ills of the health-care system.

Self-care activities can be wide-ranging, from jogging for one's health to learning to administer one's own insulin. For consumers to be involved in safe and effective self-care practices, health professionals have an obligation to provide adequate information and to teach suitable health-care measures. Such teaching would necessarily include information about the significance of symptoms in making decisions about when to seek care, and instruction in those treatments consumers might well handle on their own.[20] Health professionals have been cautious about information sharing, believing that "a little knowledge is a dangerous thing," and have often restricted the information they would release to consumers. This reluctance should be recognized; it is based on a need to protect the health professional's scope of practice. It does not necessarily protect the consumer. Consumers can only be responsible, autonomous, and health-seeking in their behavior if they have access to adequate information and resources.

Dorothea Orem has developed a conceptual model for nursing that has, as its central focus, the concept of self-care. Orem describes the need for nursing as based on the consumer's need for assistance.

> As an assisting art, nursing is the complex ability to accomplish or to contribute to the accomplishment of the patient's usual and therapeutic self-care by compensating for or aiding the patient in overcoming the conditions or disabilities that cause him 1) to be unable to act for himself, 2) to refrain from acting for himself, or 3) to act ineffectively in caring for himself.[21]

INFORMATION ABOUT THE SYSTEM

Information about the health-care system is required for at least three reasons: patients must know how to get into the health-care system when they need care; they need to know about the norms and expectations of the system when they become patients; and they need to understand the organization and structure of the system, as well as the routines and procedures that form the system of care.[22] In addition, consumers would benefit by knowing the costs of care. Canadians have had to pay scant attention to the costs of health care, because those costs are covered by national health-insurance programs. The population is only now becoming aware of the magnitude of health-care costs.

Most of the books directed toward consumer health concerns include considerable material about the various professional and occupational workers who provide care and treatment, including medical specialists and nurses. As well, the books include information about the point of entry into the health-care system, namely, the family doctor or general practitioner. But, to initiate a first contact with the health-care system in a responsible manner, consumers must state their case clearly. And they must be assertive in cases where their need may be more acute than a receptionist's assessment might indicate. Only consumers can know the extent of their pain or discomfort; only consumers can speak for the need for prompt care when required. Where the consumer cannot effectively represent his or her case, a community-health nurse or other community worker may need to assume an advocacy function to help the client (the consumer) into the treatment system.

Once consumers have gained entry into the system, they must know how to be responsible consumers: they must recognize the need to clearly outline signs and symptoms of their problem. Nurses can be instrumental in teaching patients to think through, to document, and to list their health problems, as well as to actively seek the answers they require from the physician in order to understand and to deal with that problem. Physicians and nurses frequently play a game of twenty questions with patients; some adjustment of that format for diagnosis and treatment planning might yield a more productive use of time, understanding, and commitment to the problem and its resolution. Even a young child can be taught, for example, that doctors and nurses are like detectives when they are trying to discover the health problem, and that the patient has to help them by carefully providing as many facts as possible.

One author emphasizes that the most important source of information to the physician making a diagnosis is the patient, and that the entire process of diagnosis and evaluation therapy depends on statements made by the patient. If a patient's version of the complaint is unreliable and inaccurate, diagnosis and treatment can be misdirected.[23] Therefore, greater patient teaching aimed at enhancing patient proficiency and understanding in this area can lead to better patient care. At the same time, the importance of listening skills for physicians and other health professionals must be emphasized. Patients' comments, complaints, and feedback must be heard to ensure that problems rather than symptoms are understood and treated.[24]

At least one study has indicated that, in spite of the talk about the consumer's right to information, there is considerable discrepancy between the expectations of patients regarding information-seeking in the physician-patient encounter and patients' subsequent behavior. Patients continue to play a passive role; doctors continue to dominate the relationship.[25] Consumers are not prepared to pursue information for a variety of reasons, which may include inexperience and intimidation. Health professionals would do well to provide more information routinely, even if the consumer does not appear to be seeking it.[26]

Patients also need to know the next steps in their care and treatment. If they are admitted to a hospital or other health-care institution, they need to become acquainted with the various types of personnel involved in their care and with the various departments that will become involved. Patients who will receive care in the home need to know about the various community agencies and supports available, such as homemaker services, meals-on-wheels programs, and visiting home nurses. Because of their own familiarity with available services, most health professionals assume that others will also know about these services. That assumption is not generally correct, and greater attention should be given to providing this information.

The routines and procedures in any large institution can be confusing to the uninitiated. Hospital nurses can help patients by orienting them to the hospital environment and its routines. Booklets that describe general hospital rules – visiting hours, safety of valuables, and so on – are important, but they are no substitute for the information a nurse should provide. The nurse should ensure that the information is understood. Sometimes health professionals assume that there are minimal rules in health care, particularly in comparison to hospitals of the late 1800s. For example, in 1897 the Cornwall General Hospital had these rules:

5. *Patients must be in their proper places in the ward at mealtimes and during the visits of the physicians and surgeons, and always at 8:00 o'clock at night, and no patient shall leave the hospital grounds at any time, or be absent at the hour of morning visit without special leave from the Lady Superintendent.*

10. *Every patient shall retire to bed at 9:00 p.m. from First May to First November, and at 8:00 p.m. from November to May; and those who are able shall rise at 6:00 a.m. in Summer and 7:00 a.m. in Winter.*

11. *Such patients as are able, in the opinion of the physician and surgeons, shall assist in nursing others, or in such services as the Lady Superintendent may require.*[27]

We can laugh at some of these rules – yet today there are "unwritten rules," which keep the consumer at a disadvantage. For example, the rules concerning self-discharge are not always clear to the patient; the general routines involved in physician visits to the ward are not always interpreted to the patient. Frequently, expectations regarding how much patients are to do for themselves are not clear; some patients are embarrassed or angered to learn that they are looked upon as lazy or unwilling.

Patients need to know how to succeed within the health-care system.[28] For too many patients, efforts to be a "good patient," to meet perceived obligations, and to co-operate in recovery are hampered by inadequate communication within the health-care system.[29]

Nurses must encourage patients to ask questions about diagnosis, treatments, and prognosis; nurses must also advise other staff about a patient's lack of knowledge and the patient's state of discomfort or pain. In turn, all health professionals must listen to patients and be willing to clarify or rectify their own assumptions about particular patient needs.[30] Sometimes the cause of the patient's upset cannot easily be discerned by staff or articulated by the patient. Health professionals should be sensitive to the fear patients may have of the unfamiliar and the unknown; they should be sensitive to the suffering that patients experience as a result of lost hopes and dreams.[31]

INFORMATION ABOUT DIAGNOSIS AND TREATMENT

Not all patients are able to cope with complete information about their diagnosis and treatment; but most health-care consumers want the information, for only in knowing can they exercise their autonomy. Our health-care delivery practices have fostered a sense of dependency. As a result, some consumers have not been able to change their idea that a patient should be passive and obedient. But most patients are thinking, valuing, responsible individuals who want information so they may make informed choices. These consumers want to know the details in a language they can understand. They want to be told about the anatomy and physiology of their problem, the diagnosis and prognosis, the therapy, and the predictable course of events.[32] Many of them have become quite vocal, in fact, in demanding that health professionals recognize their right to determine what happens to their bodies. Probably nowhere has this claim been more clearly articulated than in the women's movement.

In spite of these well-articulated pleas for recognition of rights to information, many patients still feel out of control of what is happening to them, often because they lack essential information about their diagnosis and treatment. Knowledge or information is power, especially when it is not shared.[33] Power can be further maintained by making the information as "mysterious and inaccessible" as possible so that only health professionals can understand what it means.[34]

There are, of course, patients who do not want information, who do not want to make treatment decisions. Some patients may want the doctor to make decisions for them, since they perceive this to be the doctor's role. Others may request a physician or nurse to make decisions because the information about their health problem is ambiguous; conflicting types of treatment might exist. There may also be times when the truth is "more than the person can bear;"[35] the patient may need time before the full details are disclosed. Charges of paternalism may be leveled against doctors or nurses who fail to disclose the full details, yet the duty to the patient may require some careful measuring of information. To force unwanted information on a patient is also to act paternalistically, and to violate that patient's autonomy.[36]

Health professionals must be sensitive to patient needs, respecting the patient's need to become dependent for a time, but always seeking to confirm the patient's potential abilities to deal with the situation and providing assurance of professional support. Interprofessional consultation is essential so that patients can receive information as they are ready for it. Anxiety can interfere with the patient's ability to hear, understand, and remember. Health professionals must work to reduce uncertainties and anxieties, providing what information is known, and remaining available to the patient.[37]

Legal Hurdles

Difficulties arise in meeting the duty or obligation to provide information to the patient. Nurses, in particular, frequently possess far more information than they are legally allowed to give. Yet they are with the patient, and therefore subject to questions, more continually than any other health professional.

Traditionally, to interpret to patients the results of medical tests and diagnoses has been considered a medical responsibility and prerogative under statutory law. As these statute responsibilities become implemented, it is not uncommon for representatives of physicians' groups, nurses' associations, and hospital associations to establish guidelines related to medical-nursing responsibilities. The guidelines then become a basis for policies in specific hospitals and health agencies.

In one province, for example, the guideline regarding the interpretation of medical tests and diagnoses to the patient states:

> *Although this is a medical responsibility, the nurse may assist when properly informed by the physician as to the plan of care. Communication between physician and nurse is very important in this area.*[38]

This type of guideline often leaves the nurse in a dilemma, since the term "properly informed" is ambiguous.

An extreme case of the nurse's dilemma is evident in the Tuma case. A nurse in Twin Falls, Idaho provided information to the patient about treatment alternatives for leukemia. When the physician made a complaint, the nurse was censured and her license revoked* because she should not have volunteered the information. Many of her colleagues agreed that she had overstepped her duties: she had included, in her discussion with the patient, infor-

---

*The nurse's license was subsequently reinstated by a decision of the Supreme Court of Idaho, not on the merits of the case but because the Idaho Nurse Practice Act does not define "unprofessional conduct." See "Selected Court Decisions," *Nursing Law and Ethics* 1 (January 1980): 7.

mation about non-traditional treatment methods. There are anomalies in this particular situation, but the case raises an important legal and ethical question: how much information can nurses safely give to patients?[39]

Because they must be extremely careful about sharing information, nurses have often become the bearers of good news only: doctors bear the bad news. This happens when patients are recovering from exploratory surgery, for example. Patients often ask the nurse about the findings of the surgery. As a general rule, nurses do not hesitate to provide welcome news – that all is well, that no cancer was found. But when cancer has been confirmed, nurses frequently feel compelled to suggest that the patient ask the doctor about the results. By referring the question to the physician, the nurse has, in effect, told the patient that the news is bad. Patients who realize this are left with no way to express their hurt, anger, or pain.

RIGHT TO THE MEDICAL RECORD

Do patients have a right to their medical records? If they are given verbal information about their diagnoses and treatments, should they be denied the right to see the written information? Since so many other persons have access to written records, is it sensible to exclude patients from such access?

Although patients have a legal right to the information on their records, the way to obtain that information is not clear. The actual documents belong to the hospital and serve as a record of a patient's health care and a means of communication amongst staff regarding that patient. Although the patient is not entitled to possess the record, in at least three provinces by statutory law, and in other jurisdictions by case law, there is legislative provision for the patient to see and to reproduce the record.[40]

But in practice, patients must rely on health professionals to communicate the contents of their charts or records. Such a practice places patients at the mercy of the health professionals' willingness to share the information. Lawyers have commonly advised that if patients request a chart, they should be allowed to see it. If patients are denied access to their charts by the hospital authorities, their only recourse is to apply to the court to have the records made available. Such an action undermines the provider-patient relationship. This is not to deny that occasional instances may arise where access may be reasonably restricted to protect patients or their families.

In December 1980, the *Report of the Commission of Inquiry Into the Confidentiality of Health Information* (the Krever Commission) was released. Although this was an Ontario inquiry, many provinces in Canada have considered the findings and recommendations relevant. Included in the report was a thorough discussion of access to one's own health records. The statute laws of Alberta, Nova Scotia, and Quebec were cited as exemplary: they establish access to health information as the general rule. Refusals of access must be carefully examined.[41]

Justice Krever outlined several arguments for the patient's access to health records:

1) patients should have access to information about themselves;
2) patients should have access so that they might be allowed to correct, by statement, any misinformation in their records;
3) patients will have greater understanding of their treatment and thereby will be better able to assist in their own care;
4) patients will be enabled to give an informed consent to release of their records to a third party when necessary;
5) patients' "trust and openess" between themselves and health providers will be strengthened.[42]

To counter the arguments that patients may be harmed by seeing their records, Krever argued that good patient care requires frankess between physician and patient.

If the patient asks to see his or her record, is informed by the physician of any risks and harmful consequences of doing so, and is nevertheless willing to run the risk, no amount of paternalism should stand in the way of right of access.[43]

Krever recommended that patients have a right to access to copies of any health information kept by the provider. In cases where refusal to access is deemed appropriate, Krever suggested, the administrator's decision should be reviewed by an independent health commissioner.

Health professionals have two responsibilities to patients who demand access to health information. First, patients should not be shown their medical records without the presence of the care-giver, who can interpret the medical jargon, the test results, and the numerous technical entries. The jargon can easily be misconstrued, thereby creating additional anxieties for the patient. Second, sometimes a request for information may indicate a lack of trust in the health professionals, a fear of being deceived. Nurses are in a vital position to alert other staff to patients' uncertainties and distrust, and to ensure that patients obtain both the information and reassurances they require.

RIGHT TO AN INFORMED CONSENT

The principle of informed consent to treatment is fundamental to individual autonomy. To provide informed consent, patients must be given sufficient information to make a decision about their involvement in diagnostic tests, treatments, and care.

The right to remain untouched by others is a basic legal right, which must be respected. There are, of course, certain circumstances under which touching will not be actionable in law – for example, where there is privilege to touch with limits, as in cases of self-defense, arrest, or when a person actually consents to being touched. Other exceptions would occur where touching cannot be avoided, for example, in a crowd.[44]

When an individual enters into a health provider-patient relationship, touching is a necessity. Yet the health-care provider is obliged to secure the consent of the patient (implied, verbal, or written) before engaging in treatment. If no consent is given, and if the health-care provider proceeds with treatment, the provider is liable for assault and battery, except in an emergency.[45]

A number of general guidelines for consent to treatment have been suggested:

1) the consent must be voluntary and genuine;
2) the consent must be informed;
3) the consent must be specific to the procedure performed;
4) it must be specific to the particular person or class of persons doing the procedure;
5) the patient must be legally capable of consenting;
6) the patient must be mentally capable of understanding the risks of undergoing or not undergoing the specified procedure.[46]

Voluntary and Genuine Consent

In medical treatment and hospital care, the principles of a voluntary and genuine consent may well be violated frequently, since the assurance of the patient's freedom from any feelings of compulsion, fear, or constraint is difficult. In hospital admitting departments or clinics, a clerk may hurriedly push a consent form in front of a patient, who may have already been waiting for some time to complete the admission process and therefore feels constrained to complete it. In the hospital ward or outpatient clinic, a busy surgeon or nurse might ask the patient to sign a consent-for-surgery form so that the pre-operative protocols can begin. Patients often feel compelled to sign. Health providers lose sight of the purpose of the consent forms; the forms are seen as an end in themselves, rather than a means to an end.[47] The end purpose is to inform the patient, not to obtain a signature.

An Informed Consent

The essential principle of an informed consent was clearly stated in an American legal case that influenced Canadian legal decisions to some degree. In *Cobbs* v *Grant*, it was decided that informed consent required "that the patient be told enough about the treatment, the alternatives, and the inherent risks of the treatment to make an intelligent choice."[48] Prior to *Cobbs* v *Grant*, the United States Court of Appeals, District of Columbia, in *Canterbury* v *Spence*, held that the patient must be informed in non-technical terms about the options and the risks of a procedure, and that the duty to inform does not depend on the patient's requesting the information.[49]

Two recent Canadian legal cases, *Kelly* v *Hazlett*[50] and *Reibl* v *Hughes*,[51] have focused on the matter of an informed consent. In *Kelly* v *Hazlett*, the court award was based upon the judgment that the patient did not understand the risks of an operation. In *Reibl* v *Hughes*, the judge pointed out that a consent given without clear reference to the risks of a procedure is misleading and is no consent at all. Further, a physician who provides information must know the patient well enough to anticipate his or her circumstances and his or her need for information about potential risks.

At issue is the matter of informing the patient of the nature and risks of treatment, and also of alternative treatments. But there must also be a proper standard of disclosure. Should disclosure standards be based on medical or consumer standards? Should it be objective or subjective?

In *Reibl* v *Hughes*, Chief Justice Laskin specified a full disclosure standard. His standard required "reference to two sources: a) the patient and what he deems to be relevant to his decision; and b) medical knowledge and material risks recognized therein."[52] He further specified that the informing doctor should reply to specific questions about risks, and voluntarily disclose the nature and gravity of the operation, including any material risks as well as any special or unusual risks.[53] Chief Justice Laskin ruled in favor of the patient; his ruling was based on the tort of negligence. Negligence is a tort based on unintentional harm or harm due to careless treatment (see Chapter Two). The physician was found negligent as a result of harm caused by a breach of duty to the patient – in this case, the duty of disclosure of risks.

The tort law of battery and assault has traditionally been the basis of the principles governing informed consent. But the *Reibl* v *Hughes* case establishes a significant precedent in Canada: the Chief Justice limited the tort of battery to situations where touching of the patient exceeds the consent given. The tort of negligence was interpreted as the failure to explain the risks of treatment.[54]

Specific Consent
A signature on one broad, general form, signed as a patient is admitted to care, does not constitute consent to all procedures. Each procedure requires consent specific to the procedure performed and to the particular health professional or class of professionals actually performing the procedure. This legal obligation to the patient can be problematic. In cases of exploratory surgery, for example, a surgeon who discovers a problem may not be empowered to proceed (unless the patient has waived the right to have risks explained, and has empowered the surgeon to proceed with the necessary treatment). The conflicts between medical goals and legal requirements become apparent. The law protects patients from surgical procedures they have not consented to – and that lack of consent may make further surgery necessary.

Nurses must know which procedures require specific written consent to fulfill the institution's legal obligations. But nurses must also be aware of the countless other day-to-day medical and non-medical procedures that should be explained to patients. Verbal or implied consent should be requested for those procedures as well, because patients need to know and need to agree.

Capacity and Capability to Consent

Every human being of "adult years and sound mind" has a right to determine what will be done to his or her body.[55] But what about those who are not adult, or are deemed not to be of sound mind?

Consent of minors to treatment has been a matter of considerable debate and concern. The standard in Canadian law is based on the capability of the minor to appreciate "fully the nature and consequences of the particular operation or treatment."[56] Statute law, which establishes the age of majority and varies by province, does not determine the child's right to refuse or consent to medical treatment.[57] In six Canadian provinces, no age of consent has been specified; four provinces have attempted, by legislation, to establish an age of consent.* The flexibility surrounding this age-of-consent law impels health professionals who treat young patients to get to know each young patient to establish his or her mental capability.[58]

There is also a need to ensure that an adult is capable of consent. Mental retardation and mental illness may render an adult incapable of an informed consent. In all Canadian provinces and territories, legislation exists that allows for the compulsory treatment of persons who are mentally ill and considered dangerous to themselves and others. In cases of mental illness or incapacity falling outside this scope, a legally appointed guardian may be required to give or refuse consent.[59]

Other conditions can affect capability of consent. For example, blindness, deafness, and illiteracy present problems; a patient whose mother tongue is not English might have difficulty giving consent. For many of these patients special provisions, such as translators, are required. For others, the problem of informed consent rests heavily on the health professional's judgment and concern.

---

*The four provinces are British Columbia, Ontario, and New Brunswick – where the official age of consent is sixteen years (subject to special conditions) – and Quebec, where the age of consent for physicians and hospitals is fourteen. Quebec has the clearest legislation in Canada. See Rozovsky, 1980, pp. 44–45 for details.

There is another exception to the rule of giving treatment only with consent. Provincial acts or regulations specifically enforce certain treatments regardless of the patient's capacity or capability to consent. Treatment for communicable diseases, such as tuberculosis or venereal disease, are compulsory and may be given despite the objections of the patient.[60] But legal authority must not be used as an excuse for insensitivity to the patient's concerns.

Nursing Responsibilities

Nurses are responsible to see that patients are informed and that they are in agreement with procedures and interactions. For legal reasons, the person doing the touching (for example, the surgeon, the anaesthetist, or the nurse) must take responsibility for ensuring that the patient is informed before proceeding with the treatment.

Health professionals who obtain a patient's consent to treatment should be concerned with more than those responsibilities imposed by law. Truth-telling and information-sharing are important to an informed consent. Concern must be focused on the patient's needs, not merely the needs of the institution and the practitioners. For example, what information does the patient need to be "informed?" How can this information be provided so that patients are able to hear and assimilate it? How do we ensure that patients have time to ask questions and not feel coerced to sign a consent form?

Nurses are involved with patients twenty-four hours a day. Because of their continual involvement, nurses are in a position to play an advocacy role and a negotiating role in securing the informed consent of the patient. The nurse is able to determine the patient's understanding of the nature of the treatment, the risks, and the alternatives; the nurse is able to inform others when patients have not understood, and to arrange for further discussion of the matter between physicians and patients; the nurse is also able to identify, and bring to the attention of others, instances where patients have not given valid consent for reasons of age, medication, or mental incompetence.[61]

SUMMARY AND CONCLUSIONS

A great many of the moral and legal rights of patients are subsumed in the patient's right to be informed. Legal rights, such as access to one's medical record and the requirements of an informed consent, must be clearly understood by nurses and other health professionals, who must know what the law demands and what moral responsibility and accountability demand. Consumer access to information about health care for health prevention and health maintenance place heavy moral obligations on health professionals to provide information, to educate, and to open up new avenues for consumer and professional participation in health care.

When professionals are providing information, paternalism may often interfere with patient autonomy. Nurses and other health professionals must constantly evaluate their interference and weigh it against the importance of an individual patient's self-determination and dignity. As one author has stated:

> The sacrifice of an individual's dignity seems to be an unnecessarily high price to pay for medical treatment.[62]

REFERENCES FOR CHAPTER 3

[1]Tom L. Beauchamp and James Childress, *Principles of Biomedical Ethics*. (New York: Oxford University Press, 1979), p. 56.

[2]*Ibid*, p. 202.

[3]Patrick Crawshaw and Betty Wong, "Achieving an Attitude of Self-Care: A Discussion Paper." Health Promotion Directorate, Health Services and Promotion Branch. (Ottawa: Health and Welfare Canada, January 1980), p. 3.

[4]Marc Lalonde, *A New Perspective on the Health of Canadians*. (Ottawa: Health and Welfare Canada, 1974), pp. 63–72.

[5]Kenneth D. Rogers, "Making School Health Education Effective." *American Journal of Public Health* 71 (January 1981): pp. 5–6.

[6]Lowell S. Levin, Alfred H. Katz, and Erik Holst, *Self-Care: Lay Initiatives in Health*. (New York: Prodist, 1979), p. 11.

[7]H. Levy, "Self-Help Groups: Types and Psychological Processes." *The Journal of Applied Behavioral Science* 12 (1976): 310–322.

[8]Carol King, "Self-Help/Self-Care Concept." *Nurse Practitioner* 5 (May-June 1980): 34.

[9]*Science* (editorial) 205: 4406 (August 10, 1979): 1.

[10]King, p. 34.

[11]David Robinson, "Self-Help in Health Care." *Journal of Medical Ethics* 6 (1980): 4–6.

[12]Levin, Katz, and Holst, p. 11.

[13]Ivan Barofsky, "Compliance, Adherence and the Therapeutic Alliance: Steps in the Development of Self-Care." *Social Science and Medicine* 12 (1978): 370.

[14]Ivan Illich, *Medical Nemesis* (London: Calder and Boyers, 1975).

[15]Crawshaw and Wong, pp. 9–12.

[16]Victor Fuchs, *Who Shall Live?* (New York: Basic Books, 1974), p. 151.

[17]Jennie J. Kronenfeld, "Self-Care as a Panacea for the Ills of the Health Care System: An Assessment." *Social Science and Medicine* 13A (1979): 264-267.

[18]David Robinson, "The Self-Help Component of Primary Health Care." *Social Science and Medicine* 14A:5 (October 1980): 415-421.

[19]Amitai Etzioni, "Individual Will and Social Considerations: Toward an Effective Health Maintenance Policy." *Annals of the American Academy of Political and Social Science* 437 (May 1978): 64; Vicente Navarro, "The Industrialization of Fetishism or the Fetishism of Industrialization—A Critique of Ivan Illich, *International Journal of Health Services* 5:3 (1975): 368-369; Kronenfeld, pp. 264-265.

[20]Robert F. Rushmer, *Humanizing Health Care: Alternative Futures for Medicine*. (Cambridge, Mass.: MIT Press, 1975), pp. 182-183.

[21]Dorothea Orem, *Nursing: Concepts of Practice*. (New York: McGraw-Hill Book Co., 1971), p. 47.

[22]Barbara W. Narrow, *Patient Teaching in Nursing Practice*. (New York: John Wiley and Sons, 1979), pp. 46-49.

[23]Rushmer, pp. 182-183.

[24]Robin J.O. Catlin, "Does the Doctor Understand What I Am Asking?" *American Journal of Public Health* 71 (February 1981): p. 124.

[25]Paul Boreham and Diane Gibson, "The Informative Process in Private Medical Consultations: A Preliminary Investigation." *Social Science and Medicine* 12 (1978): 409-416.

[26]Boreham and Gibson, p. 415.

[27]"Rules for Patients." *Hospital Administration in Canada* 14 (May 1972): 10.

[28]Barofsky, p. 370.

[29]Daisy L. Tagliacozzo and Hans O. Mauksch, "The Patient's View of the Patient's Role." In *Humanizing Health Care*. Gerald P. Turner and Joseph Mapa (Eds.). (Toronto: McGraw-Hill Ryerson, 179), p. 95.

[30]See for example, Joyce Travelbee, *Interpersonal Aspects of Nursing Practice*. (Philadelphia: F.A. Davis Co., 1971), pp. 9-16; and Dorothea Orem, *Nursing: Concepts of Practice*. (New York: McGraw-Hill Book Co., 1971), pp. 50-53. These nursing theorists are among the many who urge nurses to seek to determine the patient's conception of his or her situation and needs.

[31]Tim Wall, "Creating a Healthy Psychic Environment." *Dimensions* 57:9 (September 1980): 40.

[32]Narrow, pp. 43-45. See also Sissela Bok, *Lying: Moral Choice in Public and Private Life*. (New York: Vintage Books, 1979), pp. 232-255, for a discussion of telling the truth to the sick and the dying.

[33]John Ladd, "Medical Ethics: Who Knows Best?" *The Lancet* 8204 (November 22, 1980): 1129.

[34]Ruth McCorkle, "An Ethical Dilemma: Information Control in Cancer Cure." *Bioethics Quarterly* 2 (Fall 1980): 151.

[35]Michael J. Wilson, "Should Patients Be Told the Truth?" *Patient Counselling and Health Education* 1:2 (1978): 70.

[36]Beauchamp and Childress, pp. 207-208.

[37]McCorkle, pp. 151-153.

[38]"Guidelines for Medical-Nursing Responsibilities, 1975." Approved by the Alberta Medical Association, Alberta Association of Registered Nurses, Alberta Hospital Association, and the College of Physicians and Surgeons, Province of Alberta.

[39]Sr. A. Teresa Stanley, "Is it Ethical to Give Hope to a Dying Person?" *Nursing Clinics of North America* 14:1 (March 1979): 69-80.

[40]Ellen Picard, *Legal Liability of Doctors and Hospitals in Canada*. (Toronto: The Carswell Company Limited, 1978), p. 290.

[41]*Report of the Commission of Inquiry into the Confidentiality of Health Information*, Vol. 2, by Hon. Mr. Justice Horace Krever, Chairman. (Toronto: Queen's Printer, 1980), pp. 458, 461.

[42]*Ibid*., p. 468.

[43]*Ibid*., p. 470.

[44]Lorne Rozovsky, *Canadian Hospital Law*. (Ottawa: Canadian Hospital Association, 1979), p. 35.

[45]Walter Wadlington, "Minors and Health Care: The Age of Consent." *Osgoode Law Journal* 11:1 (1973): 115.

[46]Rozovsky. *Canadian Hospital Law*, p. 37; Lorne E. Rozovsky. "Can a Minor Consent to Treatment?" *Dimensions* 54 (May 1977): 10–12.

[47]Jan Howard, Fred Davis, Clyde Pope, and Sheryl Ruzek, "Humanizing Health Care." *Medical Care* 15 (May 1977): 15; Bradford H. Gray, "Complexities of Informed Consent." *Annals of the American Academy of Political and Social Science* 437 (May 1978): 41.

[48]K.R. Wing, *The Law and the Public's Health*. (St. Louis: C.V. Mosby, 1976), p. 113.

[49]Institute of Law Research and Reform. *Consent of Minors to Medical Treatment, Background Paper No. 9*. (Edmonton: University of Alberta, 1975), pp. 14–15.

[50]*Kelly v Hazlett* (1976), 15 O.R. (2d) 290, 75 D.L.R. (3d) 536, 1 C.C.L.T. 1 (H.C.).

[51]*Reibl v Hughes* (1980) 33 N.R. 361, 14 C.C.L.T. 1 (S.C.C.).

[52]Ellen Picard, "Consent to Medical Treatment in Canada," *Osgoode Hall Law Journal* 19:1 (1981): 145.

[53]Picard, p. 144.

[54]Picard, pp. 142–144. Also see *Zimmer v Ringrose* [1981] 4 WWR 75 (Alta C.A.), which followed the precedent established in *Reibl v Hughes*.

[55]Linda Briggs Besch, "Informed Consent: A Patient's Right." *Nursing Outlook* 27 (January 1979): 32.

[56]Picard, *Legal Liability of Doctors and Hospitals in Canada*, p. 74.

[57]Rozovsky, *The Canadian Patient's Book of Rights*. (Toronto: Doubleday Canada Ltd., 1980), p. 43.

[58]*Ibid*, pp. 44–45.

[59]In Alberta, the Dependent Adults Act (1976) makes provision for the appointment of a guardian to give consent on behalf of an incapable person.

[60]Rozovsky, p. 32.

[61]"Policy Statement on Informed Consent," Registered Nurses Association of British Columbia, Vancouver, April 1980 (see Appendix C).

[62]Beatrice J. Kalisch, "Of Half Gods and Mortals: Aesculapian Authority." In *Humanizing Hospital Care*. Gerald Turner and Joseph Mapa (eds.). (Toronto: McGraw-Hill Ryerson, 1979), p. 49.

SUGGESTED REFERENCES FOR FURTHER STUDY, CHAPTER 3

Antonovsky, Aaron. *Health, Stress, and Coping.* San Francisco: Jossey-Bass Publishers Inc., 1979.

Aaron Antonovsky, medical sociologist, proposes a new approach to the study of health and illness in suggesting that one should study health from the perspective of those factors that allow people to be healthy amidst a world of physical, chemical, microbiological, cultural, and social pathogens.

Antonovsky describes the research and the various writings that led him to the study of salutogenesis – a study of the origins of health. He discusses stressors, tension management, and generalized resistance resources, and hypothesizes that a sense of coherence is a key determinant of health. He then describes patient encounters with the health-care system to illustrate what health professionals do and can do to strengthen a sense of coherence in patients and potential patients. Antonovsky concludes with a brief discussion of the future of the health of mankind.

Bok, Sissela. *Lying: Moral Choice in Public and Private Life.* New York: Vintage Books, 1979.

Bok analyzes everyday dilemmas of truth-telling by discussing the nature and types of lying and the justifications for lying. Of particular relevance to health professionals is Chapter 15, "Lies to the Sick and the Dying." In this chapter, Bok notes the lack of attention to veracity in virtually all health-professional oaths or codes of ethics; she emphasizes that physicians' lying to patients has become more problematic because such lying increasingly involves co-workers. She analyzes the central arguments for deceiving patients – that many patients can't understand, that they do not want to know, and that they might be harmed by knowing about their condition. Bok suggests that these arguments are based on generally unfounded fears. She argues that deception of patients should be seen as an unusual step, and that the burden of justifying this action rests with the care-giver.

Crawshaw, Patrick and Wong, Betty. *Achieving an Attitude of Self-Care: A Discussion Paper.* Vancouver: Health Services and Promotion Directorate, Western Regional Office, Health and Welfare Canada, January 1980.

This discussion paper provides a rationale for greater acceptance and commitment to the concept of self-care in health-care in Canada. The concept of self-care is discussed in relation to the restorative health process and to the health-maintenance process; and five strategies for implementing the concept of self-care as a guiding principle are proposed. These strategies include a research and evaluation strategy, a health-education strategy, a professional-development strategy, and a social and political action strategy. It is emphasized that to achieve self-care as described, these five strategies must be implemented holistically.

King, Carol. "The Self-Help/Self-Care Concept." *Nurse Practitioner* 5 (May-June 1980): 34–39, 46.

King provides an excellent review of literature about self-help and self-care. She discusses the implications these patient-directed activities might hold for patients and for health professionals, particularly "nurse practitioners." She outlines Levy's typology of self-help groups and reviews the major concerns about such groups. The concept of self-care is then discussed and health professionals' concerns about self-care are summarized (including the lack of evidence to date to support the effectiveness of self-care). Controversial philosophical, political, ethical, legal, and economic issues are outlined, and King emphasizes the responsibility of nurses to become knowledgeable about self-care before either condemning or blindly supporting this consumer movement.

Levin, Lowell S., Katz, Alfred H., and Holst, Erik. *Self-Care: Lay Initiatives in Health* (2nd ed.) New York: Prodist, 1979.

This book is the outgrowth of an international symposium on the role of the individual in primary health care. The concept of self-care is discussed, and the reasons self-care has emerged as a greater public interest are outlined. Economic, philosophical, political, and legal factors that promote self-care are discussed, along with ethical issues such as manipulation of the consumer. Particular research challenges of self-care are then suggested. The book includes an extensive annotated bibliography on self-care and related topics.

Narrow, Barbara W. *Patient Teaching in Nursing Practice.* New York: John Wiley and Sons, 1979.

This book is designed to assist the nurse in integrating patient teaching into nursing practice. Narrow describes the types of settings and conditions in which teaching and learning might occur, and provides a conceptual basis for patient teaching. She includes a cogent overview of the patient's need and right to have information and understanding; she discusses the teaching-learning process in terms of assessment, planning, implementation, and evaluation. Under the discussion of assessment, Narrow provides particularly useful guidelines for assessing the patient's readiness to learn and for assessing the teaching situation. Her book should be helpful to those nurses seeking an overview of teaching and learning as well as some practical guidelines to assist them in the process.

Sklar, Corinne. "Legal Consent and the Nurse." *Canadian Nurse* 74 (March 1978): 34–37.

Sklar's purpose in this article is to assist in explaining the law of consent and to demonstrate its applicability to nursing practice. She emphasizes that nurses cannot blindly follow doctors' orders; nurses are accountable for those orders, and are legally accountable to patients for their own actions. Following brief definitions of battery, negligence, and standards of care, Sklar discusses the elements of consent: capacity, voluntariness, consent to acts performed, and informed consent. She concludes with an emphasis on the nurse's role in the consent process.

Wikler, D.I. "Persuasion and Coercion for Health: Ethical Issues in Government Efforts to Change Lifestyles." *Milbank Memorial Fund Quarterly* 56 (Summer 1978): 303–338.

Wikler examines the kinds of justifications that would be necessary for a government to institute any coercive lifestyle reform. He focuses on three goals of health-behavior reform, in each case examining the appropriateness of the goal, he also describes the problems that might arise in the pursuit of such goals. The goal of health as an intrinsic good is discussed; Wikler emphasizes the dangers of paternalistic interventions, which might involve coercion, subjectivity, or vagueness about another's decision-making ability. He describes how the goal of fair distribution of benefits raises questions of individual blame and individual liberty. He suggests that the goal of public welfare (the social benefits gained from inducing people to change self-destructive behavior) could effect a number of benefits to society. Wikler then evaluates various health-promotion strategies, such as health education, incentives and subsidies, and regulative measures, to determine the extent of coercion involved. Although Wikler predicts that there will be problems in justifying coercive action in lifestyle reform, he suggests that such reforms may nevertheless be desirable.

CHAPTER 4 The Right To Be Respected

"Respect for human rights is especially important in the health field where so much depends upon personal relationships."[1] Although few specific laws demand that health professionals respect patients, most people would agree that a patient has a right to expect respectful treatment.

> ... [It] is not enough that we in the health professions do a technically competent job of healing the patient's body; we must also do an equally competent job of safe-guarding his dignity and self-esteem.[2]

Central to the notion of respect are three moral principles: autonomy, non-maleficence, and beneficence. Autonomy refers to the personal liberty of an individual who exercises self-determination. Non-maleficence is essentially a duty "to do no harm" to a person, and is widely considered to be the duty of the health professional to the patient. Beneficence means that one acts to benefit others in a way that will contribute to their health and well-being. Therefore, in addition to treating patients as self-determining individuals, health professionals have a moral duty: to guard against actions that would cause harm to these individuals, and to act to help others.

The right to respect is basically a moral one, but it entails certain legal rights as well. There are several statutes and regulations

71

designed to protect the patient's rights of confidentiality and the patient's right to refuse treatment.

The health-care consumer's right to respect implies an obligation on the part of the health professional: the professional must see the consumer as a unique individual who has the potential to be responsible for his or her own health care. Paternalism places restrictions on a person's liberty. Although the justification for paternalism may be based in the appeal to the good of the person, the professional's interference must be carefully balanced against the consumer's ability to be responsible. Coercive practices, such as forcing patients to take pills, can seldom be justified morally or legally.

The right to respect is difficult to enforce. "Respect" includes such rights as the right to courteous and individual care, to privacy, and to confidentiality; the right to refuse to be involved in human experimentation; the right to refuse to be used as a teaching subject; the right to refuse treatment; and the right to refuse undue painful prolongation of life. This chapter will focus on the moral and legal aspects of these rights.

COURTEOUS AND INDIVIDUAL CARE

Patients who enter a health-care setting generally enter as strangers. Routines and procedures that are common to the staff of the institution are generally foreign to the patient. Health professionals who work in emergency wards, outpatient clinics, or hospital wards sometimes forget that while one new admission or contact is part of their daily task, to the average patient, this contact represents a significant and sometimes frightening and humiliating part of the life experience. Many patients have a deep-seated fear of being helpless, passive, or dependent.[3]

To treat a patient courteously and individually, the professional must address the patient by name, not by condition; must listen to the patient; must give explanations of routines and procedures; must give information about the patient's condition honestly and openly; and must tailor the care to meet the patient's individual needs and circumstances.

These requirements are not easily fulfilled, particularly in a large and specialized health center, because they involve extra time, attention, and a willingness to go the extra mile in providing individualized care. In ethical terms, this extra care is embraced in the concepts of beneficence and fidelity. Fidelity is a voluntary commitment of one person to another; it has also been described as a "faithfulness of one human being to another."[4] Such a commitment or faithfulness is predicated on a genuine care and concern, and a deep respect for humanity.

Health-care providers today have been accused of providing dehumanized and depersonalized care; not all patients feel that professionals exercise a respect for humanity. The patients' perceptions may be a result of certain behavior of health professionals:

> ...the perception of people as objects (thinging); the instrumental use and exploitation of patients and providers; coldness and indifference in social interaction; the repression and limitation of human freedom (loss of options); and social ostracism and alienation.[5]

Many of these same kinds of behavior were identified in the sixties by Esther Lucille Brown,[6] who focused on the need to individualize patient care. Since that time, the problems have increased in scope and intensity. In *Heartsounds*, Martha Lear provides numerous examples of dehumanization, a preoccupation with technology, and often a blaming of patients for their illness.[7]

The tendency of health-care professionals to unfairly blame patients, to hesitate to admit mistakes or uncertainties, to not accept patients as they are and seek to understand their behavior, would seem to be widespread. At fault is a system that does not allow for the admission of error or failure–or a system that cannot confront the harsh realities of suffering and death.

Nurses can help to turn this situation around by working towards individualized care and a greater sense of "caring." By their relatively constant involvement in patient-health-professional encounters, nurses have the opportunity and the ability to be sensitive and caring towards patients, and to remind their colleagues of the patient's need for respect.

RIGHT TO PRIVACY

There is as yet no uniformity in the Canadian laws that deal with the right to privacy. In the United States, the Fourteenth Amendment constitutionally protects a right to privacy;[8] in Canadian common law, there is no separate tort that protects this right. However, at least two provinces have protected the right to privacy in statute law.[9]

The right to privacy is also a humanitarian concern. A human's need for privacy is a necessary defense against the pressures of society and a vital condition for personal growth.[10] There are many illnesses for which privacy may be an important component of recovery.

Health-care facilities are not generally designed to maximize patient privacy. Patients who arrive in the admitting or emergency departments or move to a ward are generally in an open area and subject to questions from physicians, nurses, and other attendants. Some of these questions may be of a highly personal nature. The open physical structure in these patient-care areas is functionally convenient; unfortunately, the potential violations of patient privacy are often overlooked, particularly when health professionals behave as though cotton curtains were sound-proof barriers.

In addition, it is common practice, particularly in teaching hospitals, for many people to be present during a patient's history-taking or examination. The group may include medical students, nursing students, and other learners. Unless the patient has given permission for those not directly involved in care and treatment to be in attendance, their presence violates the patient's privacy.

Nurses can do much to foster and protect patient privacy during interviews, examinations, and treatments. They can remind others of a patient's need for privacy, and should be sensitive to a patient's need for aloneness, especially in situations of loss or grief.

RIGHT TO CONFIDENTIALITY

Confidentiality is closely related to privacy and is based in ethics and law. Health professionals have a duty to the patient based on the terms of the professional-patient relationship. Patients can best be helped when they communicate openly with professionals.

> *Part of the nursing process is to encourage the patient to express himself freely, and to share his problems and feelings with the nurse.*[11]

Patients will share information more freely if they are sure the information they give will be held in confidence.[12]

The nurse's duty of confidentiality is recognized in the Florence Nightingale Pledge for nurses and in the code of ethics of the International Council of Nurses. In the former, the nurse is directed to "hold in confidence all personal matters committed" to her keeping as well as family matters coming to her knowledge; in the latter, the nurse is directed to hold in confidence personal information and to exercise judgment in sharing such information.[13]

Sometimes the duty of confidentiality conflicts with the nurse's desire to help the patient. For example, a patient might confide suicidal intentions to the nurse; a teenager might beg the school nurse not to inform her parents of her pregnancy; a patient's wife might ask a nurse not to inform her husband of his terminal condition. In these situations, the nurse must carefully weigh seemingly conflicting duties. The nurse may at times find it necessary to breach confidentiality in the interests of the patient.

Nurses may break confidentiality for less noble reasons; for example, some nurses may be prone to gossip. Sometimes the breach is unintentional: under the pressure of their tasks (and to gain some outlet for the stressful situations with which they deal), nurses may share information too freely, and without the protection of closed quarters. While few nurses have been brought to task legally, they must recognize a moral obligation to exercise care and respect in regards to information about a patient.

The patient's right to confidentiality is protected in two ways. First, a variety of statute laws in each province include law respecting the confidentiality of health information. In most provinces, for example, the Hospital's Act imposes a fine – or imprisonment in default of payment – for persons found guilty of releasing or disclosing health information about a patient to unauthorized persons.[14] Second, under legislation regulating the practice of nursing in each province, there is a duty of confidentiality under "the concept of professional misconduct for which a nurse may be disciplined (or even lose . . . registration depending on the severity of the offense)."[15]

The Ontario Health Disciplines Act of 1974 states that professional misconduct includes

> . . . *giving information concerning a patient's condition or any professional services performed for a patient to a person other than the patient without the consent of the patient unless required to do so by law.*[16]

Health professionals must be aware that any statements of a derogatory nature made to others about patients could result in a legal suit of defamation of character.[17] Such statements, which harm an individual's good name, can only be defended if wholly true. But, as Sklar reminds us:

> *Truth is a legal defense to a charge of defamation. Truth is no defense to a breach of confidentiality.*[18]

Complete confidentiality of the patient's medical record is neither possible nor feasible. In hospitals, many individuals have access to the patient's record – physicians, nurses, physiotherapists, pharmicists, and others. In addition, government departments of health also have legal rights to access to the patient's record. As the use of computers becomes more common, it becomes increasingly difficult to protect the confidentiality of medical records because records stored in computers are too easily accessible.[19] Computerized record-keeping can benefit the patient, but an added burden is placed on computer users, who must safeguard the privacy of the patient.[20] As Justice Krever noted:

> *Computers themselves are not the problem; they have simply made the problem more clear, more immediate, affecting more of us, and putting more at stake. In the final analysis the real issue is what we store on computer systems and how we and others use it.*[21]

The Krever Commission recommended a number of measures that would ensure greater confidentiality of patient health information; in particular, the Commission dealt with computer-supported information systems in health care. The Commission suggested that those who use the systems must be responsible for protecting confidentiality:

> *...the greatest security risk is to be found not in the system's hardware or software, but rather in the persons involved in the system.*[22]

Because nurses are often in a position to act as a "guardian" of patient information on the hospital ward, in the public-health clinic, in the school, in occupational-health services, in the doctor's office, or wherever they work, they are in a key position to guard against infractions of medical record use, and they can also suggest policies and procedures that would maximize confidentiality.

RIGHT TO REFUSE TREATMENT

The law upholds the patient's right to refuse treatment, but the exercising of this right can place the health professional in a position where legal and ethical duties conflict.[23] While the physician clearly has a "professional commitment to preserve life and health, he has no legal status to require [patients] to preserve [their] own life or health."[24] Nurses have a four-fold responsibility: "to promote health, to prevent illness, to restore health, and to alleviate suffering."[25] But they also must be careful not to coerce a patient to receive treatment if the patient refuses such treatment. (The law allows several exceptions–for example, if the patient is incompetent or has a certain communicable disease.)

Patients who refuse treatment may authorize no intervention whatsoever, or they may give limited consent to a specific treatment.[26] When the patient who refuses treatment is a competent adult, the health professional is obliged to accept the refusal.

The patient's right to refuse treatment poses a problem for most health professionals: years of study and experience have generally convinced health professionals of the benefits of treatment. Health providers are tempted to act paternalistically when they genuinely feel that the treatment prescribed is in the patient's best interests. Yet the patient's self-determination and autonomy must be respected.

At the same time, the health professional should take time to discover why the patient is refusing treatment. Is the patient afraid? Does he or she understand the implications of refusing treatment? Has the patient made a truly "informed" choice?

The nurse is in a key position to evaluate patient refusals. If the refusal is motivated by fear, nurses might find ways to help the patient deal with the fear, either through their own therapeutic interventions or by alerting other health professionals to the patient's difficulty. If a patient has refused treatment because he or she does not fully understand the situation, the nurse can provide the information necessary for the patient's understanding–including the consequences of refusing treatment. For example, a hospital may not be able to maintain a patient who refuses all treatments that would likely lead to improvement, inevitable discharge, or transfer. Physicians may not feel able to continue to attend a patient who will not follow a recommended treatment plan. If the patient has made a truly informed choice, the nurse should support that decision, and ensure the patient's right to refuse treatment.

Health professionals must guard against rejecting a patient because of the decision to refuse treatment. A study of patient deviance and conformity in a hospital revealed that those patients who are deemed unco-operative often face neglect or a stigmatizing label.[27] Individual patients who make decisions that go against the health professional's goals are commonly considered incapable; much of the time, the charge is unjustified. In extreme cases, a psychiatric assessment may be ordered to determine a patient's competence. (If a patient is judged incompetent, his or her refusal of treatment presents a moral dilemma for the health professional. The special concerns of such patients – the mentally ill, the mentally retarded, children, and the senile elderly – will be discussed in Chapter 7.)

RIGHT TO REFUSE TO BE INVOLVED IN HUMAN EXPERIMENTATION

Perhaps nowhere are the ethical dilemmas of health care more glaring than in the area of human experimentation. That sick persons should be conscripted for research would seem illogical and inhumane – yet it is the sick who are needed for research purposes.[28]

Medical science is furthered by human experimentation. However exhaustive and conclusive studies on animals might be, the final demonstration of therapeutic effect and safety can be made only on human subjects.[29] Jenner found the link between cowpox and smallpox vaccination by experimenting on humans; the efficacy of blood transfusions and penicillin were proven by human experimentation.

The thought of human experimentation signals an alarm and concern about the proper treatment of human subjects. Miscarriages of justice in human research are shocking. Under the guise of scientific advances in medicine, for example, prisoners at the Buchenwald concentration camp were fed poisoned food or shot with poisoned bullets; their bodies were labelled for autopsy to determine the effects of particular poisons. Prisoners at Dachau were locked in low-pressure chambers to determine the effects of high-altitude flying, and records were kept of the behavior of the dying subjects. And prisoners at Ravensbruch were infected with streptococci, gas gangrene, and clostridium tetani, to test the effectiveness of sulfanilamide against these diseases.[30] These "experiments" were revealed at the Nuremberg trials. Three judges developed "the Nuremberg Code," a guide to the use of human subjects in research.

The Nuremberg Code lists ten basic principles for those who perform medical experiments on human beings; these principles are based on ethical and legal concepts. Some examples are:

that there must be voluntary consent of the human subject;
that the experiment must be designed to yield fruitful results, which are not procurable in any other way;
that the experiment must be conducted in a way that will avoid all unnecessary mental and physical suffering and injury;
that, by providing adequate facilities, the subject is protected from harm;
that the experiment must be conducted only by qualified persons;
that the human subject must be at liberty to discontinue participation in the experiment at any time;
that the experimenter must be prepared to end the experiment at any time if continuation is likely to result in injury (see Appendix B).

Other medical experiments have abused human subjects. Among many studies that have come to light in recent years are the Tuskegee Syphilis study, the Jewish Chronic Hospital study, the Willowbrook study, and the Milledgeville State Hospital study. A brief review of these research projects illuminates the ethical conflicts implicit in human experimentation.

The Tuskegee Syphilis study began in 1930, before the discovery of penicillin. The study, designed as a long-term investigation of syphilis, included two groups of Negro males – one group judged to be free of the disease, one group with syphilis. The men were examined periodically, and results were carefully documented. However, when penicillin was proven effective as a treatment for syphilis in 1950, the diseased group was not given treatment. Despite the criteria for human experimentation outlined in the

Nuremberg Code of 1949, and despite guidelines from the Department of Health, Education and Welfare that required a review of all new research between 1953 and 1967, the study continued. In 1969, an ad-hoc committee reviewed the Tuskegee study and agreed that it should not have begun. But the committee did not demand that it be discontinued.[31] The study continued until 1973, when adverse publicity forced its termination.

At the Jewish Chronic Hospital in Brooklyn in 1956, elderly, chronically ill patients were injected with live cancer cells to determine their rejection response. When the experimenters were summoned to answer for their actions, they stated that they had not sought an informed consent because they wished to avoid an emotional response from patients; as well, they were afraid no one would participate.[32] At Willowbrook State School in Staten Island in 1967, mentally retarded patients were deliberately injected with live hepatitis so that the experimenters could observe the disease.[33] At the Milledgeville State Hospital in 1969, patients with mental disorders were given investigational drugs; no consent was obtained from the patients or their relatives.[34]

These "experiments" represent only a fraction of the abuses in human experimentation, which occur even today. That such experiments continue to be a problem in health care is testimony to some degree of professional apathy, complacency, disregard, and lack of knowledge.

Another problem is that much serious medical therapy is experimental.[35] This anomaly arises from the fact that medicine is not an exact science. Consumers and health professionals alike have been infatuated with the potentials of medical science, and have not always paused to remember the inexactness – and therefore the experimental nature – of medicine.

Because all medical "science" is experimental, a legitimate case can be made for continuing human experimentation with proper safeguards. Many of medicine's finest techniques have not yet been proven effective, yet they are in widespread use. Is it any less risky to experiment?[36] It would seem more appropriate to candidly admit to patients some of the uncertainties surrounding various treatments, and to gain patient support in investigating the effectiveness of these treatments, than it would to proceed as though these measures had been proven effective. Certainly, procedures such as heart and renal transplants are still largely experimental, as are many drugs used in therapy, particularly cancer therapy.

Guidelines are still needed to protect human subjects in "experimental" treatment and in research.

Guidelines and Controls to Protect Research Subjects

Numerous codes of conduct in human experimentation have been developed; many are based upon the principles outlined in the Nuremberg Code. In 1964, the World Medical Association adopted the Declaration of Helsinki, which included criteria for both therapeutic and non-therapeutic clinical research[37] (see Appendix B). In 1968, the American Nurses' Association established guidelines for nursing research,[38] and in 1972, the Canadian Nurses' Association (CNA) adopted some guidelines entitled "Ethics of Nursing Research."[39] These guidelines deal with invasion of privacy, loss of dignity, loss of autonomy, and protection from risk. The CNA guidelines refer to the research subject's right to be informed, to be assured of confidentiality, and to be protected from risk; to the researcher's duty to be competent and accountable; and to the physical setting of the research (see Appendix B).

In addition, several funding bodies have established guidelines for the protection of research subjects. The U.S. Department of Health, Education and Welfare published its "Policy on Protection of Human Subjects" in 1966, and Health and Welfare Canada established general regulations specifying the ethical requirements of investigations involving human subjects. Both policies require committees to review the ethics of the research project. Such a review would be carried out by a clinical-investigation committee or by an institutional-review committee – in other words, a peer review. Although there are many difficulties with peer-review committees, particularly in-house review committees,[40] the general principle of peer review is sound.

A variety of social controls is essential to protect the subjects of experiments. Collaborative research is a significant safeguard, since members of a research team can provide a sense of balance to a research project. The editorial policies of research journals can also serve as an effective social control. For example, the journal *Nursing Research* published a policy statement in 1969, which stated:

> Nursing Research *is concerned that the rights and dignity of human subjects be considered in research. Therefore, one criteria of selection* [of articles to be published] *is evidence that rights of individuals have been protected.*[41]

Medical students, nursing students and anyone else who may be involved in research with human subjects must be made aware of the ethics of medical research.[42] Internalization of research ethics can be an important protection of patients' rights: individual researchers must be able to evaluate their work to prevent violations of the subject's rights.[43] In addition, the monitoring of research by those who care for patient-subjects is a significant safeguard.

Nurses should observe and monitor research projects within an institution or agency to detect any violations of patient rights. A nurse can ensure that voluntary consent has been given, and that patients understand they are free to discontinue their involvement in the research.

> The profession has provided moral leadership by its forthright formulation of research guidelines. What remains is for individual members of the profession to take a personal position of deep concern for the sacredness of human life and respect for the dignity and integrity of man throughout the life cycle. In addition, [nurses] must make a solemn personal commitment to protect human rights in research.[44]

The Nurse as Researcher

Researchers must be certain that the question they are examining is significant, that the study is designed to answer the research question, that the researcher is competent to do the research, and that the patient has given a valid consent and is protected from risk.

The nurse's role as researcher is not well understood by most patients. Patients are likely to assume that the researcher is a nurse practitioner, a role they can better understand. Patients might give consent to the nurse–not the nurse researcher–and might not understand the benefits and the risks of participating in research.[45]

Nurses are therefore cautioned to emphasize their researcher status and to carefully examine "the practice of combining patient care and research activities."[46] Many nurse researchers recognize the conflict inherent in the roles of helper and scientist. Nurses should be cautioned against using patient charts for data-gathering without the patient's consent. Much that is common practice in research should be scrutinized, not to create further impediments to research but rather to ensure that patient privacy, confidentiality, and consent are honored in nursing research activities.

RIGHT TO REFUSE TO BE INVOLVED AS A TEACHING SUBJECT

Traditionally, health professionals have learned their skills by a process of apprenticeship learning, which necessarily involved the use of patients in the learning process. It was commonly assumed that some hospitals existed as "training laboratories."

> *Hospitals in conjunction with universities became the major training center for a new generation of doctors. Although this situation meant that the low-income people who ended up in hospital provided clinical examples that the physician later used to cure his more well-to-do private patients, the poor at least received some sort of medical treatment.*[47]

The use of patients in teaching has sometimes resulted in physical or psychological discomfort for patients because of the lack of skill of the learner – whether that learner be a laboratory technician, a medical student, or a nurse. Because health care is a people-related service, and because certain skills must be practised on humans to be perfected, the health professional's right to use patients as teaching subjects has largely gone unchallenged.

With the introduction of new and better teaching models, the use of patients as teaching subjects has been modified. Various student health professionals are now able to practise intra-muscular injections, intravenous therapy, and cardiac resuscitation on models. But there are still many procedures and techniques that require the use of a patient as a teaching subject. What duty do patients owe towards the education of health professionals? What right do patients have to request that their care be provided by experienced practitioners only?

These questions pose some serious dilemmas for the education of all health professionals. To what degree can we expect patients to function as our live learning models? Because they are "captive" in hospital, is it fair to assume that we may use them as subjects?[48]

Suppose the practice of using patients as teaching subjects were curtailed. One result would be that the newly graduated practitioner, who has learned by using models rather than people, is suddenly given license to practice techniques on patients – with limited supervision.

The continued use of patients as teaching subjects should be balanced with greater recognition of the patient's right to self-determination. Instructors and students alike should clearly identify the learning situation to the patient, and request the patient's consent before proceeding. At the same time, they must be sensitive to the patient's condition.[49]

Some teaching hospitals believe that patients who sign the consent to admission are automatically consenting to be used as teaching subjects. In the author's view, this is an entirely unfair and presumptuous position. First, few patients are aware of the distinction between teaching hospitals and other hospitals. Second, patients do not generally choose the hospital – the physician does. Third, few patients would know they were signing away their right not to be used as a teaching subject. It is imperative that teaching hospitals provide better information to incoming patients and obtain an informed consent for use as a teaching subject. This matter is particularly critical in regards to the tasks assigned to medical interns and residents within teaching hospitals.

THE RIGHT TO DIE WITH DIGNITY

[The] crux of dying with dignity is in retaining one's individuality, be that in acceptance or denial, anger or serenity, without the humiliation of unnecessary life-prolonging machines.[50]

"The right to die with dignity" is a much-touted slogan; the phrase has many meanings. Among these meanings are two central concepts: the rights of the terminally ill patient, and the legislative aspects of the right to die.

Ivan Illich, a prominent social critic, has identified an anomaly: with the techniques and skills of modern medicine, death has come to be seen as the ultimate defeat of professional skills rather than as a normal process of life.[51] That our society is a death-denying society, and that this denial of death has affected the care and attention given to the dying, is largely undisputed. Hospital patients who are dying frequently receive fewer visits from health personnel; nurses communicate less with the dying. The hospital emphasizes treatment and cure rather than palliative care.*

---

*In her seminal book, *On Death and Dying* (1969), Elizabeth Kubler Ross draws attention to the plight of the dying person in the health-care system.

Rights of the Terminally Ill

George Annas, a leading hospital lawyer and civil-liberties spokesman in the United States, has postulated several rights that belong to the terminally ill.[52] Underlying these rights are two ethical principles, autonomy and self-determination. According to Annas, the terminally ill patient has a right to know the truth; a right to confidentiality and privacy; a right to be heard, supported, and attended; a right to refuse experimentation; a right to choose the place of death; a right to all types of treatment; and a right to choose the time of death.

As a general rule, dying patients should be told about their condition and given full details about their prognosis. They should know how long they are expected to live, the pain and disability that may occur, and the available relief. A small percentage of patients may not be able to handle such information, and there may be some justification in withholding the information for a time. But many patients experience a sense of relief when they learn the truth: matters can be discussed openly, goodbyes can be said.[53] In addition, staff can relate to the patient with a degree of honesty not possible when information is withheld. If a "conspiracy of silence" is maintained, patients invariably sense they are dying; as well, they are forced to play the game of secrecy, and therefore must bear their grief alone. The sharing of information allows patient, family, and staff to face facts honestly and openly.

The dying person has a right to confidentiality and privacy. Patients should be given information about their prognoses. When family or friends receive the prognosis before the patient does, the patient becomes isolated from the truth and from their family.[54]

The dying patient should also be assured of freedom from unnecessary examination and from other disturbances. The routines of a general hospital ward grind on, and all patients are subject to these routines. Dying patients should be protected from meaningless intrusions into their privacy and rest. Staff must realize that patients, their family, and their friends need to be alone.

Dying patients must not be deserted or unheeded because their condition is hopeless. Rather, they must be heard, supported, and attended. Staff must be prepared to hear that dying patients are *not* feeling better, but that they are feeling worse.[55] Staff need to listen and provide emotional support and comfort.

It would seem "untimely" to involve the dying in human experimentation. But patients are asked to participate in experiments for two reasons. First, experimental treatment might reveal much about the patient's medical condition. Second, health professionals might hope to learn more about what physical, chemical, or environmental measures might best support the dying. In either case, health professionals must be careful not to imply that the patient owes them a favor for their diligent life-saving efforts.

Such research, whether formal or informal, has led to the development of the hospice concept, the central focus of which is the care and well-being, rather than the cure, of the dying. The patient's right to choose the place of death is a central tenet of the hospice concept. Because most general hospitals focus on cure and recovery, a patient who is ready to accept death is often deprived of supportive care. There is a growing trend towards increasing the availability of hospice care in the home, in general hospitals, in nursing homes, in auxiliary hospitals, or in separate facilities for the dying. Because dying patients' needs are unique, those patients need constant support, ready access to pain relief, unrestricted visiting with family and friends, and ready access to chaplaincy services.[56]

The terminally ill have a right to relief from pain.[57] In addition to the pain relief possible through drugs, increased staff contact, careful positioning, and music therapy[58] have proven remarkably successful in easing pain. Such measures indicate that health professionals need to conduct meaningful research with the consent of dying patients.

A most significant right of the dying patient is the right to consent to treatment.

> ...no consent to treatment by a patient diagnosed as terminal could be considered informed if the patient was not told that his doctor viewed his condition as terminal.[59]

The dying patient has a right to be informed about all procedures and plans relating to care, and should be told about the institution's cardiac-resuscitation policy. A fair and humane approach to "no-code" orders should involve physician, nurses, patients, and family so that a clear understanding prevails and staff are able to support the patient as his or her death draws near.

Refusal to consent to treatment when the consequence is certain death is one of the more pressing legal and moral dilemmas in health-care today. One physician describes a situation where a sixty-six-year-old man refused to consent to necessary diagnostic tests or to be placed on a respirator. Other physicians assumed that the patient was mentally impaired, and tried to begin treatment. But the patient "established limits for the health care team and would not permit those limits to be transgressed."[60] In the end, the attending physician supported the man's wishes and, despite the protests of house staff, did not attempt resuscitation. The attending physician concludes:

> It is unfortunate, and I am sadly moved, that [the patient] had to expend his last measure of intellectual and physical energy to engage in ongoing debate with his physicians. But perhaps this is the price the medical system sometimes exacts from those who would assert their independence and preserve their autonomy while suffering from critical illness.[61]

Who should make the decision to withhold or limit treatment? The patient's competence must be determined, and health professionals must be prepared for ambiguities, inconsistencies, and changes in a patient's desire to refuse treatment.[62] The family's wishes, which might conflict with those of the health professionals or the patient, may further complicate the decision-making. In the end, the patient's informed consent must predominate.[63]

The dying patient's right to choose the time of death has been the subject of increasing attention and legal activity during the past decade. Historically, the physician decided when treatments should cease; the decision was a relatively simple matter. Today "the notion of 'dying' is dependent on the technology available."[64] There is little agreement about what treatments are appropriate for the terminally ill. Some advocate the continuation of treatment at all costs; others argue for early discontinuation of life-support measures. The prolongation of life by ordinary or extraordinary means, the use of reasonable or unreasonable treatments, the taking of positive steps to end a life are matters of intense debate. The center of that debate is the concept of euthanasia.

Euthanasia essentially means "a good death." How do we allow terminally ill patients to have a good death without contravening the legal and ethical duties of the health professional's practice?

The debate has been somewhat clouded by indiscriminate use of the term "euthanasia." The word has been used to refer to many types of situations, including those that involve the terminally ill, defective newborns, and suicidal persons.[65] For this discussion, the term "euthanasia" will be used only in relation to those patients who are terminally ill. Is it the patient's right to choose the time of death, thereby obligating another person to carry out a mercy killing? Or is it acceptable only to "allow" someone to die?

For a health professional to actively assist in ending a life contravenes the professional ethic to "do no harm." Such an action is also illegal in Britain, the United States, and Canada. Therefore the euthanasia debate had focused on the issue of allowing patients to die a good death – in other words, when and how to decide not to continue treatment.

Right To Die Legislation

The idea of a "living will" has been prevalent for some time, particularly in the United States. A living will is essentially a statement of a person's desire that, in the event of imminent death, life-prolonging treatments should not be initiated or should be stopped if they have already been initiated. A living will is not a mandate to health personnel; a living will is "neither legally binding nor enforceable against them."[66]

The first North American right-to-die legislation was enacted on January 1, 1977 and was called the California Natural Death Act.

> The intent of the right-to-die legislation is to protect a terminal patient against unnecessary, unwanted, and undignified medical treatment which serves only to prolong dying and cause needless suffering. It obviates application to the courts for protection against well-intentioned, but undesired medical intervention. Without legislative guidelines, the patient's right to self-determination is frequently violated.[67]

The legislation was motivated by several legal cases, for example, Karen Ann Quinlan's,[68] where measures to prolong life were maintained despite opposition from family and friends.

Neither the California Natural Death Act, nor the many right-to-die acts modelled after it, however, provide for cases such as the Quinlans', where the opposition to life-support treatments came from family. The acts authorize the withholding or withdrawal of life-sustaining measures from adult patients affected by a terminal condition only where the patient-not the family-has executed a directive in the manner prescribed by the particular act.[69] The acts help to protect health professionals who withhold treatment from civil and criminal liability and from charges of unprofessional conduct.[70]

In Ontario and Alberta, bills similar to the California Natural Death Act were introduced in the provincial legislature in the late seventies; neither bill was passed into law. There is some question about the proper jurisdiction of such legislation. Is it a provincial matter?[71] According to Lorne Rozovsky, several conditions prevail in Canadian law:

1) the patient has no legal right to heroic treatment;
2) the general rule of consent to treatment applies equally to the terminally ill;
3) if the person is incapable of consent, the law assumes consent.[72]

During the late 1970s, the Law Reform Commission of Canada began the Protection of Life Project. Its purpose was to examine law that dealt with matters of life and death and to recommend necessary changes to the Parliament of Canada. In the course of its research, the commission examined the definition of death in an attempt to resolve a question: when does death occur? That is, when can a patient be considered legally dead? With advanced life-prolonging technologies available, it has become increasingly difficult to know when a person is legally dead;[73] physicians and hospital personnel face a very real and practical problem. In 1979, the commission's study paper, called "Criteria for the Determination of Death," was released; the commission listened to comments on the study paper and then submitted its conclusions and the recommendations in a report to the Parliament of Canada.[74] The commission recommended that Parliament "establish the criteria for the determination of death by a legislative text," and incorporate those criteria in an amendment to the Interpretation Act. The amendment would define death as "an irreversible cessation of all the person's brain functions."[75]

The amendment would remove some of the uncertainty about the definition of death. Except for the Manitoba Vital Statistics Act, no provincial vital-statistics act accepts brain death as a valid definition.

Without a modified definition upon which health professionals can establish criteria for determining death, persons who are technically dead are given life characteristics, such as respiration and heart-beat, by artificial means. To keep life going can easily become an assault on the technically dead person, and upon his or her dignity.[76] Life is more than mere biological function. As one writer so aptly stated, "It isn't so much that people want to die with dignity, but rather that they want to live with it."[77]

The Law Reform Commission is currently studying euthanasia and the cessation of treatment. The commission has identified the sections of the Criminal Code that hamper health professionals' attempts to allow a person to die with dignity.[78] There appears to be a general bias in criminal law, which binds the physician or nurse to ensure that patients do not die because the care-givers have omitted treatment or therapy that could restore the patient to health, or at least prolong life for a short period.

In early discussions regarding euthanasia and the cessation of treatment, the commission indicated its concern that the U.S. right-to-die Legislation not be adopted as a model for Canada. Instead, adjustments might be made to the Criminal Code: the privacy of patients' wishes in the matter of prolonging life would be supported, as would the physician's termination of treatment in cases where there is no hope. Until the law is modified, to discontinue life-support mechanisms or to give no resuscitation orders ("no-code") with openness and freedom will continue to be a problem for many health professionals.

Nurses face a particular problem because they are with patients more constantly than is the physician. The legal uncertainty surrounding "no-code" orders is significant to nurses, who may be given a verbal "no-code" or "slow-code" order.[79]* Such orders place nurses in a severe dilemma. The nurse might believe that prolongation of the patient's life prevents the patient from dying with dignity; the nurse may wish to follow a verbal "no-code" order, but

---

*A "no-code" order means that the health professional is not to call the hospital switchboard operator to initiate a page call (or code) that would summon the resuscitation team to the patient's bedside for cardiac resuscitation. A "slow code" means that the professional should not hurry to call the operator in hope that the patient might die, but the health professionals would not be held responsible for inaction.

to do so would place the nurse in legal jeopardy. As well, the nurse may be unable to discuss the order with the patient if the physician has not discussed the "no-code" order with patient and family. While a "no-code" order has almost inevitable consequences of death, a "slow-code" order presents a more serious problem: it may cause further injury to the patient, thereby jeopardizing the quality of life if resuscitation efforts do succeed.

The patient's right to die poses one of the more acute ethical and legal dilemmas for nurses, and will continue to do so. At issue is a fundamental question raised by James Rachels: is killing any worse than letting someone slowly die?[80] Nurses, who must witness a slow and sometimes painful death of a patient, will continue to seek an answer to this question.

SUMMARY

In this chapter, issues relating to the patient's right to be respected are explored. It was noted that these rights are among the more difficult to protect, and that the ethical conflicts that arise defy easy solution. Respect hinges on the concept of patient autonomy and self-determination; it is of utmost importance that nurses examine these concepts and their own beliefs. As well, the legal dimensions of confidentiality, of refusal of treatment and experimentation, and of the right to die must be well understood.

Nurses come into contact with patients twenty-four hours a day, they have the power to turn the health-care system towards greater respect for patients. Nurses can monitor, support, intervene, and advocate for considerate and respectful care, privacy, confidentiality, appropriate use of human subjects in teaching and research, respect in cases of refusal of treatment, and dignity in dying.

REFERENCES FOR CHAPTER 4

[1]Peter M. Lazes, ed, *The Handbook of Health Education* (Germantown, Maryland: Aspen Systems Corporation, 1979), p. 322.
[2]Thomas S. Szasz, "Illness and Indignity" in *Humanizing Hospital Care*, eds, Gerald P. Turner and Joseph Mapa (Toronto: McGraw-Hill Ryerson, 1979), p. 132.
[3]George L. Engel, "The Care of the Patient: Art or Science?" in *Humanizing Hospital Care*, p. 156.
[4]Paul Ramsey, *The Patient as a Person* (New Haven: Yale University Press, 1970), p. xii.
[5]Jan Howard, Fred Davis, Clyde Pope, and Sheryl Ruzek, "Humanizing Health

Care: The Implications of Technology, Centralization, and Self-Care," *Medical Care* 15 (May 1977): 12.

[6]Esther Lucille Brown, *Newer Dimensions of Patient Care: Patients as People* (New York: Russell Sage Foundation, 1964).

[7]Martha Weinman Lear, *Heartsounds* (New York: Simon and Schuster, 1980). See, for examples, pp. 141-142, 146-148, 231-233, 323-333.

[8]L.E. and F.A. Rozovsky, "Importing Legal Concepts," *Dimensions* 57 (August 1980): 36.

[9]Corinne Sklar, "Unwarranted Disclosure," *Canadian Nurse* 74 (May 1978): 6-8. The two provinces are British Columbia (Privacy Act S.B.C., 1968, c. 39) and Manitoba (The Privacy Act, S.M. 1970, c. 74).

[10]Marilyn M. Rawnsley, "The Concept of Privacy," *Advances in Nursing Science* 2 (January 1980): 28-29.

[11]*The Nurse's Dilemma: Ethical Considerations of Nursing Practice* (Geneva: International Council of Nurses, 1977), p. 19.

[12]Sklar, p. 6.

[13]*The Nurse's Dilemma*, pp. xii, 72.

[14]See, for example, the Alberta Hospitals Act, R.S.A. 1970, c. 174, s. 35, and The Public Hospitals Act, R.S.O. 1970, c. 378, regulation 729.

[15]Sklar, p. 6.

[16]*The Health Disciplines Act*, S.O. 1974, c. 47, section 26.

[17]Sklar, p. 8.

[18]Ibid, p. 8.

[19]Arthur R. Miller, "Computers, Data Banks, and Individual Privacy: An Overview," *Columbia Human Rights Law Review* 4 (Winter 1972): 8.

[20]Ibid, p. 8.

[21]*Report of the Commission of Inquiry into the Confidentiality of Health Information*, Vol. 2, by Hon. Mr. Justice Horace Krever, Chairman (Toronto: Queen's Printer, 1980) p. 181.

[22]Ibid, p. 124.

[23]Ellen Picard, *Legal Liability of Doctors and Hospitals In Canada* (Toronto: The Carswell Company Ltd., 1978), pp. 69-70. The reader should also see *Medical Treatment and the Criminal Law*, Working Paper 26 of the Law Reform Commission of Canada, Ottawa, 1980, for a detailed discussion of the law related to a patient's refusal of treatment.

[24]Ibid, pp. 69-70.

[25]*The Nurse's Dilemma*, p. xii.

[26]Law Reform Commission of Canada, "Medical Treatment and Criminal Law," Working Paper 26 (Ottawa: Supply and Services, 1980): 70.

[27]Judith Lorber, "Good Patients and Problem Patients: Conformity and Deviance in a General Hospital," in *Humanizing Hospital Care*, p. 113.

[28]Hans Jonas, "Philosophical Reflections on Experimenting with Human Subjects," *Daedalus* 98 (Spring 1969): 237-238.

[29]World Health Organization, *Health Aspects of Human Rights with Special Reference to Developments in Biology and Medicine* (Geneva: World Health Organization, 1976), p. 28.

[30]Doris Bloch, Thomas P. Phillips, and Susan R. Gortner, "Protection of Human Research Subjects," in *Current Perspectives in Nursing*, eds. Michael H. Miller and Beverly C. Flynn (St. Louis: C.V. Mosby, 1977), pp. 14-15.

[31]Nathan Hershey and Robert D. Miller, *Human Experimentation and the Law* (Germantown, Maryland: Aspen Systems Corporation, 1976), pp. 8-10.

[32]Hershey and Miller, pp. 8-10.

[33]Bloch, *et al.*, p. 15.

[34]Hershey and Miller, pp. 7-8.

[35]Paul A. Freund. "Introduction," *Daedalus* 98 (Spring 1969): viii-xiv.

[36]This point was reinforced by studies that compared the progress of patients with ischaemic heart disease when cared for at home and when cared for at the hospital cardiac-care unit. See A.L. Cochrance, *Effectiveness and Efficiency* (The Nuffield Provincial Hospitals Trust Fund, 1971), pp. 50-54. See pages 45-66 for comparable examples.

[37]David A. Frenkel, "Human Experimentation: Codes of Ethics," *Legal Medical Quarterly* 1 (1977): 12.

[38]American Nurses Association, "The Nurse in Research: *ANA* Guidelines on Ethical Values," *Nursing Research* 17 (March-April 1968): 104-107.

[39]"Ethics of Nursing Research," *The Canadian Nurse* 68 (September 1972): 23-25.

[40]Bernard Barber, *et al. Research on Human Subjects: Problems of Social Control in Human Experimentation* (New York: Russell Sage Foundation, 1973), p. 188.

[41]"Protecting the Rights of Research Subjects," *Nursing Research* 18 (November-December 1969): 483.

[42]Bernadette Arminger, "Ethics of Nursing Research," *Nursing Research* 26 (September-October 1977): 330-336.

[43]Ibid, p. 333.

[44]Ibid, p. 333. Copyright © 1971, American Journal of Nursing Company. Quoted from *Nursing Research*, September/October, Vol. 26, No. 5.

[45]Katharyn Antle May, "The Nurse as Researcher: Impediment to Informed Consent?" *Nursing Outlook* 27 (January 1979): 37-39.

[46]Ibid, p. 39.

[47]Bonnie Bullough and Vern Bullough, "A Brief History of Medical Practice," in *Medical Men and Their Work: A Sociological Reader*, eds. Eliot Freidson and Judith Lorber (Chicago: Aldine Publishing Company, 1972) p. 95.

[48]Sheila P. Corcoran, "Should a Service Setting Be Used As a Learning Laboratory?: An Ethical Question," *Nursing Outlook* 25 (December 1977): 771-776.

[49]See, for example, the student-learning situation described by Martha Weinman Lear, *Heartsounds* (New York: Simon and Schuster, 1980), p. 373.

[50]Claire F. Ryder, "Terminal Care-Issues and Alternatives," *Public Health Reports* 92 (January-February 1977): 24.

[51]Ivan Illich, *Medical Nemesis* (London: Calder & Boyars, 1975), pp. 144-150.

[52]George J. Annas, "Rights of the Terminally Ill Patient," *Journal of Nursing Administration* 4 (March-April 1974): 21-25. See also George J. Annas, *The Rights of Hospital Patients: An American Civil Liberties Union Handbook* (New York: Avon Books), pp. 162-169.

[53]Annas, "Rights of the Terminally Ill Patient," p. 22.

[54]Ibid, p. 23.

[55]Ibid, p. 23.

[56]George J. Agich, "The Ethics of Terminal Care," *Death Education* 2 (Spring-Summer 1978): 165.

[57]George Annas, "Legalizing Laetrile for the Terminally Ill," *The Hastings Center Report* 7 (December 1977): 19-20.

[58]See, for example, S. Munro and B. Mount, "Music and Therapy in Palliative Care," *Canadian Medical Association Journal* 119 (November 4, 1978): 1029-1033.

[59]Annas, "Rights of the Terminally Ill," p. 23.

[60]Mark Siegler, "Critical Illness: The Limits of Autonomy," *The Hastings Center Report* 9 (October 1979): 12-14. Reprinted with permission of Institute of Society, Ethics and the Life Sciences, 360 Broadway, Hastings-on-Hudson, N.Y., 10706.

[61]Ibid, p. 14.

⁶²Bernard Lo and Albert Jonsen, "Clinical Decisions to Limit Treatment," *Annals of Internal Medicine* 93 (1980): 764–768.

⁶³Ibid, pp. 765–766.

⁶⁴Richard A. McCormick, "The Quality of Life, the Sanctity of Life," *The Hastings Center Report* 8 (February 1978): 30–36.

⁶⁵Milton D. Heifetz and Charles Mangel, *The Right to Die* (New York: G.P. Putnam Sons, 1976).

⁶⁶Theodore Raymond LeBlanc, "Death with Dignity: A Tripartite Legal Response," *Death Education* 2 (Spring–Summer 1978), p. 179; for further discussion and an example of a living will prepared by the Euthanasia Educational Council, see Anne J. Davis and Mila A. Aroskar, *Ethical Dilemmas and Nursing Practice* (New York: Appleton-Century-Crofts, 1978); pp. 121–122.

⁶⁷*Legislative Manual, 1978* (New York: The Society for the Right to Die, 1978), p. 5.

⁶⁸See, for example, "The Quinlan Decision: Five Commentaries," *The Hastings Center Report* 6 (February 1976), pp. 8–19; George J. Annas, "The Incompetent's Right to Die: The Case of Joseph Saikewicz," *The Hastings Center Report* 8 (February 1978): 21–23; Leonard H. Glantz, "Post-Saikewicz Judicial Actions Clarify the Rights of the Patients and Families," *Medicolegal News 6:4 (Winter 1978): 9–11.*

⁶⁹Lorne E. Rozovsky, "The Patient's Right to Die," *Dimensions* 56 (January 1979): 38–39.

⁷⁰Ibid, p. 38–39.

⁷¹John Stephens, "The Right to Die," *Legal Medical Quarterly* 1 (1977): 111.

⁷²Rozovsky, p. 39.

⁷³For elaboration on this point, see Marc Alexander, "'The Rigid Embrace of the Narrow House:' Premature Burial and Signs of Death," *The Hastings Center Report* 10 (June 1980): 25–31. According to Alexander, signs of death have always been discussed in medical writings, but it was not until the eighteenth century that the debate over the certainty of death began. Physicians became preoccupied with the uncertainty of death's signs for two reasons: they believed that rules of science could be found to establish medical authority, objectivity, and certainty regarding death, and they believed that such medical expertise could safeguard against premature burial. By the end of the nineteenth century, the verification of death had become a technical problem that could be solved by medical expertise. However, today there is sharp disagreement and debate about the definition of death.

⁷⁴See "Criteria for the Determination of Death: Working Paper 23," (Ottawa: Law Reform Commission of Canada, 1979) and "Report 15, Criteria for the Determination of Death" (Ottawa: Supply and Services, 1981).

⁷⁵"Report 15," pp. 24–25.

⁷⁶McCormick, p. 34.

⁷⁷Szasz, p. 132.

⁷⁸Sections 198, 199, and 203 of the Criminal Code are relevant:

198. *Every one who undertakes to administer surgical or medical treatment to another person or to do any other lawful act that may endanger the life of another person is, except in cases of necessity, under a legal duty to have and use reasonable knowledge, skill and care in doing so.*

199. *Everyone who undertakes to do an act is under a legal duty to do it if an omission to do the act is or may be dangerous to life.*

203. Everyone who by criminal negligence causes death to another person is guilty of an indictable offence and is liable to imprisonment for life.

[79]As a result of the concern of nursing staff at McMaster University Medical Centre, a "do not resuscitate" policy was implemented in the hospital in January 1979. The policy requires the physician to write a "do not resuscitate" order on the patient's chart, complete with relevant facts. See Aileen McPhail, Sean Moore, John O'Connor, and Christel Woodward, "One Hospital's Experience with a 'Do Not Resuscitate' Policy," *Canadian Medical Association Journal* 125 (October 15, 1981): 830–836.

[80]James Rachels, "Active and Passive Euthanasia," in *Medical Issues of Modern Medicine*, eds. Robert Hunt and John Arras (Palo Alto, California: Mayfield Publishing Co, 1977), p. 197.

SUGGESTED REFERENCES FOR FURTHER STUDY, CHAPTER 4

Agich, George J. "The Ethics of Terminal Care." *Death Education* 2 (Spring–Summer 1978): 163–171.

Agich criticizes the literature on terminal care for its underlying assumption that shifting the patient from one environment to another will solve the ethical problems of terminal care. He acknowledges the problems of care of the terminally ill in a modern medical institution, where the patient is expected to get well, and discusses three problems related to hospice care: allocation of resources, goals of hospice care, and patients' attitudes towards death. He questions the use of terminally ill patients as research subjects, and ends with a plea that nurses consider the moral and ethical aspects of care of the terminally ill.

Bandman, Elsie L. and Bandman, Bertram. "The Nurse's Role in Protecting the Patient's Right to Live or Die." *Advances in Nursing Science* 1 (April 1979): 21–35.

The authors acknowledge that nurses face ethical dilemmas in caring for dying patients, and offer a theoretical framework of rights that might serve as a reference point in decision-making. The concepts of option rights, welfare rights, and legislative rights are then discussed. Option rights are those that mark freedom of action without the interference of others; welfare rights are rights that are based on the alleviation of human suffering; legislative rights are based on justice. Four cases involving the nurse and the dying patient are then presented, and the three rights are applied to these cases.

Bloch, Doris; Phillips, Thomas P.; and Gortner, Susan. "Protection of Human Research Subjects" in *Current Perspectives in Nursing*, pp 14–31. Edited by Michael H. Miller and Beverly Flynn. St. Louis: C.V. Mosby, 1977.

The authors note the significance of research but also acknowledge that researchers may have very different conceptions and interpretations of the rights of human subjects. They review several studies in which the rights of human subjects were placed in jeopardy and discuss a number of guidelines and regulations governing human experimentation. The remainder of the article focuses on the assessment of risk and benefit in human research, noting the tendency of researchers to minimize the risk and overestimate the benefit. The invasion of privacy, a risk in many research studies, is discussed; the authors outline problems in establishing an informed consent. They conclude that responsibility for ethical behavior inevitably lies with the researcher.

Corcoran, Sheila. "Should a Service Setting be Used as a Learning Laboratory? An Ethical Question," *Nursing Outlook* 25 (December 1977): 771–776.

Service settings have always been used as a learning laboratories for nursing students, but this tradition should not prevent nursing educators or students from facing the ethical issues of this practice. With this in mind, Corcoran examines the concept of such experiential education and develops arguments for and against the continued use of service setting for teaching purposes. Arguments against continued use include the different priorities of service and education, the students' inability to fail, exploitation of patients, demands on other staff, and the marginal position of the faculty person. Arguments for continued use of the service setting include the reinforcement and integration of learning for the student, opportunities for career exploration, increased time and discussion (which benefits the client), stimulation and expanded learning for staff and faculty, and increased manpower. Corcoran concludes that the problem might be resolved by rephrasing the question to read: "Under what conditions should the servicing setting be used as a learning laboratory for nursing education?" She then argues that both the consequences and the means must be assessed, and she offers seven conditions or rules that would govern the answer.

Hayter, Jean. "Issues Related to Human Subjects," in *Issues in Nursing Research*, pp. 107–147. Edited by Florence S. Downs and Juanita J. Fleming. New York: Appleton-Century-Crofts, 1979.

Hayter analyzes a number of key issues in research on human subjects, including the recognition of self-determination through informed consent; the subject's right to refuse or withdraw from participation; the subject's privacy; confidentiality and anonymity of data; protection from physical, psychological, and sociological risks; and the securing of an informed consent. She systematically discusses circumstances that affect human rights, such as mentally or legally incompetent subjects (including the dying or the aged), captive subjects (including prisoners, students, or employees), and animal subjects. Problems of particular types of research, where full disclosure would alter outcomes or where medical treatment would be affected, are discussed; Hayter makes a distinction between withholding information and deception. Finally, she discusses the various safeguards that protect human rights in research, such as peer review committees and the role of agency staff and journal editorial boards. Nursing roles and responsibilities in research as investigator, participant, or subject are then discussed. The article provides a very thorough analysis of key issues of nursing research.

Rawnsley, Marilyn M. "The Concept of Privacy." *Advances in Nursing Science* 2 (January 1980): 25–31.

Since an improved understanding of privacy is important to understanding human nature, Rawnsley stresses the need for empirical investigation of privacy. However, before such research can occur, she stresses the need to explore the concept of privacy. She explores this concept etymologically, anthropologically, and historically, and arrives at a concept of privacy as a psycho-social reality. She then examines the legal right of privacy, concluding that in law the boundaries of privacy become defined by their disruption. Privacy as a social privilege is next explored, where privacy is seen as a scarce commodity accessed by the power of individuals to purchase it. Several psychological functions of privacy are examined: privacy as antisocial behavior, as an escape, or as a self-actualizing process. Rawnsley concludes that research approaches to privacy must go beyond spatial concepts to more broadly based concepts of privacy.

Report of the Commission of Inquiry into the Confidentiality of Health Information. By Hon. Mr. Justice Horace Krever, Chairman. Toronto: Queen's Printer 1980.

This three-volume report addresses the numerous concerns related to the practices, misuses, and problems of maintaining confidentiality of health information in Ontario between 1978 and 1980. The first volume focuses mainly on the misuse of patient's health information that gave rise to the Commission, and includes detailed case accounts of the nature and type of information supplied, as well as the means by which it was obtained. In Volume II, attention is focused on a number of organizations and their roles in the handling and processing of health information, such as the police, the Ontario Health Insurance Plan, the Hospital Medical Records Institute, the Hospital and the Individual Health Provider Organization. These systems are well described and the points of breaches of confidentiality identified. Particularly useful chapters in Volume II are Chapter 18, on the threats to privacy of computer-supported systems in health, and Chapter 23, on the patients' access to their own health information. In Volume III, issues of consent to disclosure, research, unique personal-health identifiers, and mandatory reporting of health information are discussed. In addition, the handling of student and employee health information, as well as information generated through the Workmen's Compensation Board and the Occupational Health and Safety legislation, are examined and recommendations made. The Krever Commission report is an exceptionally thorough review and analysis of the handling of health information in one Canadian province.

Sklar, Corinne. "Unwarranted Disclosure." *The Canadian Nurse* 74:5 (May 1978): 6-8.

In discussing unwarranted disclosure of health information about a patient, Sklar emphasizes the nurse's professional-ethical responsibility and legal responsibility to hold information in confidence. She outlines instances where disclosure is valid-for example, by statutory law or court order-and notes that in Canada the nurse-patient relationship is not privileged: nurses are compelled to disclose confidential information in court testimony. Types of defamation are described. Sklar concludes with several recommendations to nurses to guard against unwarranted disclosure.

Veatch, Robert M. "Death and Dying: The Legislative Options," *The Hastings Center Report* 77 (October 1977): 5-8.

Veatch's article is based on his review of eighty-five bills dealing with treatment of terminally ill patients. He underscores the need to have some policy in this area, and classifies the existing bills into three basic types: bills that would apparently legalize active killing, bills clarifying the rights of competent patients, and bills clarifying medical decision-making when the patient is incompetent. He suggests that legalized killing is opposed by the majority of lay persons and professionals. Therefore, there remains the need to assure patients that high-technology resuscitation will stop at the appropriate time, as well as the need to establish a decision-making mechanism for the incompetent. He notes the shortcomings of much of the legislation to date, and proposes some elements that should be included in a model bill to compensate for these shortcomings.

CHAPTER 5 The Right To Participate

The consumers' right to participate in making decisions that affect their health includes at least two levels of involvement: decisions that affect their direct and personal care, and the planning and evaluation of health services. The premise underlying both levels of involvement is that the people who use health services have both a moral obligation and a moral right to contribute to their care and to the planning and evaluation of that care. The obligation and right are based upon the ethical principles of autonomy and responsibility.

PARTICIPATION AS A PATIENT

In the *New England Journal of Medicine* in December 1976 Norman Cousins published an article that later became part of his book, *The Anatomy of an Illness (As Perceived by the Patient)*. Cousins describes his encounter with a severe chronic illness and the participation of his physician and himself in making decisions about his plan of care. Although his treatments and his recovery are unique, his account emphasizes the importance of patient-health-professional partnership. He states:

> *If I had to guess, I would say that the principle contribution made by my doctor to the taming, and possibly the conquest, of my illness was that he encouraged me to believe I was a respected partner with him in the total undertaking.*[1]

This notion of partnership has been too long absent from the health-professional-patient relationship. Patients are treated as passive recipients of the ministrations of health professionals in health education, in nursing-care planning, and in intervention strategies. In view of the rapidly developing technology and the number of health professions that came into being after the mid-1940s, it is not surprising that health professionals came to be seen as doers and patients as receivers. But a new generation of consumers is seeking recognition as partners in care.

> *Despite unprecedented advances in knowledge and technology...people have never been more disillusioned and discontented with health care delivery...medicine is facing a crisis in confidence; this crisis is mainly due to physicians' reluctance to communicate appropriate information to patients and to listen to their ideas.*[2]

Patient participation, in whatever setting, means that patients participate in setting goals for their care, in choosing a plan to reach those goals, in implementing the plan, and in assessing the outcomes of care. Patients must know what questions to ask about their treatment and their progress; they must know the roles of the various health professionals who work with them so that they will be clear about who to ask for information; and they must understand the ways in which they can contribute to their care and to a successful outcome of that care.[3]

The extent of patient participation will vary according to the type of patient and the severity of the illness.[4] Health professionals must take an active and dominant role in caring for patients who are seriously ill, comatose, or confused. But the patients' readiness for greater involvement must be constantly reassessed.

With the increasing numbers of chronically ill patients today – the result of a decreased incidence of infectious disease and greater life expectancy – the need for greater patient participation in care is particularly critical. These patients gradually become "experts" about their illness; they know their own limitations or handicaps. Helping to make decisions about their care is essential to the success of treatment plans and to the patients' sense of well being. Similarly, patients who are dying need to identify their needs and evaluate intervention by health professionals.

To make patient participation meaningful, the staff must legitimize and facilitate the patient's role as an active participant in care.[5] To do this, health professionals must recognize and respect the patient as a partner in care and treatment.

This partnership involves mutual decision-making. Patients must be made to feel that they are autonomous and worthy persons whose involvement is welcomed. They should be encouraged to state their expectations and their goals in seeking care. The health professional should provide information to the patient about the problem, the treatment approaches, and the health professional's own recommendation. Finally, the patient's informed "suggestions and preferences" must be heard.[6]

When health professionals allow their patient to help make decisions, they take the risk that the patient may choose an alternative that does not appear to be in his or her best interests.[7] Professionals have a "right to refuse suggestions for active intervention" that they believe would result in more harm than good, but must be willing to negotiate with patients to allow them the dignity of their choice.[8]

A patient who participates accepts some legal responsibility. Legal action is limited to cases where a lawsuit is brought by a patient against a doctor on charges of negligence; some contributory negligence may be ascribed to the patient. In effect, patients have a duty to themselves, that of a "reasonable patient in similar circumstances."[9]

Nurses should encourage patients to participate in decisions about care. Despite acknowledgement of the benefits of patient participation, the parental figure still emerges strongly in many nurses,[10] and nurses continue to make decisions for patients.

The patient's right to self-determination is fundamental. Patients have the right to determine their own best interests; they have the right to specify the nurse's role in their relationship.[11] That role may vary from nurse as surrogate mother to nurse as technician to nurse as contracted clinician, dependent upon the patient's defined need. It must be understood by both parties that nurses can decline to participate in a situation if they feel their values are compromised.[12]

Recent studies show that a significant number of patients – twenty-five to fifty per cent – choose not to comply with a prescribed therapeutic regimen.[13] The very notion of *compliance* in the context of patient care suggests that the relationship between health professionals and their patients is unbalanced – and indicates acceptance of that imbalance. Traditional medical and nursing practice has been based, to a large extent, on the authority of the health professional; that authority is based on the professional's intellectual superiority in matters relevant to health care. But intellectual superiority does not give a person the right to order others around; nor does authority give one the right to make decisions for other persons, including patients.[14] When patients choose not to comply with "authority," they may be attempting to gain some control over their treatment and thereby be recognized as contributing partners.[15]

Patient Satisfaction with Care

Patient participation necessarily involves evaluation of the care the patient receives. Patients must be involved in evaluating the care they receive and the manner in which it is delivered. Patient and nurse should review the treatment plan and together agree on the goals, care plans, and acceptable outcomes.

Patients may also be involved in evaluating the care in a particular unit. Sometimes health professionals assume that patients either do not know how to evaluate care or are too sick to do so effectively. But such assumptions are not always valid. A case in point is the patients discharged from a pulmonary intensive-care unit who were asked to evaluate their care in the unit. The patients were able to describe the routine of the unit, and identified some of the central problems of organization.[16]

Obtaining patient evaluations can be difficult, however. Some patients fear reprisals, and therefore make no negative comments.[17] Another problem is that satisfaction is difficult to measure.

Although there have been several formal studies that attempted to determine patient satisfaction, few of them provided reliable and valid means of measurement. "Thus, there is little basis for determining how successful these [studies] have been in actually measuring patient satisfaction."[18] An analysis of one hundred studies published in the past twenty-five years identifies eight elements of patient satisfaction: the art of care (the amount of caring), the technical quality of care, the accessibility and convenience of care, the financial aspects of obtaining care, the physical environment, the availability of care, the continuity of care, and the efficacy or outcomes of care.[19]

Those studies that have managed to measure satisfaction show that scores tend to be sufficiently high.[20] When assessing overall care, patients tend to respond positively, although they might indicate discontent with specific practices, for example, the communication of information about their illness and their treatment plan. Specific complaints allow providers to recognize consumer concerns and problems.[21]

Although consumer satisfaction is not synonomous with quality of care, satisfaction should be seen as one measure of quality. The health-care institution staff, the medical staff, the patients, and the patient's family hold different expectations of and perspectives on health care; no one group alone should evaluate care, nor should one single method of evaluation be relied upon. "Different aspects of care may be different in quality and have differential import across evaluators."[22]

Nursing researchers continue to explore methods that will allow patients to evaluate nursing care. Researchers are interested in both primary health-care[23] and hospital settings.[24]

Although formal evaluations are essential, the value of informal or verbal evaluations should not be underrated. Because of their frequent contacts with patients, nurses can request feedback about patients' general care, and about their nursing care.

Such information is essential to the continued accountability of the nursing profession to its clients. If nurses are serious about becoming more accountable to the patient, they must continue to extend to the patient and families these opportunities to evaluate nursing care.[25]

At the same time, they must also be committed to incorporating the patients' suggestions for change in their planning.

> *The extent to which consumer opinion can influence policy-makers and health care personnel is not only dependent upon collecting the right kind of data, it also requires that policy-makers and health personnel accept the value of the consumer's point of view.*[26]

PARTICIPATION AT THE COMMUNITY LEVEL

Consumer participation at the community level is not a new concept; "any situation in which the consumer participates in some way in decision-making related to the service he consumes" is community-level participation.[27] The consumer's right to self-determination is recognized in the concept.

Meaningful consumer participation, once an accepted facet of social life, has changed. Formerly, town meetings provided a forum for citizens to become involved in matters that affected the individual and the community.[28] As the population grew and society changed, this mode of participation became less feasible. Citizen participation gradually became limited to the political arena, where voting, letter-writing campaigns, and other activities provided a forum for change. There was little actual involvement in decision-making.[29]

During the 1960s, several events helped to change the context of citizen participation. North Americans were more affluent, were better educated, and had more leisure time. They began to demand greater involvement in decision-making. In the United States, the civil-rights movement, the "war on poverty," and community-development strategies engineered by Saul Alinsky helped to rekindle the desire to be involved. Also in the United States, legislation was enacted to attain maximum feasible participation of citizens on boards of health and in social-service organizations; a 1966 comprehensive health-planning act specified that fifty-one per cent of health-board members must be consumers.

Consumer involvement in Canadian health-care planning has been less extensive. Consumer participation flourished amongst prairie farmers and Maritime colliery workers at the turn of the century and into the 1930s, but involvement declined from the 1940s to the 1960s; federal and provincial governments have taken over many of the responsibilities once carried by families and citizen groups.

Since 1970, numerous reports have addressed the issue of consumer participation in health-care planning. A report published by the Community Health Centre in Canada advocated area-wide representation of consumers on health-centre boards and area boards, but no guidance was provided to effect such participation.[30]

Several provincial reports, however, did try to provide such guidance. The Castonguay Report, in Quebec, was one of the first to prescribe broad consumer representation at both the regional and the local level; the report recommended that non-professionals constitute a majority on boards.[31] In British Columbia, Richard

Foulkes also advocated local and regional boards composed of consumer, professional, and worker. His report notes that the public must feel it can participate in the development and implementation of new systems, but that that participation be at the "right" level.[32]

Manitoba's White Paper recommended that there be a majority of user representatives on community health-centre boards. Ideally, district boards would be composed predominantly of lay representatives, "suitably informed" for their important responsibilities, drawn from a variety of community groups.[33] In Saskatchewan, the McLeod Report recommended that advisory and planning bodies be comprised of equal numbers of physicians, allied health professionals, and lay people. The lay representation should consist of people "already informed about and capable of being informed about the problems of health care."[34]

The Health Planning Task Force of Ontario recommended that district health councils be given authority for planning and policy in geographic areas. Each council should consist of ten impartial members appointed (by the Lieutenant Governor in Council) from lists of nominees submitted by organizations and individuals in the district, and up to five representatives from the district's municipal governments.[35] Most reports that recommended predominantly lay representation stipulated advisory committees composed of health professionals.

To date, progress in implementing the ideas on consumer participation contained in these reports has been slow. Ontario has established approximately twenty-four district health councils. In British Columbia, there is some participation on regional boards, but the effects have been somewhat disappointing. In general, provincial governments seem less committed to the idea of citizen participation because of public disinterest.[36] Some have suggested, however, that the public is not apathetic. The problem, they believe, is one of ignorance: the public does not understand the role and function of public or private community agencies.[37] One of the more promising examples of consumer participation is in Quebec, where legislation calls for consumers as board members at the local level. Although "the existence of formal power does not mean that consumers hold any real power," the experience of the past five years has demonstrated to health providers that citizens and providers must work together to realize health-care goals.[38]

Citizen involvement must be tailored to the needs and purposes of local citizens.[39] The level of involvement can be described on a continuum; one extreme is professional dominance, the other consumer dominance. Several situations are possible along the continuum. At one extreme is the establishment of better mechanisms to inform the consumer about health-care programs and facilities. This is a one-way flow of communication with no feedback or negotiation. Less extreme is consultation with consumers: the consumer's view is solicited, but there is no assurance that this view will be respected. The next step is partnership, then delegated power; ultimately, citizens would control the agency.[40] There is no one best formula for consumer input, but it is essential to define the role and authority of consumers, whatever the form of their involvement.

Rationale for Consumer Participation

One fundamental function of consumer involvement is to offset the paternalism of health providers. Providers often become paternalistic not by intent but by default, and the consumer's ability to identify and articulate health-care needs, to identify the inadequacies of the system, to limit the bureaucratic nature of the organizations, to make public and private services more responsive to human need, to act as a watchdog on organizational practices, and to watch over standards of service, should not be underestimated.[41]

Consumer involvement also provides an opportunity for consumers to become better acquainted with the health-care system and to become more realistic in their expectations of that system. Involved consumers can, in turn, provide a link to other consumers, interpreting to them the system of care and increasing public understanding of the benefits and limitations of modern medicine.

In the next ten years, the types and amounts of health services available to patients will have to be examined carefully. Because consumers are ultimately affected by any decisions, they must be involved in formulating the policies that will inform the decisions. Who will live; who will die? These are no longer academic questions, but deep-seated concerns as the health-care dollar grows less elastic. That health professionals alone must make these decisions is unfair: consumers must be involved. Consumer participation brings its own kind of expertise, which complements the knowledge of the health professional.

Problems of Consumer Participation

Consumer participation in "planning and evaluating the system of health services, the types and qualities of service, and the conditions under which health services are delivered"[42] is not achieved with ease. A number of problems complicate adequate and meaningful consumer participation. Foremost among these are lack of consumer interest, the cumbersome structural features of the system, difficulty in selecting and training consumer representatives, and a lack of consumer self-confidence that is often reinforced by the behavior of health-care providers.

Apathy is probably the greatest stumbling block to consumer participation. The lack of interest may stem from the growing technical complexity of the medical system, from skepticism, or from lack of immediate concern for health.[43] Other reasons for lack of interest may be:

1) that health services are not used routinely;
2) that individual health problems are not attributed to health institutions;
3) that health care has not been generally accepted as a community problem;
4) that discrepancies in care among different socio-economic groups are not highly visible;
5) that the perceived legitimacy of the medical profession negates the need to be involved.[44]

Consumer participation is also prevented, to some extent, by the complex structure of the health-care system. Information exchanges, social contacts, and professional roles are highly structured and consumers are naturally isolated by such structures.[45] One author suggests that for consumers to be involved effectively, they must be involved with the larger health-care system, not just with their local health facility, and that there must be "career possibilities" in that involvement.[46]

The selection and training of participating consumers is another common problem. Frequently only the "right" kind of people are selected for boards or committees – that is, people who have financial backing, particular expertise, or "connections." Since the mid-sixties, those who are not represented on such boards and committees – the poor, members of the counter-culture, and the "victims" – have expressed growing dissatisfaction. Many agency administrators have tried to develop representative boards, but not without difficulty. Who truly represents the consumer? The question is compounded because health-care consumers form a transitional group, a non-cohesive group that lacks homogeneity. Most consumer representatives are appointed, although a few counties and municipalities fill board vacancies with elected municipal officials. In agencies where a wide-ranging representation of consumers has been sought, the number of people selected and the diversity of backgrounds have often encumbered effective board functioning.

To participate meaningfully on boards and committees, consumers must have some orientation to the organization and some background information and understanding regarding the central problems and issues of that system. Health professionals must develop and provide orientation programs and information so that consumers can make informed choices. Many health professionals do not know how to educate board members effectively, and some seem unwilling to learn. As well, health professionals are frequently reluctant to relinquish the power that knowledge and decision-making gives them.

Professional resistance to consumer involvement is a real impediment to participation. To date there is limited acceptance of the idea that professionals and consumers can work together. There is a prevailing attitude that "consumer participation" means that inexperienced people learn the hard way what experts knew all along.[47]

To participate effectively, consumers must feel competent and capable of working with professionals. At times the behavior of the professionals reinforces consumers' lack of self-confidence, which undermines any contributions consumers might make.[48] In a tongue-in-cheek article in a recent issue of the *American Journal of Public Health*, two writers outline a number of ways in which providers "'contain' and render ineffective" consumer participation. The writers cite overwhelming the board with data, scheduling meetings during a weekday, using professional jargon, and avoiding questions and confrontation as examples.[49]

Professionals also resist consumer representation on health-professional regulatory boards.

Opponents of public membership claim that nonprofessionals cannot understand board activities since they do not understand or have the knowledge of practise needed to serve on a board. Others assert that

*consumers will only interfere with normal business activities of boards.
Still others ask who the public represent and question their purpose in
seeking membership on health professional boards.*[50]

NURSES AND CONSUMERS

Nurses must view consumers as partners in planning for and
evaluating health care, whether that be personal health care or
health care for the community. Nurses who are involved in pri-
mary-care community clinics will need to be aware of the problems
and prospects of consumer participation in planning and evaluating community health-care programs; they must learn to be more
adept at working with consumer groups. When consumers work on
hospital and nursing-department committees, there will be greater
accountability. For example, consumer board members may serve
on patient-care committees and be involved in reviewing critical-
incident reports. In nursing departments, consumers may be
involved on standard-setting and policy committees, on audit committees, and on staff development committees.[51]

Consumers are also beginning to participate in professional
nursing associations. The Canadian Nurses Association Board now
has three lay (consumer) representatives; several provincial associations, by choice or by mandate, are including consumers in their
governing councils.

TOWARDS PARTNERSHIP

*The consumer movement of the 1970s can be seen as an outgrowth of the
1960s, a period marked by challenges to existing social institutions and
mores. Also challenged in that period was the traditional paternalistic and
authoritarian relationship between the professional and the client.*[52]

Partnership involves mutual goals, trust, and information-sharing.
For the health professional, partnership is a new and largely
uncharted course, but a course well worth pursuing. It will require
the development of consultation and negotiation skills and of new
and carefully designed educational materials; and there must be a
willingness to reach agreement without compromising professional standards.

REFERENCES FOR CHAPTER 5

[1] Norman Cousins, *Anatomy of an Illness (As Perceived by Patient)* (New York: W.W. Norton and Company, 1979), p. 48.

[2] David S. Brody, "The Patient's Role in Clinical Decision-Making," *Annals of Internal Medicine* 93 (1980): 718–722.

[3] Marcella Z. Davis, "The Organizational, Interactional, and Care Oriented Conditions for Patient Participation in Continuity of Care: A Framework for Staff Intervention," *Social Science and Medicine* 14A (1980): 39–40.

[4] Beatrice J. Kalisch, "Of Half-Gods and Mortals: Aesculapian Authority," in *Humanizing Hospital Care*, eds. Gerald P. Turner and Joseph Mapa (Toronto: McGraw-Hill Ryerson, 1979), pp. 44–56.

[5] Davis, p. 44.

[6] Brody, pp. 719–720.

[7] Kalisch, p. 55.

[8] Brody, p. 720.

[9] Lorne E. Rozovsky, "The Patient's Duty to Himself," *Dimensions* 56 (December 1979): 27–28.

[10] "The Health Care Consumer: Compliant Captive," *Nursing Outlook* 23 (January 1975): 21.

[11] Sheri Smith, "Three Models of the Nurse-Patient Relationship," in *Nursing Images and Ideals*, eds. Stuart F. Spicker and Sally Gadow (New York: Springer Publishing Co. 1980), pp. 176–187.

[12] Smith, pp. 182–186. Smith describes the surrogate-mother role as one of unlimited commitment and ultimate responsibility for the patient; the role also involves an obligation to determine what is best for the patient. The tehnical model is based on nursing as a clinical science, and the nurse provides scientific care: objective, non-judgmental, and non-interfering. The contracted-clincian model assumes the patient is capable of self-determination; the nurse-patient relationship is based on an agreement between nurse and patient. The patient contracts with the nurse to have specific care provided by the nurse: the nurse incurs this obligation to provide that care.

[13] Brody, p. 721.

[14] John Ladd, "Some Reflections on Authority and the Nurse," in *Nursing: Images and Ideals*, eds. Stuart F. Spicker and Sally Gadow (New York: Springer Publishing Co., 1980), pp. 160–175.

[15] David E. Hayes-Bautista, "Modifying the Treatment: Patient Compliance, Patient Control, and Medical Care," *Social Science and Medicine* 10 (May 1976): 233–238. Note: studies have demonstrated that the patient-health-professional agreement makes it easier to solve problems. See Barbara Starfield, Christine Wray, Kellian Hess, Richard Gross, Peter Birk, and Burton C. D'Lugoff, "Influence of Patient Practitioner Agreement on Outcome of Care," *American Journal of Public Health* 71 (February 1981): 127–131.

[16] Karin Kirchhoff, "Let's Ask the Patient: Consumer Input Can Improve Patient Care," *Journal of Nursing Administration* 6 (December 1976): 36–40.

[17] Virgina Nehring and Barbara Geach, "Patient's Evaluations of Their Care – Why They Don't Complain," *Nursing Outlook* 21 (May 1973): 317–321.

[18] John E. Ware, Allyson Davies-Avery, and Anita L. Stewart, "The Measurement and Meaning of Patient Satisfaction," *Health and Medical Care Services Review* 1 (January – February 1978): 1–3.

[19] Ware, *et al*, pp. 4–5.

[20] Lawrence S. Linn, "Factors Associated with Patient Evaluation of Health Care," *The Milbank Memorial Fund Quarterly* 53 (Fall 1975): 534.

[21] David Locker and David Dunt, "Theoretical and Methodological Issues in Sociological Studies of Consumer Satisfaction with Medical Care," *Social Sciences and Medicine* 12 (1978): 286-287.

[22] Jay L. Lebow, "Consumer Assessments of the Quality of Medical Care," *Medical Care* 12 (April 1974): 334. See also Avedis Donabedian, *The Definition of Quality and Approaches to its Assessment* (Ann Arbor: Health Administration Press, 1980), pp. 24-25 for a discussion of the ways in which clients contribute to defining and judging the quality or "goodness" of care.

[23] See for example Nancy Risser, "Development of an Instrument to Measure Patient Satisfaction with Nurses and Nursing Care in Primary Care Settings," *Nursing Research* 24 (January-February 1975): 45-52; Peggy-Anne Field, "Sources of Client Satisfaction with Nursing Care," unpublished paper, McGill University, School of Nursing, November 1978.

[24] See for example Beverly Safford and Rozella Schlotfeldt, "Nursing Service Staffing and Quality of Nursing Care," *Nursing Research* 9, No. 3 (1960): 149-154; Wilda R. Routhier, "Tool for the Evaluation of Patient Care," *Supervisor Nurse* (January 1972): 17-27; Darlene Pienschke, "Guardedness or Openness on a Cancer Unit," *Nursing Research* 22, No. 6 (1973): 484-490; Karran M. Thorpe, "Validation of Patient Satisfaction with Nursing Care," unpublished Master of Nursing thesis (Edmonton, University of Alberta, 1981).

[25] Gwen D. Marram, "Patients' Evaluation of their Care - Importance to the Nurse," *Nursing Outlook* 21 (May 1973): 323-324.

[26] Locker and Dunt, p. 290.

[27] Ann T. Slavinsky and Vivian Romanoff, "Consumer Participation," *Journal of Nursing Administration* 2 (May-June 1972): 14-18.

[28] Thelma McCormack, "Citizen Participation: A Background Paper for the OMA Task Force," in *Report of the Special Study of the Medical Profession in Ontario*, Edward A. Pickering, Project Director (Toronto: Ontario Medical Association, 1973), pp. 2-3.

[29] Herbert Harvey Hyman, *Health Planning: A Systematic Approach* (Germantown, Maryland: Aspen Systems Corporation, 1975), p. 241.

[30] *The Community Health Centre in Canada*, John E.F. Hastings, Chairman (Ottawa: Information Canada, 1972), pp. 50-51.

[31] Claude Castonguay, "Reorganization of Health and Social Services in Quebec," *Canadian Journal of Public Health* 62:3 (May-June 1971): 192-198.

[32] Richard G. Foulkes, *Health Security for British Columbians* 1:3 (Province of British Columbia, December 1973), pp. 1-3.

[33] *White Paper on Health Policy*, Cabinet Committee on Health Education and Social Policy, S.A. Miller, Chairman (Government of Manitoba, July 1972), pp. 39-40.

[34] J.T. McLeod, *Consumer Participation, Regulation of the Professions, and Decentralization of Health Services*, A report submitted to the Minister of Health, Saskatchewan (Regina, Saskatchewan, August 1973), p. 49.

[35] *Report of the Health Planning Task Force*, J.F. Mustard, Chairman (Ontario Ministry of Health, January 1974), p. 28.

[36] H. Philip Hepworth, *Community Multi-Service Centres* (Ottawa: The Canadian Council on Social Development, 1976), p. 101.

[37] Hepworth, p. 102.

[38] Jaques Godbout, "Is Consumer Control Possible in Health Care Services? The Quebec Case," *International Journal of Health Services* 11 (1981): 151-167.

[39] Jay O. Yedvab, "Consumer's Role in Defining Goals, Structures and Services," *Hospital Progress* 55 (April 1974): 59.

[40] Rudolf Klein, *Notes Toward a Theory of Patient Involvement*, a Commissioned

Paper to the Community Health Centre Project (Toronto: Canadian Public Health Association, 1972), p. 2. See also Eugene Feingold, "Citizen Participation: A Review of the Issues," in *The Citizenry and the Hospital* (Durham, N.C.: Duke University, 1974), pp. 12-13.

[41] Hepworth, p. 103.

[42] "Consumer Rights in Health Care," *Canadian Consumer* 4 (April 1974): 1.

[43] Klein, pp. 10-11.

[44] Michael Lipsky and Morris Lounds, "Citizen Participation and Health Care: Problems of Government Induced Participation" *Journal of Health Politics, Policy, and Law* 1 (Spring 1976): 90-91.

[45] Warren R. Paap, "Consumer-Based Boards of Health Centers: Structural Problems in Achieving Effective Control," *American Journal of Public Health* 68 (June 1978): 579-580. See also Wim. J.A. Van Den Heuval, "The Role of the Consumer in Health Policy," *Social Science and Medicine* 14A (October 1980): 423-426.

[46] Paap, p. 581.

[47] McCormick, pp. 30-31.

[48] Eleanor Palo Stoller, "New Roles for Health Care Consumers: A Study of Role Transformation," *Journal of Community Health* 3 (Winter 1977): 176.

[49] Allan B. Steckler and William T. Herzog, "How to Keep Your Mandated Citizen Board Out of Your Hair and Off Your Back: A Guide for Executive Directors," *American Journal of Public Health* 69 (August 1979): 809-812.

[50] Dale B. Christensen and Albert I. Wertheimer, "Consumer Action in Health Care," *Public Health Reports* 91 (September-October 1976): 409.

[51] Ellen M. Lewis, "Consumers as Members of Nursing Committees," *Nursing Administration Quarterly* 4 (Spring 1980): 11.

[52] Christensen and Wertheimer, pp. 406-407.

SUGGESTED REFERENCES FOR FURTHER STUDY, CHAPTER 5

Brody, David S. "The Patient's Role in Clinical Decision-Making," *Annals of Internal Medicine* 93 (1980): 718-722.

The traditional concept of the physician-patient relationship is described as one where the patient is in a passive role. Brody suggests that this imbalance of power is perpetuated by a number of factors, including an information gap, a social gap, and the attitudes of both patients and physicians. The increased demand for participation and the potential for consumers to participate at different levels are noted. Four steps to encourage mutual participation are then outlined, and potential advantages of participation to the physician, the patient, and the outcome of care are discussed. Brody suggests that the degree of patient participation will vary according to the physician and the patient, but that physicians should experiment with varying degrees of patient participation.

Christensen, Dale B. and Wertheimer, Albert I. "Consumer Action in Health Care," *Public Health Reports* 91 (September-October 1976): 406-411.

A brief historical background on consumer participation is provided in this article as a prelude to describing several modes of consumer action that would make the market more responsive to consumer demand. Because the consumer's main bargaining tool, economic control (the refusal to purchase health services) is not effective, the consumer is forced to use other means to elicit a response from the medical marketplace, such as collective consumer representation, public-interest research groups, and third-party payment plans. Major legislative attempts to involve consumers in planning for health services in the United States are discussed, and the problems of consumer representation on regulatory boards are noted. The authors discuss three methods of participatory democracy for consumers on these boards: containment, co-operation, and co-determination; they urge that attention be directed toward making co-determination possible.

Cousins, Norman. *Anatomy of an Illness (as Perceived by a Patient)*. New York: W.W. Norton & Co., 1979.

In six short chapters, Cousins describes his various encounters with the health-care system as patient, observer, and journalist. The first chapter, originally published as an article in *The New England Journal of Medicine*, describes his experience in the treatment of a chronic disease. In the remaining chapters Cousins describes his perspectives on the use of placebos; observes creativity, longevity, and the treatment of leprosy; reflects on holisitic healing and health; and interprets the response of physicians to his article. Throughout the book he stresses two central themes: the capacity of the human body to work towards regeneration and restoration, and the importance of the health professional's attempt to engage the patient's ability to mobilize forces of mind and body in turning back disease.

Godbout, Jacques. "Is Consumer Control Possible in Health Services?: The Quebec Case," *International Journal of Health Services* 11 (1981): 151–167.

As part of a health- and social-system reform in Quebec in the past two decades, approximately eighty CLSCs (local community service centers) have been developed to provide primary care. A unique feature of the CLSC is its mandated citizen-majority board. Godbout discusses the extent of consumer participation in the CLSCs; his information is based on his study of six CLSCs in Montreal. He discusses consumer involvement in three distinct phases of CLSC development, describes the socio-economic characteristics of citizen members, discusses relationships between the CLSC providers and their boards, and describes the consumers' effect on output and changes in the provision of service. Godbout suggests that despite the partial neutralization and limitations imposed by the system in which they exist, the CLSCs are a significant addition to the system and hold great potential for meaningful user and provider partnership.

Locker, David and Dunt, David. "Theoretical and Methodological Issues in Sociological Studies of Consumer Satisfaction with Medical Care," *Social Science and Medicine* 12 (1978): 283–292.

The authors provide a review of some of the studies in consumer satisfaction, with a focus on the theoretical and methodological aspects of these studies. They review studies of general-practitioner care, primary care, hospital care, and outpatient care; in all these areas, care receives high ratings of satisfaction. Methodological issues are then reviewed, including global evaluations, ways to measure satisfaction with each aspect of care, and composite measures derived from separate responses; the need for better measurement is emphasized. The nature of consumer assessments of care is discussed; the authors point out that little is known about how consumers make their assessments. Three purposes of consumer-satisfaction studies are then identified, and the authors conclude with some directives for further research.

Paap, W.R. "Consumer-Based Boards of Health Centers: Structural Problems in Achieving Effective Control," *American Journal of Public Health* 68 (June 1978): 578–582.

Paap discusses consumer-based boards of health centers, and focuses particularly on those factors that hinder effective consumer control and perpetuate provider and health-professional control. Several factors mitigate against informed involvement and control by consumers, among them lack of integration into the information networks, failure to appreciate the critical importance of timing, and limited contact with providers and health professionals on a steady basis. In addition, Paap suggests, internal organizational factors, such as role ambiguity of the consumer board member, also limit consumer power. Paap argues that the emphasis on training consumers to be board members is misdirected unless structural changes occur that would accommodate consumer control.

Rozovsky, Lorne E. "The Patient's Duty to Himself," *Dimensions* 56 (December 1979): 27–28.

Rozovsky emphasizes that the primary duty in health care is based in the relationship between patients and the health facility and staff. The patients' duty is secondary, and occurs when patients bring lawsuits against the provider on charges of negligence. The provider may then bring, as defense, the patients' duty to themselves–the duty to act as a "reasonable patient in similar circumstances." If patients have breached that duty, they may be assessed a portion of the final settlement on the basis of contributory negligence. Rozovsky summarizes a Canadian legal case involving contributory negligence; he defines the patients' duties and gives specific recommendations for health providers' protection in legal suits of this nature.

Silver, G.A. "Community Participation and Health Resource Allocation," *International Journal of Health Services* 3 (1973): 117–131.

Silver contends that there is a need to accumulate evidence of the value (or lack of value) of consumer participation and control in effecting improved decision-making in health care. Although health professionals have access to a wide range of techniques to improve their decision-making, consumers are now demanding greater input in the decisions that affect their health services: the stage appears set for confrontation. Silver suggests that there is no need for conflict because both professionals and consumers can be well-served by improving professional accountability and by obtaining the consumer's concepts of what services are needed. The issues, he suggests, are a greater recognition of client wishes and a greater development of professional accountability without interfering with professional freedom. He provides several examples of successful consumer participation in effecting health-resource allocation through attention to these issues.

Van den Heuval, Wim. J.A. "The Role of the Consumer in Health Policy," *Social Science and Medicine* 14A (1980): 423–426.

This article provides a summary of recent literature in consumer participation. The author briefly describes some changing ideologies in health care, and examines the pros and cons of the concept of "consumer" as applied to health care. He then reviews several trends in and approaches to consumer participation, and discusses the difficulty of the consumer's role. He draws several conclusions (based on his review of the literature), and suggests the need for a new theoretical model of the consumer in health care.

CHAPTER 6 The Right to Equal Access to Health Care

According to the Consumers' Association of Canada, the consumer should have a

> right to equal access to health care (health education, prevention, treatment and rehabilitation) regardless of the individual's economic status, sex, age, creed, ethnic origin, and location.[1]

The right to equal access to health care is based on the ethical principle of justice. Justice relates to the allotment of goods or services to persons; distributive justice refers to a fair distribution of benefits and burdens within a society, including a fair distribution of health care. The impetus, in recent years, to establish health care as a basic human right implies that all persons should have equal access to health services.

That health care is a basic human right has been claimed both explicitly and implicitly in a number of national and international documents. One of the most commonly cited bases of a right to health care, in this case as a part of social security, is contained in the United Nations Universal Declaration of Human Rights (1948), Articles 22 and 25.

> [Everyone has] the right to social security and is entitled to realization...
> of economic, social and cultural rights indispensable for his dignity and
> the free development of his personality. (22)

115

*Everyone has the right to a standard of living adequate for the health and
well-being of himself and his family, including food, clothing, housing
and medical care and necessary social services, and the right to security in
the event of unemployment, sickness, disability, widowhood, old age or lack
of livelihood in circumstances beyond his control.*[2] *(25; see Appendix D.)*

The "International Covenant on Economic, Social, and Cultural
Rights" (1966) includes a statement that recognizes "the right of
everyone to enjoyment of the highest attainable standard of physical and mental health."[3]

These declarations and convenants are not legally binding documents. Yet such statements have been instrumental in raising the
claim of a right to health care – and sometimes (misguidedly) a right
to health. The right to health, while obviously an ideal, poses
problems for those who would attempt to fulfill the implied obligation. Genetic endowment, housing, income, and numerous other
hereditary and societal factors are determinants of health. Our
concept of health is broad, and it would be unrealistic to assume
that society can work with a concept of health that is infinite in
scope and addresses itself to both a right to health and a right to
health care.[4] As a society we may be able to "guarantee access to
health services but not health itself."[5]

Consumers' claims to health education, prevention, treatment,
and rehabilitation services would seem to be legitimate. These are
the parameters that define health services. Given these parameters, is there a right to health care, and to equal access to health
care, in Canada?

CANADIAN HEALTH CARE

This question of a right to health care has created tension in the
development of the Canadian health-care system. Before Confederation, the emphasis on individual responsibility for health and
health care was in keeping with the rugged individualism so much a
part of a pioneer spirit in a new and developing country. Self-
sufficiency and family or neighbourly support were the hallmarks
of the early settlers.[6]

As the population of the young country grew, it became necessary, particularly in urban centers, to provide occasional assistance
to persons in need when families or neighbours were unable to

help. In establishing ways to provide help, English-speaking settlers relied on English Poor Law traditions, which placed the major responsibility for care on the local municipality. French-speaking settlers relied on the church. Primary responsibility still rested on the individual; municipal or parochial resources were secondary. The belief in the market-economy ideology, which holds that all are free to exchange goods and services without the need for state interference or regulation, remained strong.[7]

In 1867, when Canada became a Dominion, the British North America Act reflected these traditions and priorities; health and welfare were not seen as matters of substantial concern.[8] The federal government was given the power to act in health matters that required broader control, such as quarantine and marine hospitals: provincial governments were given the power to establish, maintain, and manage hospitals, asylums, charities, and eleemosynary institutions in and for the province (see Appendix D).

Shortly after Confederation, the health and welfare needs of the population became acute. The individualism of the rural pioneer collapsed in the face of growing urbanization and industrialization. Self-sufficiency had become "insufficient," and could not counter loss of family support, dependence on factories for employment, and the community interdependencies that the new age required. After three depressions, the population's reliance on industry and the citizens' inability to do much about employment were obvious.[9]

In the early 1900s the debate about individual versus state responsibility in matters of health and welfare began in earnest. Other countries were instituting health insurance and general public-welfare programs; for example, Bismarck introduced his health-insurance program in Germany in 1891.

In rural Canada, where population was sparse and medical personnel unavailable, the need for health-care resources was acute. Saskatchewan began to make some provisions for health services; those provisions affirmed the government's right and responsibility to make health services available to citizens. The Rural Municipalities Act was revised in 1916 to allow municipalities to use tax monies to pay a physician a retainer fee to keep a physician in their midst. Shortly thereafter the Union Hospital Act was passed; the act allowed municipalities to combine their resources to build hospitals. Several other provinces followed Saskatchewan's lead.[10]

The federal government was also beginning to act. The Department of Health was formed in 1919; as well, several isolated attempts were made to provide provinces with disease-control resources. The federal Liberal party raised the need for health insurance in 1919 as part of their party platform, but it remained for an interested health minister, a committed bureaucrat, and a young scholar to commence the planning.[11] In the early 1940s, the federal government began to develop plans for health-and-welfare programs in Canada.

In 1941, President Roosevelt and Prime Minister Churchill met and issued the Atlantic Charter, which contained the statement that "people should be free from fear and from want."[12] This ideal was to echo through the Western World and provide impetus for greater social justice. Health-care began to be thought of as a right.

In 1945, plans for social security in Canada were presented to a conference of provincial premiers. These plans contained proposals for an integrated system of health and welfare, including health insurance and income security, for Canadians. The plans represented the ideal of equal access to health care for all Canadians, and included provisions to improve the health status of the Canadian people.[13]

Unfortunately, the country was not yet ready for so bold, imaginative, and costly a program. The integrated plan was rejected, and the federal government was forced to find ways to influence provincial planning for health services in a limited and piecemeal fashion. In 1948, the provinces were offered National Health Grants, which would assist them in conducting health surveys as a basis for health-program planning, in building hospitals, and in establishing various services, including mental-health, public-health, and venereal-disease control services. Ten years later, prodded by the provincial governments, who were already active in providing such services, the federal government moved to establish the Hospital Insurance and Diagnostic Services Act. The Act made provision for the payment of hospital in-patient and certain out-patient services for all Canadians. Both programs were introduced amid the continuing debates of individual versus state responsibility and federal versus provincial responsibility.

Meanwhile, the provinces were still working on their own to effect medical-care insurance, particularly Saskatchewan, under Tommy Douglas's leadership. The federal government appointed the Royal Commission on Health Services to examine the health-care needs of Canadians and to recommend ways to improve existing health-care services.[14]

The Report of the Royal Commission on Health Services in Canada (the Hall Commission) contains a clear statement of the concepts of individual responsibility and public responsibility in health care. Within the Health Charter for Canadians, in the early pages of the report, is contained the following statement:

> *The achievement of the highest possible standards for all our people must become a primary objective of national policy and a cohesive factor contributing to national unity, involving individual and community responsibilities and actions. This objective can best be achieved by a comprehensive, universal Health Services Programme for the Canadian people.*[15]

The Charter lists the principles that should form the basis of such a health-services program.

The Canadian government introduced a medicare program based on the recommendations of the Hall Commission in 1968. Four principles were upheld as the basis for medicare: universality, comprehensiveness, portability, and public administration.[16] The Medical Care Act was seen as the final step in a more comprehensive care program; it established, in principle, the right to health care and, in principle, the right to equal access to health care for the Canadian people.

THE CONTINUING TENSION: IDEALS VERSUS REALITIES

Rights in principle are not equivalent to rights in practice. Despite the good intentions of policy-makers, equal access to health care has not become a reality.[17] In the mid-forties, when the social-security proposals were introduced, the intent was a "basic minimum standard of living to be provided by the state in case of social insecurity"–essentially, equality of condition.[18] This type of equality remained a guiding ideal until the late sixties.

Since 1968, there has been continuing dialogue and debate about the government's responsibility to provide health care. Rising costs in health care make questionable the government's ability to maintain the health and social-services programs established in the late 1960s.

During the late sixties and early seventies, numerous reports and documents that outlined the need for cost containment, for a system of integration, and for greater control of professions were produced by federal and provincial governments. As well, other problems of the recently completed "system"[19] were described and analyzed. In 1974, the federal health minister released a working paper entitled *A New Perspective on the Health of Canadians* (the Lalonde Report), which emphasized the need for greater individual responsibility in health care; the paper pointed specifically to diseases that were connected to lifestyles.

Again, the responsibility for health was being placed on the individual. The concept of "equality of condition" was being replaced by the concept of "equality of opportunity." With equality of opportunity, the onus is on the individual to take the opportunities available in society,[20] including opportunities to stay healthy or to avail oneself of health services. By 1977 the federal government had withdrawn from the open-ended cost-sharing and conditional grant agreements with the provinces–those joint federal and provincial arrangements that supported hospital and medical insurance. The agreements were replaced by the Established Programs Financing Act, which provides a block grant to each province, and also transfers tax monies to the provinces. The provinces, with only limited federal directive or accountability, can decide how to spend their health-care dollars. But this new freedom also means that much of the health-care dollar is in competition with other provincial dollars; inequities in health services between provinces may become marked.[21] Progress toward the right of equal access to health care for Canadians (even defined as equality of opportunity) stands in jeopardy.

By 1979, more potential barriers to equal access to health services became apparent. Many doctors began to opt out of the medicare programs; other doctors pressed the issue of balance billing or extra billing. The federal government commissioned a review of Canada's national-provincial health programs to determine if the goals of reasonable access, universal coverage, comprehensive coverage, portability, public administration, and uniform terms and conditions–in short, the principles of the health programs– were sufficient, and the extent to which these goals were being met.[22] The review supported the principles of Canada's health programs and suggested a partial return to federal-provincial cost-sharing to relieve interprovincial inequities. And, because extra billing was thought to violate the principle of reasonable access to care, the report urged that physicians be prevented from using the tactic.[23]

By 1982 these issues, as yet unsettled, were the subject of heated exchange between the federal government and the provinces, and between provincial governments and the physicians. The issues raised in these exchanges have much to do with the more general problem of the allocation of scarce resources. How does a government, a people, decide what is a fair share of funds and resources for health care, for particular health programs, and for individuals in those health programs?

SCARE RESOURCE ALLOCATION

Canadians are not alone in their worry about the allocation of health resources. Rising costs and the inevitable realization of the limited quantity of health-care dollars have begun to plague most Western nations, some of which do not have national health-insurance programs. But while Canada's spending has been moderate in relation to other nations,[24] there are limits to what money can do. As David Mechanic, a prolific writer on health- and medical-care policy, has stated:

> Containing costs is only part of the problem. The challenge is to do so while providing reasonable access to medical care that is effective and humane.[25]

Complicating the problem is the fact that there is "no scientific way" to decide what proportion of the tax dollar should be spent on health care.[26] These decisions are based on economic and political factors, and especially on the values of a people. In the past, the Canadian people have supported values that emphasized equal access to health care. Do they still? What values will structure the decisions ahead? How will we ration services?

There are at least three levels of resource allocation related to health services. First, we must decide how much money actually goes to health care. The competition is between health care and other services, such as education, housing, highways, defense, and any number of other governmental programs. The Established Programs Finance has rendered almost obsolete the concept of "the health-care dollar;" all services are in competition for a limited amount of money.

Once a certain amount is allocated for health care, there is the problem of deciding how much each health-care program receives. The Lalonde report emphasized this level of resource allocation by demonstrating that a substantial amount of money is directed toward treatment and curative services, much less money to prevention. Further, within curative programs, different age groups and different types of illnesses receive different amounts of funds. For example, less has been spent on health care for the elderly than on services for young or middle-aged adults; less has been spent on services for the mentally ill or for drug rehabilitation programs than on provision for life-saving surgeries.

Finally, after we decide how much money a program will receive, we must sort out priorities within that program. Who should have coronary-bypass surgery or renal dialysis if services are not available to meet all needs? Should access to these costly services be a function of ability to pay for the services? Canadians have generally been uninformed about health-care costs and allocation problems of this nature. Most Canadians are never forced to decide if they can afford coronary-bypass surgery, nor to count the financial cost of a loved one's life-prolonging treatment.[27]

One philosophy of distributive justice proposes that, when there is not enough money to provide the services everyone wants or needs, society's least advantaged should be taken care of first.[28] If this philosophy were implemented on a government-program level, greater attention would be paid to human services and less to programs that benefit the corporate structure; if implemented at the health-program level, more monies would be spent on programs for the aged or for native people, and less on exotic life-saving technologies or on white middle- and upper-class abortion services. Those with the greatest need for services, although they might have the fewest financial resources, would have access to health services equal to the services available to those who can pay.

Politicians, policy-makers, and planners must recognize the inevitability of rationing in health services, and become more explicit about the choices that must be made. In many cases, decisions are made with limited planning and deliberation regarding the most sensible approach to rationing.

Rationing of health care is not a new concept; it is built into our health-care system and can occur on at least three levels: the patient level, the professional level, and the administrative level.[29] Rationing affects the health professional differently at each level, but the general effects regarding equal access to health care are the same. When patients must pay hospital-user charges, extra-billing charges, or pay the physician directly, restrictions are imposed: some patients cannot afford these charges. The services they may purchase are limited. Health professionals may ration services, based upon their professional judgment of the patient's suitability for treatment (for example, age as a factor in renal dialysis or cardiac surgery). At the administrative level, the government may decide which diseases and conditions are eligible for care and which are not.

Paul Ramsey, an ethicist, has described the agonies of sparse medical resource-allocation decisions in his account of the Seattle Swedish Hospital's renal-dialysis program. Since the available resources would allow only a few patients to enter the program, a lay committee was given the responsibility of deciding who, among all those medically eligible, would benefit. He points out that "at any given time and place, the medical profession faces the problem of having to choose who will live and who will be allowed to die." Ramsey emphasizes the need for greater public involvement in such decisions.[30]

Medical advances have created a situation that poses acute analytical and social problems in regards to the notion of a right to health care.[31] Perhaps the Canadian system will have to begin by discussing a right to a certain minimum standard of health care, rather than a right to the best care that is available. Or perhaps we will have to allow some inequities in access to health care to foster innovative treatments and research. In the end, it may not be reasonable to suggest that equality in health care can occur while inequalities in wealth and income appear to be morally acceptable.[32] But some attention should be devoted to a definition of the least that should be guaranteed to everyone in health care.[33]

RESPONSIBILITIES OF NURSES AND OTHER HEALTH PROFESSIONALS

To nurses, the conflicts between ideals and realities regarding access to health care may seem somewhat removed from the more poignant issues of patient rights. It might be more comfortable to assume that these conflicts are the responsibility of others; but such an assumption is insular and not realistic. All those involved in health care in Canada must be informed of the issues and ready to take some responsibility in influencing and in being involved in some of the difficult allocation decisions ahead.

Nurses are involved in providing needed services to remote areas, for example, in the north, where nurses provide comprehensive, community-based health services to help people attain and maintain their health. Although nurses are generally accepted as physician-substitutes (by other health professionals and by the public) in northern Canada, this is not the case in the rest of the country. In addition to occasional instances where substitution for physicians is practised, nurses have unique contributions to make in primary care (patient care that includes first-contact care plus health promotion and maintenance, and complete and continuous care). The caring and health-counselling basis of nursing provides a much-needed skill in primary care, and offers potential benefits not only in regards to better access to care, but also in regards to quality of care.[34]

Nurses must be prepared to advocate with and on behalf of individual patients and patient groups for better access to care. Often, in the course of patient care, a nurse may become aware of inequities and/or discrimination in the provision of health services, for example, underservice or inadequate service. These inequities must be brought to the attention of persons able to effect change. Frequently those patients who are most affected are not able to voice their concerns, or cannot make their problems known. Health professionals who advocate for these patients need both courage and persistence; as well, advocates must be aware of their own intents and personal values. Underserved or poorly served patients do not need a misguided reformer; they need help from someone who is well-acquainted, with the particular situation and the health-care system in general, one who is willing to risk, one who truly represents the patients' interests or can assist patients in representing their interests.

Nurses must also maintain competence to ensure consumers equal access to care. Nurses across the country are grappling with issues of accountability and are concerned about the structuring of continuing education programs, which will ensure adequately qualified personnel. Standards of nursing practice and nursing education have been developed by a number of provincial nursing associations, and by the Canadian Nurses' Association. As difficult as these endeavours may be to participants and onlookers alike, they are critical to the assurance of quality of care in nursing practice and in health care, for unless we develop adequate standards, we have limited bases for evaluation of practice.

SUMMARY

The right to health care, and the right to equal access to health care, are discussed in this chapter with particular attention to the Canadian health-care system. The development of the Canadian system is reviewed with an intent to emphasize the values that underline the system and the emerging ideals of equal access to health care. These ideals have not been realized, and the current conflicts between federal and provincial governments and between professions and governments threaten these ideals.

The conflicts are symptomatic of the more general question of the allocation of scarce resources. How should a society determine what constitutes sufficient resources for health care? How can citizens choose between health-care programs, and decide what individuals will receive benefits within health programs? It is suggested that it might be beneficial to establish some standards in health care. Nurses and other health professionals, as well as the general public, need to become more involved in making choices about health care and in formulating acceptable standards for care.

REFERENCES FOR CHAPTER 6

[1]"Consumer Rights in Health Care," *Canadian Consumer* 4 (April 1974): 1.

[2]Ian Brownlie, ed., *Basic Documents on Human Rights* (Oxford: Clarendon Press, 1971), p. 111.

[3]*Ibid*, p. 204.

[4]Daniel Callahan, "Health and Society: Some Ethical Imperatives," *Daedalus* 106 (Winter 1977): 26.

[5]John S. Millis, "Wisdom? Health? Can Society Guarantee Them?" in *Moral Problems in Medicine*, ed. Samuel Gorovitz *et al* (Englewood Cliffs, N.J.: Prentice-Hall Ltd., 1976), p. 486.

[6]For a more detailed account of the development of the Canadian health-care system, see Carl A. Meilicke and Janet L. Storch, eds., *Perspectives on Canadian Health and Social Services Policy: History and Emerging Trends* (Ann Arbor: Health Administration Press, 1980).

[7]Andrew Armitage, *Social Welfare in Canada: Ideals and Realities* (Toronto: McClelland and Stewart Ltd., 1975), p. 18.

[8]Elisabeth Wallace, "Origin of the Social Welfare State in Canada, 1867–1900," *Canadian Journal of Economics and Political Science* 16 (1950): 386–387.

[9]*Ibid*, p. 387.

[10]Sylva M. Gelber, "The Path to Health Insurance," *Canadian Public Administration* 9 (June 1966): 211-212.

[11]For a fascinating account of this period in Canadian health-care history see Malcolm G. Taylor, *Health Insurance and Canadian Public Policy* (Montreal: McGill-Queen's Press, 1978), Chapter 1.

[12]Robert E. Asher *et al*, *The United Nations and the Promotion of General Welfare* (Washington, D.C.: The Brookings Institute, 1957), p. 178.

[13]*Proposals of the Government of Canada*, Dominion-Provincial Conference on Reconstruction (Ottawa, August 1945), pp. 27-31.

[14]*Royal Commission on Health Services in Canada, Vol. 1*, Justice Emmett Hall, Chairman. (Ottawa: Queen's printer, 1964), p. 3.

[15]*Ibid*, p. 11. Reproduced by permission of the Minister of Supply and Services Canada.

[16]Lee Soderstrom, *The Canadian Health Care System* (London: Croom Helm, 1978), pp. 132-133.

[17]See Robin F. Badgley and Catherine A. Charles, "Health and Inequality: Unresolved Policy Issues," in *Canadian Social Policy*, ed. Shankar A. Yelaja (Waterloo: Wilfred Laurier University Press, 1978), pp. 71-86. See also Anne Crichton, "Equality: A Concept in Canadian Health Care: From Intention to Reality of Provision," *Social Sciences and Medicine* 14C (1980): 243-257.

[18]Crichton, p. 245.

[19]For a summary of some of these major reports and studies, see John Browne, "Summary of Recent Major Studies of Health Care in Canada," in *Perspectives on Canadian Health and Social Sciences Policy*, eds. Carl A. Meilicke and Janet L. Storch (Ann Arbor: Health Administration Press, 1980), pp. 293-305.

[20]Crichton, pp. 245-248.

[21]R.J. Van Loon, "From Shared Cost to Block Funding and Beyond," *Journal of Health Politics, Policy, and Law* 2 (Winter 1978): 454-478. See also Malcolm Brown, "The Implications of Established Program Finance for National Health Insurance," *Canadian Public Policy* 6 (Summer 1980): 521-532; Geoffrey R. Weller, "The Determinants of Canadian Health Policy," *Journal of Health Politics, Policy and Law* 5 (Fall 1980): 405-418.

[22]*Canada's National-Provincial Health Program for the 1980s: 'A Commitment for Renewal,'* Justice Emmet Hall, Chairman (Ottawa: Supply and Services, 1980).

[23]*Ibid*, Chapters 2 to 4.

[24]Eugene Vayda, Robert G. Evans, and William R. Mindell, "Universal Health Insurance in Canada: History, Problems, Trends," *Journal of Community Health* 4 (Spring 1979): 217-231.

[25]David Mechanic, *Future Issues in Health Care* (New York: The Free Press, 1979), p. xi.

[26]*Ibid*, p. 91.

[27]See for example Robert Stinson and Peggy Stinson, "On the Death of a Baby," *Atlantic* 244 (July 1979): 70-72; Duane Stroman, *The Quick Knife: Unnecessary Surgery in the U.S.A.* (Port Washington, N.Y.: Kennikat Press, 1979), p. 149.

[28]John Rawls, "Justice as Fairness," in *Contemporary Issues in Bioethics*, eds. Tom L. Beauchamp and LeRoy Walters (Belmont, California: Wadsworth Publishing Co., 1976), pp. 44-46.

[29]Mechanic, pp. 91-103.

[30]Paul Ramsey, *The Patient as a Person: Explorations in Medical Ethics* (New Haven: Yale University Press, 1970), pp. 242-252; see also Renée C. Fox and Judith Swazey, *The Courage to Fail: A Social View of Organ Transplants and Dialysis* (Chicago: The University of Chicago Press, 1974), Chapter 9.

[31]Charles Fried, "An Analysis of 'Equality' and 'Rights' in Medical Care," *Hospital Progress* 2 (February 1976): 45.

[32]*Ibid*, pp. 44–47. See also Charles Fried, "Equality and Rights in Medical Care," *The Hastings Center Report* 6 (February 1976): 29–34.

[33]For example, see Gerald Rosenthal and Daniel M. Fox, "A Right to What? Toward Adequate Minimum Standards for Personal Services," *Milbank Memorial Fund Quarterly* 56 (Winter 1978): 1–6.

[34]Phyllis E. Jones, *Nurses in Canadian Primary Health Care Settings: A Review of Recent Literature*. Literature Review Monograph 2 (Toronto: University of Toronto, Faculty of Nursing, 1980).

SUGGESTED REFERENCES FOR FURTHER STUDY, CHAPTER 6

Armitage, A. *Social Welfare: Ideals and Realities*. Toronto: McClelland and Stewart, Ltd., 1975.

Armitage describes the dynamics of welfare policy and programming in Canada, and notes that society's emphasis on economic independence and self-reliance leads to less-than-full support for humanitarian social-welfare values. The need for income redistribution is discussed, and various methods of redistribution are carefully outlined. Armitage describes the federal-provincial aspects of social welfare, income-security provisions, and personal and community social services; he also discusses trends in social-welfare research and social-development policy.

Callahan, D. "Health and Society: Some Ethical Imperatives." *Daedalus* 106 (Winter 1977): 23–33.

Callahan states that every major social change forces a confrontation with values. In the past, because of the lack of effective measures of care and cure, a fatalistic approach to illness was common. Today, as new treatments are developed and greater effectiveness of care has become a reality, we are being forced to confront many philosophical and ethical questions. For example, what constitutes a good life? How much health is necessary for a good life? Callahan suggests that with a broadened definition of health, demands for a right to health and health care, and a scarcity of resources, it becomes important to examine these ethical questions. The answers are necessary to an allocation of resources to health programs.

Crichton, Anne. "Equality: A Concept in Canadian Health Care: From Intention to Reality of Provision." *Social Science and Medicine* 14C (1980): 243–257.

Crichton states that the intention to provide greater equality for the health of Canadians (since 1940) has not been realized. She analyzes this failure and describes various concepts of equality. She then suggests that Canadians have moved from a concept of "equality of condition" to one of "equality of opportunity." The structures and processes involved in translating ideologies (such as equality) into practice are described with specific reference to health policy in Canada. Crichton concludes with a discussion of the challenges facing Canada's health-care system.

Fried, Charles. "Equality and Rights in Medical Care." *The Hastings Center Report* 6 (February 1978): 29–34.

Fried suggests that recent major advances in medical technology have led to problems with the notion of a right to health care. He provides a number of arguments in the on-going debate on equality and rights in health care. He first describes the concept of a right, and notes the confusion regarding rights to health care (and equality in health care) and equality of health. To clarify his argument, Fried uses the example of articifical implantable hearts: should there be an insistence on equality, these would pose a problem. Fried proposes that perhaps the right is better described as a right to a certain *standard* of health care. While acknowledging that even this standard would be relative and changing, he proposes that analysis and research may assist policy-makers in recognizing irrational practices; he outlines several of these irrationalities in health-service delivery.

Meilicke, Carl A. and Storch, Janet L. eds., *Perspectives on Canadian Health and Social Services Policy: History and Emerging Trends*. Ann Arbor: Health Administration Press, 1980.

This book of readings focuses on the historical development and the current issues and trends of the Canadian health and social-services system. The introduction analyzes five major eras in the Canadian social-security policy; Part One is devoted to an historical development of personal social services and income security; Part Two deals with health services. In Part Three contemporary policy issues and trends are examined. Each part is prefaced by a brief commentary on the set of articles. The composite of perspectives in these articles provide the reader with a broad understanding of policy dynamics in Canadian health and social services.

Taylor, Malcolm G. *Health Insurance and Canadian Public Policy: The Seven Decisions that Created the Canadian Health Insurance System*. Montreal: McGill-Queen's University Press, 1978.

In this book Malcolm Taylor provides a brilliant analysis of the development of Canada's health-insurance system and of health policy-making at federal and provincial levels of government. Seven major decisions have been selected for analysis; three federal and four provincial. Each decision is analyzed according to the basis of the decisions, the immediate effects, and the long-term outcomes of these decisions. The book is an invaluable source of information regarding the development of the Canadian health-care system.

Thomas, Lewis. "On the Science and Technology of Medicine." *Daedalus* 106 (Winter 1977): 35–46.

Thomas notes that massive expenditures in the past twenty-five years to improve health have fallen short of the mark and he suggests three possible reasons: the health of the nation has suddenly deteriorated; the technology of dealing with health problems has undergone a major change; the nation has been caught in a series of errors. Thomas shows that no disintegration of health has occurred in the population since 1950, that new technologies tend to be half-way technologies rather than decisively effective technologies for prevention or cure, and that public expectations about the positive benefits of medicine are not realistic, thereby creating excessive demands on the health-care system. He suggests that the public should be better informed about the limits of medicine; he also suggests that we need to determine how much the public is willing to invest in health care.

CHAPTER 7 Special Rights Concerns

This chapter is devoted to an examination of specific rights concerns in health care. These special concerns arise because patients are disadvantaged (and, therefore, particularly vulnerable to abuses in health care) or because of particular problems experienced at either end of the life cycle. Issues of reproduction, the rights of children, rights of the mentally disadvantaged, rights of aged persons, and rights of native people are among these special concerns.

These five categories do not include all the special moral and legal dilemmas of patient care, but have been selected because of their relevance to nurses and to nursing practice. Health professionals have special obligations to these patients.

ISSUES OF REPRODUCTION

Several important and controversial legal and moral issues are included under the general topic of issues surrounding reproduction. These include issues of contraception and abortion; control of genetic quality; control of the process of procreation; and treatment of pregnant parents.

Contraception, Sterilization, and Abortion

Contraception Nurses frequently provide contraceptive information to couples through premarital education programs, family

129

planning clinics, physician or out-patient clinics, or post-partum teaching sessions. Nurses have an obligation to be diligent in keeping their own knowledge current and accurate, and to be sensitive to individual patients and respectful of their decisions. They also must know the physician's preferences and organizational policies with respect to their freedom to provide information. Further, they must be true to their own moral or religious convictions. These latter may be conflicting and competing duties.

In situations where nurses are prevented, by their own constraints or by organizational directives, from providing a breadth of contraceptive teaching to patients, they would be remiss if they did not at least advise patients where such information and assistance can be obtained.

Sterilization As a means of birth control, sterilization has become a fairly common practice. Health professionals who work with patients requesting sterilization must ensure that procedures are carried out competently, and that the patient is informed about the effect of the surgery and the likelihood of its permanency. Many physicians and institutions insist on obtaining spousal consent for voluntary sterilization, particularly when the patients are women. The insistence on spousal consent appears to be motivated by the uncertainty in case law regarding proper consent for sterilization.[1] Nurses exercise responsibility toward their patients by ensuring that patients are well-informed about the procedures, and by working toward fair policies regarding spousal consents.

Abortion Abortion can be defined as "the deliberate causing of the death of a fetus, either by directly killing it or (more commonly) by causing its expulsion from the womb before it is viable. . . ."[2] Abortions may be sought for a number of reasons; for example, maternal cardiac complications; psychological trauma or suicidal condition; pregnancy caused by rape; inadvertant use of fetal-deforming drugs; and personal or family reasons.[3] Patients and health professionals face legal and moral questions regarding abortion, as well as personal and religious value conflicts.

The legal status of abortion in Canada changed in 1969 with amendments to Section 221 of the Criminal Code. Prior to these amendments, abortion was illegal. Although the abortion law is federal, its enforcement is a provincial responsibility. Under present legislation, abortion is permissible if continuation of the pregnancy would endanger the woman's life or health. Further, the following criteria must be met:

a) the abortion must take place in a hospital accredited by the Canadian Council on Accreditation;

b) it must be approved by the hospital's therapeutic abortion committee;

c) the physician performing the abortion must not be a member of the therapeutic abortion committee;

d) the therapeutic abortion committee must review the case at a meeting and reach a decision by a majority vote.[4]

No guidance has been provided by the Parliament of Canada in defining the phrases "endanger" and "life or health." Health may be defined broadly, to include physical health, psychological health, and mental health. "The therapeutic abortion committee may be as liberal or conservative as it sees fit, as long as it is fair and reasonable in its approach."[5] Thus, Canadian abortion law has been applied in a "highly erratic and apparently arbitrary way."[6]

Religious perspectives on abortion vary from a conservative stance (traditionally ascribed to the Roman Catholic Church) to a liberal stance. Conservative anti-abortionists argue that abortion is never acceptable; they occasionally concede that it is permissable only if it is required to save a pregnant woman's life.[7] Liberal pro-abortionists argue that a woman should have free choice in the matter. Between these two extremes is a continuum of religious positions.

Moral arguments surrounding abortion center on at least two main themes: the status of the fetus, and the problem of conflicting claims.[8] At what point in fetal development (from conception to birth) does the fetus acquire the characteristics that would prohibit homicide? How does one determine the nature and the timing of personhood?

Some suggest that all members of the species *homo sapien* (in a genetic sense) are persons and are entitled to protection against homicide; others hold that the actual or potential possession of personhood (someone possessing a particular set of characteristics) is the critical factor. Yet others suggest that such rights are contingent upon the age of the fetus (rights grow gradually through the nine-month gestation), and still others propose an actual time (for example, birth) when a fetus becomes a person.[9]

The conflict of claims is often subsumed by another debate: the pregnant woman's right to choose versus the fetus's right to life. The woman's "right-to-choose" argument may be based on the notion of a woman's property rights over her body, on the notion of self-defense of the mother who may be harmed if she is required to bring an unwanted fetus to term; or on the concept of autonomy, which implies the right to make decisions about one's body and one's person.[10]

A number of authors involved in the moral debate opt for a limited number of criteria for abortion, suggesting that abortion should not be impermissible, but neither should it be always permissible.[11] Some have argued that the critical issue is not the moral status of the fetus or the conflicting claims to rights, but that abortion is a practice whose justification is a social issue. This utilitarian perspective holds that abortion be judged permissible in terms of its consequences for society as a whole. If the consequences of allowing abortion are generally superior to the consequences of not allowing abortion, then abortion should be permitted, either as a rule or in particular cases.[12]

Society will likely continue to debate the acceptability of abortion in general, and particularly of abortion on demand. In the United States the debate on abortion is on-going, as evidenced by events of the past decade. A 1973 Supreme Court decision ruled that a woman has a constitutional right to an abortion, but in 1977 the question of the state's obligation to pay for abortions was raised in the courts, and it was decided that there was no constitutional obligation to pay in the absence of "compelling medical reasons" for the operation.[13] In 1981 the debate resurfaced with an attempt to have Congress define the meaning of life as it related to the Fourteenth Amendment.[14]

In Canada the debate is less open, but the issue of abortion is no less significant; its politics and morality are clouded with emotionalism. As noted earlier, the application of Canadian abortion law is "erratic and arbitrary." A recent study of the application of abortion law in Canada noted that:

> [there are] *sharp disparities in the distribution and accessibility of therapeutic abortion services; a continuous exodus of Canadian women to the United States to obtain this operation; and delays in women obtaining induced abortions in Canada.*[15]

Robin Badgley, chairman of this study, noted that these disparities are a reflection of the way in which Canadian society has dealt with "a socially sensitive issue involving much stigma and fear."[16]

Some nurses may be placed in a situation of religious or moral conflict by their involvement with abortions; they should remove themselves from the conflict by transfer or job change. It is difficult to provide good care, to fulfill one's responsibility to the patient, in situations of moral conflict. Several professional nurses' associations have gone on record in support of nurses changing jobs in such situations or withdrawing care. For example, the position of the Registered Nurses' Association of Nova Scotia is cited in the Badgley report:

> The RNANS recognizes that nurses as individuals may hold certain moral, religious or ethical beliefs about therapeutic abortion and may be in good conscience compelled to refuse involvement. The RNANS supports the right of the nurse to withdraw from a situation without being submitted to censure, coercion, termination of employment or other forms of discipline, provided that in emergency situations the patient's right to receive necessary care would take precedence over exercise of the nurse's individual beliefs and rights.[17]

In addition, provincial human-rights commissions, staff associations, and union contracts offer a means of conciliation in resolving these concerns.[18]

Nurses who work with patients who receive abortions owe those patients a special duty of care, consideration, and protection of confidentiality. They must be particularly aware of the patients' need for information and for supportive counselling.

The Control of Genetic Quality

As a result of recent advances in genetic research, the attempt to control genetic quality has become one of the more controversial legal and moral issues of the past decade. Several aspects of genetic control involve nurses directly: genetic screening, genetic counselling, prenatal diagnosis, and in-vitro fertilization (IVF).

Genetic Screening Prospective parents are screened to ascertain if either parent is the carrier of a genetic disease; the results of the screening may be used to prevent any disease from being passed on to the child. Newborn children are also screened, in order that any diseases revealed by the screening can be treated. The actual technology of genetic screening is better presented elsewhere.[19] This discussion will focus on issues that arise in the course of screening that pose dilemmas for nurses.

One issue is the matter of consent for genetic screening, which is a diagnostic procedure. Before any medical treatment or diagnostic test, the patient must give permission to proceed; therefore, the general principles governing patient consent must be applied in genetic screening. Information given should include the nature and purpose of genetic screening; the possible consequences of screening; the risks of undergoing or not undergoing the tests; finally, the patient should be advised that many tests are as yet inexact and may yield inaccurate results.[20]

The patient's right to information in general poses particular problems when that patient has had a genetic screening test. Is it moral to provide information to a patient who is presently symptom-free but whose test reveals an untreatable genetic problem? Should the patient be told all, or should some information be withheld? Most practitioners would agree that information should not be restricted, but that it must be supplied with care and sensitivity. Nurses can be particularly instrumental in providing support and follow-up to those confronted with a dismal diagnosis.

Another issue is that of confidentiality of information obtained from genetic screening. Who should have access to the information – the spouse, the relatives, the employers, the insurance company? One could argue a case for release of information to each of these. Yet, one of the nurse's responsibilities to the patient is to maintain confidentiality. An important consideration, therefore, is the terms, agreed to before the screening process, between the health-care practitioner and the patient about the release of information; careful adherence to the patient's wishes in providing results is essential. If the health professionals are obliged to release information to other persons or agencies, for whatever reason, that obligation must be communicated to the patient before screening, so that he or she can refuse to be screened.[21]

A fourth problem is whether it is acceptable to perform screenings on infants. How many tests should be done? And who should consent to these tests? While no easy answers are available to guide the nurse in dealing with these dilemmas, the utmost care and attention must be given to the infant, who is totally vulnerable. Sometimes raising these questions with fellow-workers may be the nurse's greatest contribution to finding answers.

Genetic Counselling Genetic screening and genetic counselling are in many ways related. Safeguarding confidentiality, paying attention to patient's rights to information, and respecting the personal decisions of patients are important aspects of genetic counselling. Patients must not feel coerced to choose abortion.[22] In addition, the nurse's role in supporting patients as they make a decision to risk procreation or not, and as they live with the consequences of that decision is an essential part of counselling. Patients confronted with test results that indicate a genetic problem need someone to listen to them and to help them understand their choices.

Prenatal Diagnosis of Genetic Disorder A growing and increasingly sophisticated technology is available to medicine: the ability to diagnose certain genetic disorders with relative accuracy prior to birth. This technology uses amniocentesis, ultrasound, and other techniques. The introduction of the new technology has raised a number of significant legal and moral concerns about the risk to the fetus, the consequences of inaccurate results, the potential for coercive counselling, and the protection of privacy.[23]

Health professionals who work with patients undergoing these tests must ensure that patients are informed about all possible risks, benefits, and uncertainties of the various procedures; that the results of the tests should not dictate the continuation or termination of pregnancy; and that patients receive emotional support that will see them through the pregnancy and beyond, or that will enable them to cope with the voluntary termination of the pregnancy by abortion. The nurse can ensure that these tasks are accomplished, and has a responsibility to work toward policies, regulations, and provisions that guarantee these patient rights and needs.

Control of the Process of Procreation The reality of "test-tube babies" brings with it new potential for genetic manipulation. In-vitro fertilization (IVF) has been accomplished without a clear public perception of the reasonable limits of such practice. The public is beginning to question the basic right to have one's own biological child at any expense; the rights of potential embryos to survive when the one suitable embryo is implanted; the risks of clinical IVF research to the potential offspring; the unnaturalness of such procreation; the ramifications of the surrogate mothering that is made possible by IVF; and the potential for cloning.[24]

Nurses involved with these frontier efforts in medical science do not have specific guidelines to help them decide what is best for their patients. However, two general principles – the right to information and the right to respect – are highly applicable guidelines. As in prenatal diagnoses, the nurse should ensure that the patient has adequate information about the procedure, including the risks, and that the couple's "case for IVF" is heard with due respect. The question of equal access to such technology is a matter to be determined by society. As yet, there are few available or adequate means to determine the social implications of these technologies.[25]

Care in Childbirth

The final topic to be discussed in this section on issues in reproduction is the care of parents in the childbirth experience. Childbirth is a most significant human event and it is no wonder that disputes have arisen regarding the role of medicine in the birthing process. These disputes are of a long-standing nature. In the 1850s people debated the use of chloroform to relieve pain in childbirth; in the 1950s the move towards natural childbirth challenged medical practice.[26] The debate continues today on the issue of home delivery versus hospital delivery.

Individuals and groups dissatisfied with modern birthing practices complain that these practices are too frequently geared to high-risk pregnancy and delivery rather than normal birth.[27] As a result, many parents feel they are subjected to unnecessary obstetrical policies and routines that interfere with their sense of autonomy and control; they feel their sense of self-respect, esteem, and appreciation of the experience are diminished.[28]

Rights of pregnant parents have been discussed in a popular Canadian book, *The Rights of the Pregnant Parent*, by V.H. Elkins. These rights include: the right to a supportive doctor, the right to a baby who is safe from X-ray damage, medication effects, and so on, the right to childbirth education, the right to a shared childbirth experience (participation by both parents, explanations offered and choices given), the right to childbirth with dignity (a sense of control over one's experience), and the right to family-centered maternity care.[29]

Nurses have traditionally been very involved in prenatal, natal, and postnatal care, and therefore are in a position to influence the direction of care and to safeguard patient rights. To effect the establishment of birthing centers, safer home deliveries, and greater use of midwives, the support of nurses is required. Nurses safeguard patient rights by attention to patients' informational needs and by respecting the capabilities and motivations of the expectant parents.[30]

RIGHTS OF CHILDREN IN HEALTH CARE

The year 1979 was declared the International Year of the Child. During the year, much discussion focused on the rights of children. Included in the United Nations Declaration of the Rights of the Child were the child's right to affection, love, and understanding; the right to adequate nutrition and medical care; and the right to special care for the handicapped child. These rights call for some special obligations on the part of health providers. A number of specific concerns related to children in health care are the care of defective newborns, the age of consent, the problem of children as subjects in research, and rights of access to good health care.

Care of Defective Newborns

With the advent of genetic counselling, prenatal diagnosis, and selective abortions of abnormal fetuses, a new attitude is developing toward the care of defective newborns. Although history is replete with examples of infanticide for abnormal neonates, a more humane approach to care and treatment of defective children had evolved; that humane approach is challenged by the newer technologies.[31] As one author predicted in 1974, there has been an increase in the number of parents who instruct physicians not to keep a seriously defective baby alive.[32]

This changed and changing situation poses some acute moral and ethical dilemmas for nurses who work with neonates and their parents. At issue are at least two questions of major import. Who should decide if the neonate is to be kept alive? And what constitutes responsible care and treatment of the neonate?

One much publicized case concerned the parents of a mongoloid infant with duodenal atresia; the parents refused to allow any surgery on their child. Since then, the parents' right to decide has been strongly challenged: the burden the parents bear "might prevent them from being able to consider adequately the independent rights of the infant as a unique individual."[33] Their conflicting interests should be recognized, and some other means found to represent the distinct interests of the child. But neither physicians alone, nor the courts, nor committees appear able to represent the child. Health professionals must ensure that the rights of the neonate are protected. At the same time, the parents need support and they need to know what options are available to them; for example, if they are not able to accept the child, it can be made a ward of the government. Nurses must "mobilize nursing resources for as long as they are required by the family whatever decisions are made."[34]

A second major issue is the care of the neonate for whom passive euthanasia has been chosen. The law forbids mercy killing, but death by withdrawal of treatment is often "slow and arduous." Nurses must work to provide as "comfortable an existence as possible for the infant."[35] Passive euthanasia can be tragic for the infant, the parents, and the staff; nurses are urged to learn about and be involved in the ethical debate surrounding the care of these babies, to effect a more satisfactory resolution of this problem.

The Age of Consent
The right of a minor to consent to medical treatment is not clearly delineated in Canadian law.[36] The law does not render a minor incapable of giving an informed consent; nor does it establish that such a consent is valid.[37]

As discussed in Chapter 3, four provinces have attempted to set an age of consent. By regulation under the Public Hospitals Act, Ontario has set the age of consent at sixteen years for surgical operations in public hospitals; British Columbia has established sixteen years as the age of consent for medical, dental, or psychiatric treatment; New Brunswick has set sixteen as the age of consent to treatment; and Quebec permits a person of fourteen to consent to "medical care and treatment, required for his health."[38] In other provinces there is considerable variation in the criteria governing a minor's consent to treatment. There are three exceptions to the minor's inability to give consent:

a) in emergency situations;
b) when the minor is emancipated (self-supporting and living outside of parental control);
c) when the minor is considered a "mature minor" by reason of his or her understanding and independence of action.[39]

Health professionals are generally uneasy with the uncertainty and flexibility surrounding the age of consent. Many would find it more comfortable to have some uniform rule that defined minor patients. A natural reaction to this insecurity has been that parental consent is often sought before medical treatment will be provided.[40] But, as one Canadian lawyer has emphasized, the key to the consent should not depend upon legal capacity, but on mental capacity. The patient must understand the nature of the procedure, the risks of undergoing that procedure, and the alternatives to the particular procedure.[41]

Assessment of mental capacity requires a subjective assessment and judgment by physicians, nurses, and other health professionals. Informed consent is not synonymous with signing a consent-to-treatment form. Even minors who are not legally allowed to sign should be given an explanation congruent with their ability to understand. At least one study has suggested that age seven might be a generally appropriate age of capacity to understand.[42]

Particular problems arise with regard to the care of adolescents. Adolescents who need contraceptive devices, abortion services, or treatment for communicable diseases or drug or alcohol abuse may be unwilling to have parents involved. These circumstances are among the most troublesome for health providers and their patients, and involve the balancing of consent rights against the need to protect minors from their lack of experience and possible poor judgment. In addition, the issue of confidentiality between the health professional and the patient becomes problematic.

When terminally ill children or adolescents ask to have life-sustaining treatment discontinued, health professionals and parents alike are faced with a moral dilemma. Experience has shown that if a child refuses treatment to hasten death, efforts toward intervention are generally ineffective. Careful consideration should be given to the benefits of continuing treatment.

Consent by proxy is another problem when treating minors. Parents–the child's guardians–are generally considered capable of providing consent. However, the courts have assumed guardianship of children whose parents have not given a consent to certain kinds of treatment, for example, blood transfusions. It is recognized, therefore, that the child's right exists independently of the parents.[43] Thus, the issue of proxy consent can be blurred.

Research and Children

At least three major issues are relevant to the debate over the involvement of children in biomedical research: the research imperative, the concept of proxy consent, and the question of risks and benefits.[44] These three issues will be discussed briefly.

If the outcomes of a given therapy are accurately predictable, there is no need for research. But if the outcome of a therapy is not predictable, that therapy is essentially research.[45] Because children differ from adults in their physiological responses to diseases and to various therapies, such as drugs, health professionals cannot always learn how to treat children by doing research on adults.[46] Therefore, the involvement of children in research is imperative for the benefit of other children and society.

A second key issue is the concept of proxy consent. Do parents have a right to volunteer their children for experimentation pur- poses? Some have argued that proxy consent in experimentation is not acceptable; consent in such acts of generosity, they say, can only be given by the individual involved in the experiments.[47] Others argue that parental consent is valid for non-therapeutic medical research if there is negligible risk and pain, and if the research is conducted with attention to patient safety.[48] However, even with acceptable parental consent, two conditions should prevail. Chil- dren should not be encouraged to participate against their will.[49] Further, they should be free to discontinue participation if they change their minds.

A third issue is the question of the risks and benefits to the child involved in research. The research design must be adequate and the risks to the child minimal. Beyond low or minimal risks, all such research should be questioned and subject to intense methodologi- cal and ethical review. The potential benefits to medical knowledge and to future treatment of children must be explicit and reasonably sound. Further, as Charles Fried points out, children as research subjects should "benefit" in knowing they have been involved in a useful act of generosity.[50]

Access to Care

Parents have a legal duty to provide health care to their children as a necessity of life, as specified in the Criminal Code of Canada. This right to health care, supported by the UN Declaration of Rights of the Child and by various children's bills of rights, is often in conflict with parental self-interests and judgments. If parents neglect to fulfill their duty to provide health care to their children, the state may intervene.[51] Because state intervention frequently leads to a breakdown in parent-child relationships, more positive ways to ensure good health care for children must be sought.

In 1978, a Task Force Report of the Canadian Council on Children and Youth was released under the title *Admittance Restricted: The Child as a Citizen in Canada*. Among the many areas of concern examined in this report was the child's need for health care. The report noted that the public-health movement between 1880 and 1920 had a most immediate and positive effect on the lives of Canadian children, and deplored the lack of particular attention paid to specific issues of child health in the past decades. A plea is made for a health policy that focuses on the child's basic environment (the family) and on ways to improve family functioning to support healthy development. Several ideas were suggested. For example, families whose children are at risk should be given support, as should new parents; support should be given to general health promotion, and to health care for handicapped children.

The right of the child to health care is meaningless unless universal health programs are available and unless children have access to these programs.[52]

Children who are admitted to health-care institutions must receive humanized care – care that takes into account their particular needs as children. For many children the presence of a parent is a critical factor in humane care. In spite of the evidence supporting this need, hospitals have been slow to support parental involvement in care.[53] Parents must be encouraged, supported, and educated to be the greatest possible help to the hospitalized child; in turn, the parents' needs must also be met.

RIGHTS OF THE MENTALLY DISADVANTAGED

The mentally disadvantaged include all those persons who are disabled through mental retardation or mental illness. These people merit special care and attention because they are not always able, intellectually or emotionally, to understand the process of their illness and its treatment; nor do they always grasp the consequences of their care.

Although this discussion focuses mainly on the mentally ill patient, many of the ethical and legal concerns that arise in caring for the mentally ill arise, as well, in the care of mentally retarded patients. Health professionals tend to underestimate the abilities of both groups. Mentally retarded patients are sometimes treated as a single group; not enough attention is paid to disparate degrees of retardation, and little attempt is made to capitalize on the abilities of individual patients. Professionals also tend to forget that the person labelled mentally ill is not ill all the time: mentally ill people have periods when they are well and "normal." These oversights often lead to charges of paternalism against health professionals.

Of the many issues related to the rights of the mentally disadvantaged, three will be discussed briefly; commitment and care of the mentally ill, the right of these patients to refuse treatment, and the ethics of behavior modification and behavior influence.

Commitment and Care of the Mentally Ill

Only for two types of illness does society demand compulsory treatment: communicable disease and mental illness. The argument for protecting the public from communicable disease is rarely disputed, but the motive for compulsory treatment – commitment to mental hospitals – of the mentally ill is less clear. Is it to protect society from the dangerous behavior that sometimes is a result of mental illness, or is it to provide needed treatment for ill persons who are not always able to appreciate their illness?[54] The public is confused about the motives for committing people to mental hospitals, perhaps because the goals of such hospitals are not obvious. Historically, mental hospitals have been used to reduce the threat to public safety and social order.[55]

Numerous cases can be cited to demonstrate past and present inadequacies in the laws governing commitment.[56] Much of the descriptive terminology – "competence," "danger to self and others" – is not clearly defined and health professionals have sometimes extended these terms beyond reasonable limits. As well, many people think too much power is vested in the psychiatrist, the doctor, and sometimes the family to commit a person. During the past twenty years in Canada, attempts have been made to limit the grounds of committal, to establish independent review boards, and to shorten authorized detention periods. The changes aim to protect the civil liberties of the patient while ensuring that treatment will be available.

In the United States, the involuntarily institutionalized patient has a right to treatment; that treatment implies certain minimum standards.[57] In Canada, no specific right is laid out, yet an obligation is assumed.

During the past two decades there has been a trend to reduce the in-patient population of the mental hospital in order to provide more suitable and more humane care. However, such de-institutionalizing practices, without adequate attention to the development of community programs to provide rehabilitation and support for the mentally ill, are in themselves dehumanizing.[58]

Increasingly, advocates for the mentally ill are identifying these problems and are urging that the choice should not be institutionalization versus non-institutional care but rather that innovative, non-institutional programs should be developed while also improving institutional care.[59]

The Right to Refuse Treatment

The mentally ill patient's right to refuse treatment is a subject of continued litigation in US courts, and of debate in North American medical literature. The "reformist zeal" of mental-health advocates who attempt to promote safeguards to civil liberties is often in direct conflict with the realities of psychiatric practice. Psychiatric care providers argue that mentally ill patients are not a minority group whose civil rights are denied; because the patients are lacking the full range of mental capacities to allow them to decide what is in their best interest, it is not a question of civil rights.[60]

Apprising a patient of his 'rights' when he is delusional and hallucinating, is an act of bureaucratic madness when he lacks the capacity to comprehend what is being read to him.[61]

Advocates for the mentally ill argue that our society values the right of the individual to self-determination, to personal liberty, and to be as free as possible from coercive powers of the state, yet we single out mentally ill people and deny them "the respect and dignity afforded others,"[62] including the right to an informed consent.

The benefits of the litigation and the debate is the gradual change from "a highly paternalistic and inappropriately weighted position of the physician's 'best judgment'" to a more careful assessment of patient competencies to make treatment decisions.[63] These changes mean that patients not likely to injure themselves or others should be allowed to refuse treatment – that is, they have a right to self-determination.

Behavior Modification and Behavior Influence

There are a number of treatment methods that modify individual behavior. These include psychotherapy, direct stimulation to the brain, psychopharmacology, and behavior therapy or behavior modification. As these technologies have become more sophisticated and more available, they have introduced several moral questions.

Some degree of behavior control is essential to the functioning of society. Parents teach children to control their bowels, to develop socially acceptable eating habits, and to conform, in other aspects, to social standards. Without such control, a society would not be possible. The attempt to control destructive or pathological behavior, which is an extension of the attempt to promote conformity, raises some complex questions. Because the definition of mental illness has become increasingly broad, the number and types of behaviors assigned to the care and treatment of health professionals has also expanded, in turn, health professionals are given increased opportunity to abuse the power to control or modify behavior.

In most respects the ethical issues related to behavior modification differ from the ethical issues associated with other educational and therapeutic approaches only in degree.[64] But the public is confused about the proper meaning of the term "behavior modification." As well, there is confusion about the value judgments used to determine which behaviors to modify. Finally, because the techniques work quickly, because they may be used on a patient when that patient is not aware of it, and because aversion conditioning involves discomfort, there has been some public outcry.[65] The public is asking a number of questions. Are behavior-modification techniques significantly successful? Do the procedures involve dehumanizing practices? Do the ends justify the means?[66]

There are also questions about the use of psychopharmacologic drugs to influence behavior, a practice that has become particularly widespread since the 1940s and the 1950s. Drugs are widely disseminated and readily available; other techniques, such as psychosurgery, electrode transplant, or even psychotherapy, are used less frequently.[67] A person's autonomy can be severely restricted by some drugs, which destroy the individual's ability to think rationally.

In all these treatment methods, health professionals must balance individual rights and needs against the collective good. To make decisions, health professionals need guidelines that preserve autonomy but that also recognize the importance of treatment for mentally ill patients. At least two sets of guidelines are available. Erica James and Richard Allon provide guidelines that apply specifically to behavior-modification techniques. Their guidelines advocate accurate documentation of methods and results; the tailoring of methods to the needs of the individual; careful monitoring of programs and equipment; assurance of patient dignity; public education; and research.[68] Gerald Dworkin's guidelines deal with behavior control. According to Dworkin, health professionals must avoid treatment methods that are destructive to the patient's ability to reflect rationally, that affect the personal identity of the patient, or that rely on deception. Methods of influence that are not physically intrusive and that call for active participation on the part of the patient are preferrable. In short, methods that support the dignity and self-respect of those being influenced should be chosen.[69]

Implications for Nursing
Nurses who care for the mentally ill face a number of dilemmas. They are a prime source of information about patients and about how various treatment regimes affect patients' behavior. This information can be used for the benefit of the patient – or it can be used to serve the needs of the nurse or the institution. For example, a medication plan may be used not to help the patient, but to punish non-compliant behavior or simply to make the patient easier to manage. Or other health professionals might try to use the nurse as a double agent: a nurse who legitimately obtains information from a patient may then be required to provide that information to a third person without the patient's awareness or permission.

Even the fundamental patient-care activities of most psychiatric treatment centers can pose problems for nurses. How much should the nurse interfere with the patients' liberty of action – their freedom, their privacy, their autonomy? Coercing patients into going for walks or joining others in the patient lounge are daily tasks for most nurses. When is the activity in the patients' interest? When is it justified only because the ward functions more smoothly if the patients co-operate? How do nurses obtain a patient's consent?

These very common dilemmas show that nurses must be involved in discussing problems, in developing guidelines, and in seeking to balance patients' treatment needs; and nurses must respect the patient's rights and autonomy.

RIGHTS AND THE ELDERLY

Elderly people who enter the health-care system encounter the same problems facing the average health-care consumer, but with a number of qualifying conditions. Our society generally regards the elderly as a low-status group, and the elderly are therefore subject to numerous difficulties as patients. Their rights to information, to respect, to participation, and to equal access to care take on added significance.

Elderly patients often have trouble getting information about preventive strategies because health professionals are geared to treat acute ailments: they largely ignore the potentials of early detection and treatment, and the possibilities for preventing premature aging and disability.[70] An aged patient's right to information is also jeopardized by declining auditory and memory abilities. To fulfill the principles of an informed consent, health professionals must pay careful attention to the environment in which they seek that consent: it should be free from external distractions and group pressures. The patient should know the professional who requests consent; the approach should not disrupt the patient's established routines. Finally, non-written (for example, tape-recorded) consents should be permissible.[71]

Individual care and privacy are critical in the care of the elderly. The tendency to view the aged as a uniform group is destructive to individual care and to human dignity.[72] Health professionals should not determine what constitutes appropriate care on the basis of the patient's age, but rather on the basis of the patient's abilities. Elderly patients should have a choice in the type of institutionalized care that will be provided, and the institution must suit the needs of the patient. This last fact is often ignored: the needs of the institution take precedence over the needs of the patients. Conformity of patients in nursing homes does not occur because all aged patients are basically alike, but because the way in which their care is managed results in similar behaviors.[73] Over-medication perpetuates this conformity.

Privacy is a critical issue in long-term care for the elderly. Aged patients who have lost the privacy of their homes need a place where their privacy will be respected. Facilities for the aged are designed and managed to focus on groups of patients: group eating and group activities can be over-emphasized, and often there is not adequate allowance for privacy.

> *The psychological reality of aging is very private.... Again and again, older men and women in nursing homes or other institutions are forced to participate in programs so utterly meaningless in nature that their effect is depressing.*[74]

Access to good health care is a pressing problem for the elderly. As a group, the aged are underserved, and too frequently the care they receive is not geared to their needs.[75] In comparison to university hospital settings, nursing homes or other institutions for the elderly are low-prestige organizations, and some physicians visit nursing-home patients irregularly and infrequently.[76] Nor are elderly patients given enough time and attention in out-patient office visits. The aged sick generally have multiple pathologies, and drug-related illnesses are common; therefore, proper assessment, diagnosis, and treatment are time-consuming and challenging. Better understanding of these conditions must be attained through research, and health professionals must be better educated about the needs of the elderly. As well, suitable payment methods for physicians will have to be found to provide incentives for them to spend adequate time with the elderly in assessment, diagnosis, and treatment.

In today's society the elderly are subject to many prejudices and individuals are looked upon not as individuals but as stereotypes. Because society values youth, activity, and efficiency and denies suffering and death, older people are isolated and often neglected, and they begin to question their self-worth. Sickness sometimes becomes a safety valve, allowing them to retreat from a situation where they have no clearly defined roles to a more legitimate role, being sick.

The sick role provides an individual with a defense against shame engendered by desertion and banishment, but only for a short time.... while a short-term illness may help older persons offset their rolelessness, a long term illness makes it acceptable to permanently banish the elderly to institutions.[77]

Implications for Nursing

Nurses have the potential to fill a glaring gap in health services for the elderly. To satisfy the needs for prevention, for early detection, and for access to primary health services are well within the scope and capability of nursing's function. In a brief to the *Health Services Review* in 1979 (the federal government's Hall Commission), the Canadian Nurses' Association emphasized the role nurses can play in making health care more accessible to the elderly.[78]

Nurses can also play a key role in ensuring that elderly patients can give an informed consent. Most elderly patients, especially those in long-term care settings, know and trust their nurses; similarly, nurses are well-acquainted with their patients and can identify times and circumstances in which a truly informed consent is not possible. Nurses can help other health professionals choose a suitable time and place to talk to patients.

Increased privacy for the elderly is also a goal nurses should work toward. The institutional setting may not always be conducive to privacy, but nurses can find innovative ways to create greater privacy.

Much remains to be done to make nursing homes, other long-term care settings, and community-care programs more conducive to patient respect and patient comfort. It is important that each sick elderly person be cared for in an appropriate setting. Placement decisions should take into account the patients' preferences.[79] Nurses have the capacity to work collectively and individually for needed changes in governmental and institutional policies.

RIGHTS OF NATIVE PEOPLE

The term "native people" is used to describe a wide diversity of Indian and Inuit people, some of whom "have a high degree of continuity with their traditional culture" and some who are acculturated to Euro-Canadian society.[80] The right to equal access to health care and the right to participate are critical to native people.

Under the terms of the BNA Act, Section 91, the provision of services for native people, is the responsibility of the federal government. In fact, two federal departments have much to do with the health care of the native people – Health and Welfare Canada (Medical Services Branch) and Indian Affairs and Northern Development. Historically, federal responsibilities for native people have been carried out under the auspices of various federal departments, leading to fragmentation of health services and discontinuities in socio-economic and educational development.[81] In the early sixties, National Health and Welfare stated that one of its objectives was to ensure that Indians receive health care of the same quality as that enjoyed by the rest of the country, and to try to make the standard of health of the Indian people nearly equal to that of other Canadians.[82] But, twenty years later, evidence of such accomplishments is lacking. According to a recent survey of Indian Affairs and Northern Development, entitled *Indian Conditions*, health services are more accessible to those in need, but the health status of the Indian people is not nearly equal to that of other Canadians. Indian death rates are two to four times the national average; neonatal mortality is approximately sixty per cent higher than the national average; violent deaths are three times the national average; suicides in the fifteen-to-twenty-four age group are six times national rates; and alcoholism continues to be a severe problem.[83] The survey concludes:

Health conditions which can be improved by medical care have improved; those influenced by social and living conditions have not.[84]

These survey findings clearly demonstrate that health is not equivalent to equal access to medicine;[85] there must also be equal access to other services, such as housing, sanitation, and education. The disparity in socio-economic conditions between native Canadians and other Canadians starkly emphasizes the absence of equality of condition.[86]

Nurses have been in the forefront of provision of health care to many native Canadians, and in many respects the type of "holistic" health care provided through the Nursing Stations is better than the services available to other segments of rural Canada. The relationships many of the northern nurses have with native patients assist in establishing the kind of rapport necessary to deal with the broader social issues affecting health care.[87] Yet the change from traditional native health practices to more modern Canadian practices is not without confusion:

> For most people, comprehending the complexities of germ theory and preventive medicine is low in priority when their energy and attention is focused on the social, political, and economic upheavals occurring around them.[88]

The fragmentation of services for native persons across government departments has added to a sense of confusion, mistrust, and conflict.

Natives are demanding that their right to participate be respected. They want to determine the direction of their cultural change, and they want to be involved in health policy-making and health-services planning. For example, in 1969, when the government's White Paper on Indian Policy was released, there was an accompanying storm of Indian protest and comment. Despite consultation with Indian peoples in developing the policy paper, the government had seemed to ignore much of the native input, and had offered some unilaterally determined recommendations.[89]

It has taken some time for Euro-Canadians to realize that the use of paternalistic practices in working with native people is injurious and self-defeating. A Sister of Providence has identified this error:

> To me, our most serious mistake was the conviction that the more we could make our native students think, look, and act like white people, the better it would be for them in their later life. We thought we were doing them a favor by bringing them our culture, our religion, our language. We failed to see the merit of helping them enrich their own culture, of bettering their own level of existence, of working with them instead of for them.[90]

A new Indian Health Policy, released by the Government of Canada in 1979, emphasizes the need for greater involvement of Indian people in the "planning, budgeting, and delivery of health programs." Health professionals working with native people are committed to work towards implementing consumer participation at the community level.

SUMMARY AND CONCLUSIONS

The groups identified in this chapter as those in need of special attention and concern are parents in their reproductive role, children, the mentally disadvantaged, the elderly, and native persons. These patients require special protection because of their vulnerability, the result of rapid technological changes, societal values, physical or emotional handicaps, or structural barriers.

The particular health-care problems of these groups stem from wide-ranging inequities; therefore, resolution to these problems demands far-reaching reforms. However, there is much that nurses (and other health professionals) can do, working individually and collectively, to better health care for these patients. Some suggestions to safeguard patient's rights are included in this chapter; others will be discussed in Chapter 8.

REFERENCES

[1] Doris Wilson, "Voluntary Sterilization: Legal and Ethical Aspects," *Legal Medical Quarterly* 3:1 (1979): 13–23.

[2] Joel Feinberg, "Abortion," in *Matters of Life and Death*, ed. Tom Regan (New York: Random House, 1980), p. 183.

[3] Tom L. Beauchamp and LeRoy Walters, ed., *Contemporary Issues in Bioethics* (Belmont, California: Wadsworth Publishing Co., Inc. 1978), p. 187.

[4] Lorne E. Rozovsky, *Canadian Hospital Law*, 2nd edition (Ottawa: Canadian Hospital Association, 1979), pp. 109–111.

[5] *Ibid*, p. 112.

[6] John Badertscher, "Religious Dimensions of the Abortion Debate," in *Ethics in Medicine: Historical Perspectives and Contemporary Concerns*, eds. Stanley Joel Reiser, Arthur J. Dyck, and William J. Curran (Cambridge, Mass.: MIT Press, 1977), p. 447.

[7] Beauchamp and Walters, p. 187.

[8] Feinberg, pp. 183–184.

[9] *Ibid*, pp. 191–198.

[10] *Ibid*, pp. 203–212.

[11] See for example Sissela Bok, "Ethical Problems of Abortion," *Hastings Center Studies* 2 (January 1974): 33–52; Judith Jarvis Thomson, "A Defense of Abortion," *Philosophy and Public Affairs* (Fall 1971): 47–66; Joel Feinburg, pp. 183–217.

[12] Beauchamp and Walters, p. 193.

[13] "Four Big Decisions," *Time* 116 (July 14, 1980): 9.

[14] "The Battle Over Abortion," *Time* 117 (April 16, 1981): 20–21.

[15] *Report of the Committee on the Operation of the Abortion Law*, Robin F. Badgley, Chairman (Ottawa: Supply and Services, 1977), p. 17.

[16] *Ibid*, p. 17.

[17] *Ibid*, pp. 287–288. Reproduced by permission of the Minister of Supply and Services.

[18] *Ibid*, p. 34.

[19] For a cogent account of the technology of genetic screening see George J.

Annas and Brian Coyne, "Fitness for Birth and Reproduction: Legal Implications of Genetic Screening," *Family Law Quarterly* 9 (1975): 463–489.

[20]Lorne Elkin Rozovsky and Faye Rozovsky, "Public Health and the Law," *Canadian Journal of Public Health* 72 (January–February 1981): 15–16.

[21]Annas and Coyne, pp. 486–487.

[22]Gina Bari Kolata, "Mass Screening for Neural Tube Defects," *Hastings Center Report* 10 (December 1980): 8–10.

[23]John C. Fletcher, "The Morality and Ethics of Prenatal Diagnosis," in *Genetic Disorders and the Fetus*, ed. Aubrey Milunsky (New York: Plenum Publishing Co., 1979), pp. 621–635. See also Tabitha M. Powledge and John Fletcher, "Guidelines for Ethical, Social and Legal Issues in Prenatal Diagnosis," *The New England Journal of Medicine* 300 (January 25, 1979): 168–172.

[24]LeRoy Walters, "Human In Vitro Fertilization: A Review of Ethical Literature," *Hastings Center Report* 9 (August 1979): 23–43. See also Margaret O'Brien Steinfels, "In Vitro Fertilization: 'Ethically Acceptable' Research," *Hastings Center Report* 9 (June 1979): 5–8.

[25]Ora L. Strickland, "In Vitro Fertilization: Dilemma or Opportunity," *Advances in Nursing Science* 3 (January 1981): 41–51.

[26]Cornelius L. Katona, "Approaches to Antenatal Education," *Social Science and Medicine* 15A (January 1981): 25–33.

[27]Valmai Howe Elkins, *The Rights of the Pregnant Parent* (Ottawa: Waxwing Productions, 1976), pp. xi, 38.

[28]*Ibid*, p. 185.

[29]*Ibid*, pp. 88–228.

[30]Heather Rothwell, "Pregnancy–A State of Ignorance," *Midwives Chronicle and Nursing Notes* 91 (February 1978): 28–30.

[31]John Fletcher, "Attitudes Toward Defective Newborns," *Hastings Center Studies* 2:1 (January 1974): 21–32. See also Bok, pp. 49–50.

[32]Fletcher, p. 31.

[33]Natalie Abrams and Lois Lyon Neumann, "Human Rights and Ethical Decision-Making in the Newborn Nursery," in *Bioethics and Human Rights*, ed. Elsie L. Bandman and Bertram Bandman (Boston: Little, Brown and Co., 1978), p. 159.

[34]Carolyn Sara Roberts, "Ethical Issues in the Treatment of Neonates with Severe Anomalies," *Nursing Forum* 18:4 (1979): 352–365.

[35]*Ibid*, pp. 363–364.

[36]Corinne Sklar, "Minors in the Health Care System," *The Canadian Nurse* 74 (September 1978): 20.

[37]Lorne E. Rozovsky, "Can a Minor Consent to Treatment?" *Dimensions* 54 (May 1977): 10. For background information on the consent of minors to treatment, see *Consent of Minors to Medical Treatment, Background Paper No. 9*, Edmonton: Institute of Law Research and Reform, University of Alberta, 1975.

[38]Rozovsky, p. 12.

[39]Sklar, p. 19.

[40]Ellen Picard, "A Child's Right to Health Care," *Dimensions* 56 (May 1979): 60–61.

[41]Rozovsky, p. 11.

[42]Charles E. Lewis, Mary Anne Lewis, and Muriel Ifekwunigue. "Informed Consent by Children and Participation in an Influenza Vaccine Trial," *American Journal of Public Health* 68 (November 1978): 1079–1082.

[43]*Admittance Restricted: The Child as a Citizen in Canada* (Ottawa: Canadian Council on Children and Youth, 1978), p. 72.

⁴⁴William G. Bartholome, "Central Issues in the Debate Over Involvement of Infants and Children in Biomedical Research," in *Research on Children: Medical Imperatives, Ethical Quandaries, and Legal Constraints*, ed. Jan van Eys (Baltimore: University Park Press, 1978), p. 69.

⁴⁵Wataru W. Sutow, "Therapeutic Research as a Necessary Mode of Management," in *Research on Children*, p. 25.

⁴⁶Martha Freeman, "Federal Regulations: Their Growth and Intent," in *Research on Children*, p. 128.

⁴⁷Bartholome, p. 73; John Holt, "The Right of Children to Informed Consent," in *Research on Children*, pp. 8–16.

⁴⁸Bernard M. Dickens, "The Use of Children in Medical Experimentation," *Medicolegal Journal* 43 (1975): 169.

⁴⁹Jean Hayter, "Issues Related to Human Subjects," in *Issues in Nursing Research*, eds. Florence S. Downs and Juanita Fleming (New York: Appleton-Century Crofts, 1979), p. 126.

⁵⁰Charles Fried, "Children as Subjects for Medical Experimentation," in *Research on Children*, p. 113.

⁵¹Picard, p. 60.

⁵²*Admittance Restricted*, p. 72.

⁵³"Issues in Humanizing Care for Children," *American Journal of Public Health* 68 (September 1978): 831–832; and Carol B. Hardgrove and Rosanne Kermoian, "Parent-Inclusive Pediatric Units: A Survey of Policies and Practices," *American Journal of Public Health* 68 (September 1978): 847–850.

⁵⁴Lorne E. Rozovsky, "Civil Commitment of the Mentally Ill," *Dimensions* 55 (November 1978): 38.

⁵⁵Gerald N. Grob, "Rediscovering Asylums: The Unhistorical History of the Mental Hospital," *Hastings Center Report* 7 (August 1977): 33–41.

⁵⁶See for example Stewart Page, "The Case of Tim Crawford: Mental Health Legislation Five Years Later," *Legal Medical Quarterly* 2:1 (1978): 24–28; George J. Annas, "O'Connor v. Donaldson: Insanity Inside Out," *Hastings Center Report* 6 (August 1976): 11–12; Marge Reitsma, "Civil Liberties and the Mentally Ill," *Canada's Mental Health* 21 (November–December 1973): 10–11.

⁵⁷For a summary discussion of these minimum standards see Kenneth R. Wing, *The Law and the Public's Health* (St. Louis: C.V. Mosby, 1976), pp. 47–51. See also Erica L. James and Richard Allon, "Legal Issues and Behavior Modification: A Canadian Perspective," *Canadian Psychological Review* 20 (October 1979): 177–178.

⁵⁸Federico Allodi and Henry B. Kedward, "The Evolution of the Mental Hospital in Canada," *Canadian Journal of Public Health* 68 (May–June 1977): 219–224.

⁵⁹James M. Smith, "Madness, Innovation, and Social Policy," *Hastings Center Report* 7 (October 1977): 8–9.

⁶⁰See for example Lawrence R. Tancredi, "The Rights of Mental Patients: Weighing the Interests," *Journal of Health Politics, Policy and Law* 5 (Summer 1980): 199; Harvey Shwed, "Social Policy and the Rights of the Mentally Ill: Time for Reexamination," *Journal of Health Politics, Policy and Law* 5 (Summer 1980): 194.

⁶¹Shwed, p. 195.

⁶²Jack Himmelstein, "The Right to Refuse Psychotropic Drugs," *Hastings Center Report* 3 (June 1973): 9.

⁶³Lawrence R. Tancredi, "The Right to Refuse Psychiatric Treatment: Some Legal and Ethical Considerations," *Journal of Health Politics, Policy and Law* 5 (Fall 1980): 521.

[64]Philip Roos, "Human Rights and Behavior Modification," *Nursing Digest* 3 (March–April 1975): 48.

[65]James and Allon, p. 176.

[66]Roos, p. 48.

[67]Robert M. Veatch, "Drugs and Competing Drug Ethics," *Hastings Center Report* 2 (January 1974): 68–80; Gerald L. Klerman, "Psychotropic Drugs as Therapeutic Agents," *Hastings Center Report* 2 (January 1974): 81–93.

[68]James and Allon, pp. 180–181. See also Nicholas N. Kittrie, *The Right to be Different: Deviance and Enforced Therapy* (Baltimore: The Johns Hopkins Press, 1971), pp. 400–408 for a therapeutic bill of rights.

[69]Gerald Dworkin, "Autonomy and Behavior Control," *Hastings Center Report* 6 (February 1976): 27–28.

[70]Jerome Hammerman, "Health Services: Their Success and Failure in Reaching Older Adults," in *Dominant Issues in Medical Sociology* ed. Howard D. Schwartz and Cary S. Kart (Don Mills: Addison-Wesley Publishing Co., 1978), p. 467.

[71]Although the guidelines suggested here were originally proposed for consent to research on the elderly, they are appropriate to informed consent to treatment. See Kathleen Kelly and Eleanor McClelland, "Signed Consent: Protection or Constraint?" *Nursing Outlook* 27 (January 1979): 42.

[72]Thomas Halper, "The Double-Edged Sword: Paternalism as a Policy in the Problems of Aging," *Milbank Memorial Fund Quarterly* 58 (Summer 1980): 488.

[73]David Skelton, Address to the Edmonton Branch, Victorian Order of Nurses Annual Meeting, Edmonton, February 23, 1981.

[74]Matthew Ies Spetter, "Growing Old in America: Can We Restore the Dignity of Age?" in *Bioethics and Human Rights*, ed. Elsie L. Bandman and Bertram Bandman (Boston: Little, Brown and Co., 1978), p. 203.

[75]Hammerman, p. 467.

[76]Elizabeth Gustafson, "Dying: the Career of the Nursing Home Patient," in *Dominant Issues in Sociology*, p. 47.

[77]Cornelia Beck, "Mental Health and the Aged: A Values Analysis," *Advances in Nursing Science* 1 (April 1979): 80–83.

[78]"Putting 'Health' into Health Care," Submission to Health Services Review '79 (Ottawa: Canadian Nurses Association, February 1980), pp. 19–20.

[79]For an example of a model for patient placement that takes into account patient preferences, see K.S. Bay, P. Overton, F.P. Harrison, S.M. Stinson and S.L. Hazlett, *Patient Classification by Types of Care: A Research Report on the Development and Validation of the PCTC System* (Edmonton: Health Services Administration, Faculty of Medicine, University of Alberta, 1979), p. 225.

[80]E. Palmer Patterson, "Native People and Social Policy," in *Canadian Social Policy*, ed. Shankar A. Yelaja (Waterloo, Ont.: Wilfred Laurier University Press, 1978), p. 184.

[81]G. Graham-Cumming, "Health of the Original Canadians, 1867–1967," *Medical Services Journal of Canada* 23 (1967): 127.

[82]Allen Booz and Hamilton Canada Ltd., *Summary Report on a Study of Health Services for Canadian Indians* (Toronto: McClelland and Stewart Ltd., 1975), pp. 16–20.

[83]*Indian Conditions* (Ottawa: Department of Indian Affairs and Northern Development, 1980), pp. 3, 15–22. For a narrative account of Indian conditions, see Paul Grescoe, "A Nation's Disgrace," in *Health and Canadian Society*, eds. David Coburn, Carl D'Arcy, Peter New and George Torrance (Don Mills: Fitzhenry and Whiteside Ltd., 1981), pp. 109–122.

[84]*Indian Conditions*, p. 8.
[85]Aaron Wildavsky emphasizes this point when he accuses Americans of goal displacement–health is often seen as equivalent to equal access to medicine. See Aaron Wildavsky, "Doing Better and Feeling Worse: The Political Pathology of Health Policy," *Daedalus* 106 (Winter 1977): 106.
[86]Equality of condition is described as "basic minimum standard of living to be provided by the state in case of social insecurity–if there should be need for social support." See Anne Crichton, "Equality: A Concept in Canadian Health Care: From Intention to Reality of Provision," *Social Science and Medicine* 14C (1980): 245.
[87]John P. O'Neil, "Health Care in a Central Canadian Arctic Community: Continuities and Change," in *Health and Canadian Society*, pp. 139–140.
[88]*Ibid*, p. 140.
[89]Patterson, pp. 180–183.
[90]Sr. Jean LaBissoniere, *Providence Trail Blazers* (Edmonton: Sisters of Providence Centre, 1978), p. 134.

SUGGESTED REFERENCES FOR FURTHER STUDY, CHAPTER 7

Admittance Restricted: The Child as a Citizen in Canada. Ottawa: Canadian Council on Children and Youth, 1978.

This book is the report of a task force that investigated the place of the child in Canadian society. It provides a broad overview of national and provincial policies that affect the quality of life for children in Canada. Four main principles underlie this investigation: 1) the rights of children; 2) support for the family; 3) equality of opportunity; 4) individuality of the child's interest. The report examines policy and practice in relation to children's needs, and stresses the need for economic support, the need for health care, the need for protection, and the need for education. A separate chapter focuses on the needs of native children. The report concludes by suggesting a number of changes to existing systems and institutions designed to make them more responsive to the needs of children and families.

Annas, George and Coyne, Brian. "Fitness for Birth and Reproduction: Legal Implications of Genetic Screening." *Family Law Quarterly* 9 (1975): 463–489.

As a prelude to a discussion of legal issues in genetic screening, the authors provide a sound overview of the technology of genetics and genetic screening, including patterns of dominant and recessive inheritance, detection of genetic diseases in the fetus, and the screening of children and adults for genetic disorders. They then discuss legal issues that surround test results of prenatal diagnosis, such as false positives (a test that concludes the fetus is affected when in fact it is not) and false negatives (a test that concludes that the fetus is not affected, when in fact it is). A number of legal cases are discussed, including those that arise from the birth of a defective infant following amniocentesis, the abortion of a healthy infant following amniocentesis, and a failure to perform amniocentesis. Neonatal screening and the screening of children and adults are then discussed, and matters of confidentiality in genetic screening are underscored. The authors stress the challenge for legislatures to carefully determine what role is appropriate for the government to take in regulating and fostering genetic advances.

Beck, Cornelia. "Mental Health and the Aged: A Value Analysis," *Advances in Nursing Science* 1 (April 1979); 79–87.

In this article, Beck explores the question of why there has been a lack of concern for mental illness in the aged, and emphasizes the need to be more attentive to this group of individuals. Beck believes that neglect of the aged is a result of society's valuation of youth and work and denial of death and suffering. She describes senility as a misunderstood and too easily explained cause of mental illness in the aged, and notes that the bases of senility are isolation caused by sensory deprivation and social isolation. She then suggests that sickness becomes a safety valve for the elderly, and that treatment of mental illness in the aged must be geared to their needs. Since mental illness is an outgrowth of the elderly's situation in society, Beck emphasizes the need for basic changes in values.

Caldwell, Janice M. and Kapp, Marshall B. "The Rights of Nursing Home Patients: Possibilities and Limitations of Federal Regulation," *Journal of Health Politics, Policy and Law* 6 (Spring 1981): 40–48.

The authors describe the background of patients' rights concerns, with particular attention to the legal rights of nursing-home patients. They discuss new proposed federal regulations in the US, and outline a number of changes in specific provisions of the regulations to elevate patients' rights, to protect against transfer of rights, to strengthen patients' rights to access to outsiders, to formalize the concept of resident councils, to limit involuntary transfer, and to provide for some patient and family involvement with federal and state surveyors for purposes of expressing opinions and concerns. The limits to the establishment of regulations are also discussed, and the authors conclude that these regulations can protect dependants from abuses only to a small degree: compassion and respect for individuals (which cannot be regulated) are the key to protection.

Dworkin, Gerald. "Autonomy and Behavior Control." *The Hastings Center Report* 6 (February 1976): 23–28.

Dworkin suggests that if individual autonomy is accepted as possible and desirable, then the possibility that various techniques of controlling and influencing behavior will affect autonomy in different ways may be an important variable in the debate surrounding behavior control. To this end, he offers a concept of autonomy that includes authenticity and independence. He suggests a number of guidelines for the preservation of autonomy in behavior control, such as methods of influence that support self-respect and dignity, and methods that require active participation by the individual. He disapproves of methods destructive to the individual's ability to think rationally, methods that affect the personal identity of individuals, methods that rely on deception, methods that are physically intrusive, and methods that do not restrict the time in which the changes take place.

Elkins, Valmai Howe. *The Rights of the Pregnant Parent.* Ottawa: Waxwing Productions, 1976.

Elkin's book is directed to couples who want to make the present obstetrical system work for them. In the beginning chapters, Elkins describes approaches to obstetrical care in other countries, misconceptions about labor, and problems with the medically managed birth. She then describes ways in which delivery-room practices can be modified to accommodate more acceptable birthing practices. The remaining chapters propose various parental rights: to a supportive doctor, to a healthy baby, to childbirth education, to a shared birth experience, to childbirth with dignity, and to family-centered maternity care. In the final chapters, Elkins emphasizes the parents' responsibility to demand these rights, and the health professional's responsibility to be sensitive and supportive to the parents' rights.

Feinberg, Joel. "Abortion" in *Matters of Life and Death*, pp. 183–217. Edited by Tom Regan. New York: Random House, 1980.

Feinberg addresses the question, "Under what conditions, if any, is abortion morally justified." He looks at two key philosophical issues: the status of the fetus – that is, when do fetuses become people? – and the problem of conflicting claims between the woman and the fetus. Feinberg outlines several approaches to the concept of personhood and describes the various perspectives on moral personhood. In discussing the issue of the woman's claims, he refutes the notions of property rights and self-defense in favor of bodily autonomy, but even then he suggests that only a limited number of criteria should be accepted as justifiable for abortion.

Indian Conditions: A Survey. Ottawa: Minister of Indian Affairs and Northern Development, 1980.

This report consolidates information documenting changes in the social, economic, and political conditions of the Indian people in Canada during the past ten to twenty years. The five chapters of the report describe social, economic, and political conditions, government programs, and off-reserve conditions. Each chapter includes a summary of conditions in the 1950s and 1960s; recent changes, perspectives and comments from Indian leaders and government officials; and a discussion of the implications of the information presented. Although the report deals mainly with quantifiable aspects of living and material conditions, it is an excellent resource summary of factual information. For example, the section on health in the chapter on social conditions provides graphic illustrations and a discussion of key health indicators.

James, Erica L. and Allon, Richard. "Legal Issues in Behavior Modification: A Canadian Perspective." *Canadian Psychological Review* 20 (October 1979): 175–183.

The authors suggest that those who use behavior-modification techniques must become more sensitive to the emerging legal concepts surrounding these modes of treatment. While acknowledging the lack of direct effect of US judicial decisions in Canada, they suggest that these decisions may well have an impact on the development of standards for behavior modification in Canada. They outline some general concerns of behavior modification and then discuss legal issues, citing American law and recent judicial decisions related to ethics, patients' rights, due process, and informed consent. Nine guidelines for use of behavior-modification techniques are proposed to accommodate the social and legal concerns raised by the US experience.

Johnson, Freddie Louise Power. "Response to Territorial Intrusion by Nursing Home Residents." *Advances in Nursing Science* 1 (July 1979): 21–34.

Johnson describes the concept of territoriality as "that conscious or unconscious behavior which is characteristically displayed in individual territory to indicate possession or ownership." According to Johnson, this concept is significant to health professionals working in any institution, particularly nursing homes. She provides a model of the sequential development of territoriality in the institutionalized aged, and reports on a study conducted in a nursing home to examine territorial behavior. Residents' territorial behavior was found to vary according to type of room accommodation, sex, and previous occupation. Johnson underscores the nurse's central position in influencing patient privacy and ameliorating the negative effects of intrusion by showing respect for the resident's preference for the immediate environment and offering as much choice as possible. She further suggests that architects who design nursing homes should consider resident's individual territory.

Patterson, E. Palmer. "Native Peoples and Social Policy," in *Canadian Social Policy*, pp. 167–185. Edited by Shankar A. Yelaja. Waterloo, Ont.: Wilfrid Laurier University Press, 1978.

Patterson notes the re-emergence of the native people as an important segment of Canadian society, and describes Canadian Indian history and social policy to demonstrate the problems native people have encountered in Canadian society. He highlights various government legislation and government policies that have been directed towards natives in their traditional status, in a transitional status, or with the goal of assimilation, and notes the inadequacy of these models. Native people are seeking a new identity and want greater involvement in determining the future directions of their cultural change. Finally, he urges the Canadian native people not be seen as a "problem" amenable to "solution" but rather as a distinctive and vital part of Canadian life.

Roberts, Carolyn Sara. "Ethical Issues in the Treatment of Neonates with Severe Anomalies," *Nursing Forum* 18:4 (1979): 352–356.

Roberts explores the ethical positions and the locus of decision-making surrounding care of severely deformed neonates. She first notes the societal problem of scarce resource allocation and then provides a brief overview of various ethical perspectives regarding the value of life and the duty to preserve life. In discussing the matter of who should decide whether treatment should be withheld from a severely defective neonate, she reviews arguments for committee, state, physician, and parental decision-making, concluding that the parents have an *a priori* claim. She notes the problem of conflicting interests of parent and child, but emphasizes that, to exercise their duty of care, nurses must accept parental prerogative. Finally, she urges nurses to become involved in the continuing debate regarding the proper treatment of newborns with severe birth defects.

Sklar, Corinne. "Minors in the Health Care System." *Canadian Nurse* 74 (September 1978): pp. 18–20.

Sklar provides an overview of the law related to minors in the health-care system and notes two basic principles of law: 1) that the law attempts to protect children from their own immaturity in matters of consent; 2) that the state will assume a protective role to a minor when parents neglect their duties. Sklar reviews consent to treatment and points out the ambiguity of common law in this respect; she emphasizes the need to assess the minor's capacity to appreciate the nature of the proposed treatment. (There are two exceptions: emergency cases, and cases concerning an "emancipated minor" or a "mature minor.") Various provincial statutes that deal with the consent of minors are reviewed, and Sklar provides some general guidelines to nurses engaged in the care and treatment of these children.

Social Issues in Human Genetics: Genetic Screening and Counselling Ottawa: Science Council of Canada, August 1980.

The proceedings of a workshop sponsored by the Science Council of Canada are summarized in this report, which begins with a discussion of the state of the art of genetic services in Canada. Included in this discussion is a brief summary of a survey of genetic services in Canada. Problems in genetic screening are then discussed, including problems of a more general nature, such as informed consent in screening; and problems specific to particular genetic conditions, such as screening for Duchenne's muscular dystrophy or cystic fibrosis. Methods for genetic decision-making are then explored. The summary discussion suggests that the development of perspectives on Canadian genetic services have just begun, and that guidelines sensitive to local conditions and needs may be appropriate.

Strickland, Ora L. "In Vitro Fertilization: Dilemma or Opportunity?" *Advances in Nursing Science* 3 (January 1981): 41–51.

Using the example of Louise Brown's birth as the signal of an important scientific breakthrough, the author briefly describes the technique of In Vitro Fertilization (IVF) as a prelude to analyzing the ethical, moral, social, and legal questions of this new technology. She notes the anomalies of treating a clinical defect by IVF versus greater attention to prevention of the defect; and of aborting potentially healthy babies versus devoting resources to IVF. Problems of the experimental nature of IVF are reviewed, and the dilemmas of the unnatural aspects of IVF discussed. Strickland questions the possible implications IVF may have for women, the family, and society; she urges nurses to become informed about the opportunities and the dilemmas of IVF.

Tancredi, Laurence R. "The Right to Refuse Psychiatric Treatment: Some Legal and Ethical Considerations." *Journal of Health Politics, Policy and Law* 5 (Fall 1980): 514–522.

Prior to the mental-health law movement of the 1960s and the 1970s in the US, patients involuntarily committed to mental institutions were deemed not competent to make the kinds of decisions that the average citizen could make in everyday life, including the right to refuse treatment. Tancredi outlines the changes that have occurred during the past fifteen years, and notes judicial cases based on the right to be protected from cruel and unusual punishment and the right to privacy. Recent court cases that have begun to refer to the principles such as a right to self-determination, to autonomy, and to psychological identity will be problematic until fundamental ethical questions are resolved. He suggests that greater attention should be given to the practical matter of the effectiveness of existing treatments and the nature of undesirable side effects, as well as the issue of competency in making treatment decisions.

Thomson, Judith Jarvis. "A Defense of Abortion." *Philosophy and Public Affairs* 1 (Fall 1971): 47–66.

Thomson's argument begins with the premise that the fetus is a human person from the moment of conception, with a right to life. She then discusses the mother's right to decide what shall happen in and to her body. To demonstrate the problem of fetal dependence and the mother's lack of consent in many cases, Thomson provides a hypothetical situation: a man discovers an unconscious violinist with a fatal kidney ailment strapped to his body upon awakening one day. She discusses the various perspectives on a woman's right to decide and argues that a woman should be able to defend her life against the threat posed by an unborn child, that the right to life does not guarantee the use of another person's body, that there may be some cases in which the unborn has a right to the use of its mother's body, and that the fetus is a person for whom the mother has a special kind of responsibility. She concludes that although abortion is not impermissible, it is not always permissible.

CHAPTER 8 Nurses, the Organization of Health Care, and Patients' Rights

The preceding chapters have focused on the issues of patients' rights, and were based on the premise that increased awareness and understanding of these rights can lead to a new and better health professional-patient relationship.

The nursing profession has the potential to effect patient rights in health care and to promote humanized care, "care that enhances the dignity and autonomy of patients and health professionals alike."[1] Because there are more nurses than other health professionals, because they work throughout the health-care system, and because they have sustained contact with patients, nurses have the potential to establish new models for health professional-patient relationships.

Despite this tremendous potential, nurses are often hindered in their attempts to promote patient rights and to provide humanized care. A number of constraints – structural, social, and behavioral – are apparent. Among the structural constraints are the division of labor in health care, the size of health-care organizations, and the organization of nursing services. Social and behavioral constraints originate from poor physician-nurse relationships and from the problems nurses experience because they are members of a profession largely composed of women.

161

STRUCTURAL CONSTRAINTS

The Division of Labor in Health Care

As noted in Chapter 1, a very complex and hierarchial division of labor has developed in health care in response to advancing technologies. Health-care personnel have become highly specialized to increase their abilities to care for patients.

This specialization has led to a problem: who should head the team of specialists? By long-standing tradition, the medical practitioner has been and continues to be the "captain" of the patient-care team. This tradition was highly appropriate when the physician functioned as a semi-independent agent. But today, the physician is the leader of a diverse health-care team; "this unique axial position breeds enormous inefficiencies and costs."[2]

Much has been written about the problems of a physician-dominated health-care system. Some writers have decried the waste of physicians' time and talent on tasks that could readily be performed by persons with lesser training;[3] others have suggested that physicians, because they dominate the health-care team, are able to control all other health professionals and para-professionals. That control is detrimental to both the team[4] and the patients.

In a physician-dominated health-care structure, patients sometimes have difficulty in getting the care they need. For example, patients who need surveillance or reassurance may not have reasonable access to supervision or counselling because the physician may be too busy or is otherwise unable to provide such care; because the physician must see the patient first, the patient has nowhere to turn to gain supervision or counselling. Other patients may not be able to get the care they need because they are not able to obtain information about their diagnoses or treatment since the physician controls the information.

Physician dominance also creates problems for other health professionals when they perceive that their own "dignity and autonomy" are not respected. Physicians often fail to acknowledge the expertise other health professionals bring to patient care, and fail to allow them to share in decision-making about patient care.

The structure of our health-care system does not promote equality of professionals. The fee-for-service systems that have become part of Canadian medicare tend to promote a single entry point to the system – the physician – and to foster on-going physician supervision of patients. Although the health-insurance system has brought numerous benefits to providers and consumers, it has also been the cause of numerous structural barriers to professional equality and to better consumer access to care. In 1979, when the Hall Commission invited submissions to its review of the Canadian health-insurance program, the Canadian Nurses Association submitted a brief calling for legislative changes to the existing hospital and medical insurance programs that would

> ...*allow the emergence of a health insurance program which would stimulate the development of primary health care services, permit the introduction of new entry points and promote the appropriate utilization of qualified health personnel.*[5]

Authority and Health Bureaucracies

The proliferation of large health-care organizations is another constraint on the attention paid to patients' rights. Large-scale organizations–bureaucracies–are designed to provide service according to universal rather than particular criteria.[6] Unanticipated consequences of bureaucratic organizations can be apathy, rigidity, alienation of employees, an over-reliance on rules and regulations, and resistance to change.[7] And, because bureaucracies require large numbers of health professionals, who will have varying backgrounds and expertise, conflicts of goals and interests can occur. Health professionals often experience conflicting demands in a bureaucracy: the rules and the hierarchial chain of authority may produce situations of conflict with the professionals' "service ideal."[8]

Another problem with bureaucracies is that they often have no one single line of authority. Hospitals "have two and sometimes three separate lines of command."[9] Authority is shared by the board of trustees, doctors, and administrators; the trustees and administrators form one line of control, the doctors another. With two lines of control, co-ordination is often difficult, and other health professionals employed by the organization find themselves responsible both to doctors and to supervisors. This formal dual-authority structure has been particularly problematic for nurses.[10]

Nursing staff are required to take orders both from supervisors, who are part of the bureaucratic chain of command, and from physicians, who are outside the bureaucratic chain of command.

Each line of authority represents a separate system, although the two systems overlap – thus creating competing and conflicting demands.[11] The bureaucratic system emphasizes the maintenance of the organization; the medical system emphasizes the provision of service.[12] The physicians, the medical resident, and the intern "function as individuals and are individually responsible for their actions," while the nurse is an agent of the institution and obliged to report and record activities.[13] The nurse, therefore, must handle physician-nurse conflicts by reporting through the proper channels, while the physician has free movement to approach the hospital administrator. This anomaly creates a dilemma for nursing in that it "places the nurse in the position of being forced to use tact, flattery, or even subterfuge in her role as co-ordinator between a bureaucratic system and a free-wheeling artist."[14]

In a sense, the nurse on the unit represents to the patient both the administration and the physician.[15] Nurses are expected to assume great responsiblity for patient care or cure, but they have limited authority from the organization and limited communication from the physician. To cope with a dual-authority system that demands increasing responsibility, nurses may routinize tasks since rules and routines sometimes protect nurses from the arbitrary whims of supervisors or doctors.[16]

Excessive rules and routines can degrade professional functioning, and can lead to inadequate attention to patients and their rights. Thus nurses' attempts at self-preservation in the bureaucracy may conflict with patients' rights.

Nurses are trying to deal with the conflicts they experience in bureaucracies. One attempt is the trend toward unionization of nurses. Nursing unions essentially provide a collective body of nurses, who can negotiate with the administrators of large and complex organizations. Through such collective action, nurses have achieved better salaries and better general working conditions, two essential elements to attaining dignity and autonomy for the care giver. More equitable salaries for nurses have become a reality; now attention is being directed toward working conditions, for example, problems of staffing and of workload. Two major Canadian hospitals (the Mt. Sinai Hospital in Toronto and the Vancouver General Hospital) were the settings of recent disputes about adequate staffing and overwork.[17] The nurses involved in disputes of this nature may be seeking more humanized care for their patients and themselves by calling attention to inadequate staffing and unsafe patient care. Through their professional associations, nurses must work towards improving standards of patient care through a variety of means, including the establishment of formal standards of care and the development of patient classification systems to establish appropriate staff-to-patient ratios. Staff associations or unions can complement the activity of the professional associations in these endeavours by supporting better staffing practices in nursing.

Through their unions, nurses are also seeking greater participation in managerial decision-making. Recent Canadian studies have shown that nurses feel they ought to have a greater say in making decisions that directly affect their practice. Nurses' rights statements depict this need to become more involved. Nurses want the right to challenge, to be heard, to participate, to advocate for patients' rights, and to hold their own beliefs.[18] Although managers are bewildered by, and possibly even resistant to, the nurses' demands for greater participation, they must be aware that patients' needs cannot be met if the care providers have many unmet and unrecognized needs.[19] If nurses feel less than human, how can they ensure that their patients will be treated as humans?[20]

There is no question that nurses' needs and nurses' rights may frequently be at odds with patients' needs and patients' rights. It has been suggested that "a professional role confers a privilege not a right" because rights belong to the helpless (the patient), not the powerful.[21] However, nurses are themselves in a relatively powerless position in the health-care hierarchy and need to be recognized as persons with needs. It is essential to pay attention to the caregivers needs, although such attention should not be demanded at the expense of the patient. Nurses will have to become increasingly skillful at negotiating for their needs in situations that do not compromise patient care.

Organization of Nursing Care

The organization of nursing care involves different types and levels of nurses, and there are various models for the delivery of nursing care. The structure of nursing care has had an effect on nurses and patients alike.

At the turn of the century, there was only a small number of practical nurses in relation to the number of professional nurses.

Then, as a result of World War II, auxiliary workers were hired. These workers, recruited to augment nursing staff, became known as nursing aides and nursing auxiliaries.

Initially, the nursing profession did not support the idea of using these new workers in hospitals. But the benefits of having intermediate workers were eventually acknowledged, and more nursing aides were sought. During the mid-1940s and the 1950s, nurses were

> ...delegating much of their former work to practical nurses, aides, and maids, while continually taking on new duties assigned to them by physicians and administrators of hospitals.[22]

Generally, the tasks delegated by nurses were those they downgraded, such as bed-making and housekeeping duties.[23] To delegate such tasks is common: other professional groups also redefine their functions upward and slough "off their dirty work, that is, their less technical or less rewarding tasks."[24]

Many professional groups have successfully discarded selected functions, but the nurses' attempts to delegate certain functions to auxiliary workers has created substantial on-going problems. Some of these problems arise because the difference between the nurse and the auxiliary worker is a difference in degree of responsibility, not a difference of occupation. Furthermore, the auxiliary worker and the registered nurse "comprise parts of one another's work environment; thus concerns about comparative status are accentuated."[25] This confusion of roles is a problem for both nurses and patients. Another problem is that nurses may come from very different educational programs (for example, diploma nurses and baccalaureate-degree nurses) and the division of labor is sometimes determined by the type of expertise the nurse has developed through education. Again, the distinction is not always clear to patients or to other staff.

As the kinds of nurses increased, there was a trend away from individualized nursing care (which was modelled on private-duty nursing) to functional nursing care, so that large numbers of patients could be cared for. One nurse would make all the beds, one would handle all the medications, another did all the treatments, and so on. Functional nursing care eventually evolved into team nursing, an arrangement that gave staff the "psychological support" of working in a small group. The search for a satisfactory way to organize nursing care has continued and appears to be influenced by the trends of the particular time-period, by the needs and capabilities of the organization, by the needs of the nurses, and (one would hope) by the needs of the patients.[26] Primary nursing is gradually becoming the vogue today: a nurse is accountable for one or more patients for the entire length of their stay on the nurse's unit. Primary nursing appears to represent an attempt to return to individualized nursing care; it focuses on the nurse as professional practitioner and provider of humanized care.[27] Primary nursing has been trumpeted as a means of providing greater job satisfaction for nurses, and therefore a means of reducing turnover in nursing staff.[28] It also has the potential to improve the quality of patient care by making nurses full partners in the health-care system.[29]

For this more independent and patient-oriented model of nursing care to flourish, at least two things must happen. The organization must be "prepared to accept the nurse as a full-fledged professional capable of self-direction and self-discipline."[30] As well, the nurse must be prepared to provide more patient-centered care. Primary care has been heralded as a means to achieve individualized patient care. But there have been few concrete indications that better care is provided through this model.

Perhaps the model of care is not nearly as important as the motives underlying the model. There is a great need, within the health-care system, for models of caring. Nurses may yet function as the "ideology bearers," the repositories of therapeutic values and beliefs regarding patient care.[31] Their firm commitment to patients' rights and to humanized patient care could set the tone throughout the health-care system.

SOCIAL AND BEHAVIORAL CONSTRAINTS

Physicians and Nurses

The patterns of the relationships that can exist between physician and nurse limit attention to patient rights and the provision of humanized care. These patterns have been set by structural factors and by differences in social status.

In a classic article, the behavior patterns that exist in the nurse-physician relationship are called a "game." The central characteristic of the "game" is that the nurse takes much initiative and responsibility while appearing to remain passive, allowing the physician to make the recommendations.[32] The "game" exists because both players perceive the dominance and omnipotence of the physician, and it is perpetuated by all those factors that cause nurses to defer to physicians. (One of those factors is the sexual-role stereotype.) That this "game" is not in the best interests of the patient is clear.

More than a century ago, Florence Nightingale was bold enough to suggest that the nurse has a good base from which to advise the doctor, since the doctor rarely sees the patient more than once a day.[33] Dr. Helen Mussallem, former executive director of the Canadian Nurses Association, refers to a "reverse-Cinderella syndrome" that occurs in hospital wards. In the daytime, the responsibilities of the doctor and nurse are fairly clear – and the nurses' responsibilities are limited. At night, particularly in understaffed or rural hospitals, the same nurse is "capable" of suturing, delivering babies, and instituting various forms of therapy.[34]

Another aspect of the physician-nurse interaction does not function in the patients' best interest. Nurses often act to defend the physician. Such behavior can occur when a patient complains about a doctor, or when a nurse excuses a physician's absence. Protecting a fellow professional in the face of a patient's complaint blocks further communication with that patient. Patients need to be able to talk about their concerns.[35] Some very real examples of nurses excusing physician behavior are provided by Martha Lear. For example, one infiltrated intravenous occurred because the medical resident failed to listen to the patient and the nurse excused the resident's behavior to the patient; in another example, the nurse allowed the resident to sleep through a critical but reversible stage of a patient's illness.

> *"Listen, I am getting very sick," he said. "Where is a doctor?"*
> *"I'm sorry Dr. Lear. They're all busy. They said they'll get here as soon as they can." Apologetic. She took his blood pressure. It struck him how often nurses seemed to be apologizing for doctors. He wondered if nurses ever had apologized for him.*[36]*

Nurses need to question, to speak out both individually and collectively about the quality of care. Too many nurses continue to succumb to the advice that "no prudent nurse will discuss physicians or criticize their methods."[37]

> *To raise questions about the quality of care is a bad thing for a nurse to do. To keep quiet about it is a good thing. That's how the ethics fall down.*[38]

The patterns of interaction between physicians and nurses clearly require change. Perhaps if doctors and nurses changed their attitudes, the patterns would also change. More likely it will be necessary to change organizational structures to bring about attitudinal and behavioral changes. However the changes are achieved, it is important that further walls of separation between patient and physician are avoided.[39] A mutual respect between physician and nurse must be established. Each must have confidence in the other's person and profession; each must be willing to support the other in the provision of quality patient care without compromising the patient, the recipient of care.

Nurses as Women
Most nurses are women. Many nursing leaders believe that the powerlessness of nurses in the health-care system today is a result of the powerlessness of women in society.[40]

This problem is not limited to the 1970s or the 1980s. Florence Nightingale states:

> *I would earnestly ask my sisters to keep clear of both jargons now current everywhere... about the 'rights' of women which urges women to do all that men do, including the medical and other professions, merely because men do it and without regard to whether this is the best that women can do; and of the jargon which urges women to do nothing that men do, merely because they are women.... Surely woman should bring the best she has, whatever that is... without attending to either of these cries.*[41]

Historically, women were involved in both the care and cure functions of patient care; it was only with the founding of medical associations that women were denied participation in the cure function and were relegated to helping with the care function.[42] And women, by their traditionally subordinate role in society, posed little threat to this imbalance of power.[43] (Nightingale does not escape blame: she helped to establish male surgeons as superior to nurses in Scutari.[44])

That women defer to men, then, appears to be part of a cultural norm that is beginning to change. For the sake of the patient, nurses and physicians must develop relationships that are more collaborative and collegial.

The voice of nursing has been "sadly muted at the level where policies and decisions that govern the provision of health care are made."[45] For a profession closely associated with people and their health, such silence is odd, but it persists because many nurses consider political action unprofessional, unwomanly, and unnecessary.[46] Helen Mussallem argues that nurses must seek representation on planning bodies and encourage formal co-operation between professional associations and government agencies.[47] Nurses must not maintain silence, but must be prepared to commit themselves publicly to their beliefs about nursing, health, and society.[48] Opinions based on sound conclusions must be offered in the right place at the right time.[49] The professional association must bring pressure on governments and other groups.[50]

STRATEGIES TOWARD HUMANIZED CARE

There is much that needs to be done to correct the structural, social, attitudinal, and behavioral aspects of the health-care system that interfere with attention to patients' rights and the promotion of humanized care. Many of these corrections require change of structure, attitudes, and behavior over time; meanwhile, some interim strategies are required.

Six strategies are suggested here; three relate to changes within a particular health-care organization and three are system-wide strategies. Strategies within a particular organization are

a) the implementation of patients' advocacy programs;
b) the development of means for ethical deliberation;
c) the implementation of in-service education directed toward humanized care.
Strategies throughout the system are:
d) the development of new service-delivery modes to meet patients' needs for care;

e) greater lay- and health-professional involvement in policy development and planning;

f) system-wide education in ethics and law for health professionals.

Because of their numbers, and because they serve throughout the health-care system, nurses can be instrumental in lobbying and co-operatively planning for these needed strategies to promote more humanized care.

Strategies within Organizations

The Ombudsman: the Patient Representative Nurses have frequently been viewed as the health professional who could best serve as patient ombudsman. But during the past two decades a new worker has emerged, particularly in hospitals; the worker is known variously as the patient representative, the patient advocate or the patient ombudsman.* The existence of this new worker constitutes a rather uncomfortable (but completely realistic) admission on the part of the hospital that the presumed focal point of the institution's attention – the patient – now requires someone who can represent his or her interests.

The patient can easily become lost in the complex organization of a hospital. "At any given time and place in a hospital today, it is not unusual to find no one who really knows the patient."[51] The position of the patient ombudsman has developed to co-ordinate the "normally fragmented bits and pieces of a patient's hospital experience"[52] and to represent, or advocate for, the patient as required.

The ombudsman will seek out those individuals who have problems; talk to patients to identify the source of difficulty; determine appropriate action to provide suitable care; negotiate institutional

---

*Patient-representative programs in the US began to emerge in hospitals in the 1950s and the 1960s, often as an expansion of the public-relations function of the hospital. In the 1970s the concept gained momentum, and in 1971 the Society of Patient Representatives was formed. See Janet L. Storch, "Consumer Rights and Nursing," unpublished Master's thesis (Edmonton: University of Alberta, Division of Health Services Administration, 1977), Chapter 6; and "Essentials of Patient Representative Programs in Hospitals," (Chicago: Society of Patient Representatives, American Hospital Association, 1978), p. 2.

red tape on the patient's behalf; provide information about the organization and its services; refer patients to other departments; and provide a very essential follow-up, to ensure that satisfactory service has been rendered.[53]

The ombudsman provides to the institution a centralized, consistent patient-grievance mechanism; a central source of information and referrals; a monitor for patient experience and perceptions; a monitor for problems in departments or staff; and a research and documentation center for obstacles requiring change.

A patient representative must have qualifications similar to those of a parliamentary ombudsman in Canada.[54] The patient representative must be independent to be effective. Ideally, patient representatives should report to the executive director or board of directors, for although the representatives act on behalf of the hospital, they are there to represent the interests of the patient and must be free to do so. Finally, the position requires much tact and skill in dealing with others. Given the complexities of hospital structure and staff relationships, patient representatives must be able to deal with all types of staff as well as all types of patients.

Many assume that patient representatives would not be necessary if health-care providers did their jobs properly. This is a naïve assumption. Conflicting duties and conflicting demands arise in any highly specialized institution; even when jobs are properly performed, there are conflicts. For example, good medical care is not always synonomous with good patient care. Someone must speak up for patients who are caught between conflicting goals.

The patient representative cannot replace genuine care and concern for patients and patients' rights by all staff. However, the patient representative can complement staff care, for the presence of a patient representative may serve to sharpen the health providers' awareness of patient "abuse;" the representative may also serve as a powerful role model and educational tool.

The Nurse as Advocate Nursing leaders have increasingly identified patient advocacy as part of nursing's role and function. Some have maintained that advocacy has always been the nurse's role, and that the advent of the patient representative poses a threat to nurses. Others acknowledge that nurses have not been the best advocates, and that they require the stimulus of a patient representative to assist them in this role. Yet others suggest that the advocacy role is potentially incongruent with the nursing role.

Those who support the nurse as advocate argue that nurses, because of their sustained contact with the patient, are in a position to advocate on the patient's behalf, and that advocacy is an essential part of nursing. At least one Provincial Nursing Association has gone on record with a statement on patient advocacy,* which states that the nurse's "prime responsibility as a patient advocate is to educate consumers with regards to their rights and alternatives," and to speak for and assist clients in the attainment of these rights. Many nurses are not true advocates, however, because they fear risk-taking and involvement.[55] Advocacy may "require making unpopular decisions, having disagreements with physicians and other personnel, and committing oneself to a very great extent in the personal lives of clients."[56]

One author has argued that the same traits that place nurses in an advocate position are detrimental to an advocacy relationship. For example, intimate and daily contact with patients may create some difficulties in advocacy, particularly when the nurse is identified as part of the problem.[57] Those who argue against the nurse as the natural patients' rights advocate maintain that nurses need broader powers to advocate effectively, for example, access to chiefs of all staffs, ability to delay discharge, and freedom to monitor hospital committees. They argue that nurses should treat the job of patient advocate as a specialized role and function; it requires a new power base, and nurses will need further education to equip them for the role.[58]

Leah Curtin reconciles these divergent views when she suggests that nursing should not be distinguished by its care functions but rather by its philosophy of care, which should be "human advocacy." Curtin's concept of advocacy is more than legal advocacy or health advocacy: it is based on the shared humanity of nurse and patient.[59] Therefore, the nurse's attention to patient's needs for information, respect, participation, and access to care should be based on the nurse's concerns for the patient as a fellow human being worthy of respect. Such a concept of the nurse as advocate can only be enhanced by the development of patient ombudsmen in the health-care system.

Mechanisms for Ethical Deliberation The need for some group of

---

*Registered Nurses' Association of Ontario, April 1977 (see Appendix C).

people in the hospital to teach and advise on ethical matters is becoming increasing urgent. Many hospitals have ethics committees; others have prognosis committees or critical-care committees.[60] These committees may review ethics in individual patient-care decisions or policy decisions (for example, research ethics or the allocation of scarce hospital resources); some serve as counselling committees to the terminally ill and their staff. (These last might be asked to confirm a prognosis such as, "No reasonable possibility exists for the patient to return to a cognitive, sapient state."[61])

Hospital ethics committees were established in the United States largely in response to the Karen Ann Quinlan case;[62] one judgment in that case proposed the establishment of a committee to "make, review, or advise in decisions regarding the care of the terminally ill."[63] By asking for an "ethics committee or like body," the judge suggested that mechanisms other than court systems should deal with conflicts of this nature.

Ethics committees that are set up to confirm prognoses can be dangerous: the responsibility for the prognosis becomes diffused amongst committee members, who have immunity from the consequences of their decisions. Ethics committees should teach, support, and advise; they can discuss patient "problems" on nursing units, provide advise on the protection of research subjects, on decisions surrounding treatment of defective neonates, comatose patients, or dying patients, and on the care of the mentally ill or other patients in need of special protection. Ethics committees can cut through emotionalism and help to clarify values.

In addition to a hospital ethics committee (or like body), nurses, physiotherapists, respiratory therapists, and other health professionals should establish intra-unit committees and/or inter-unit ethics conferencing ("ethics rounds")[64] as a method of teaching and support for those endeavoring to provide humanized care under difficult circumstances.

In-Service Education Programs Hospital-wide education programs can also help to humanize patient care. Orientation programs should include instruction about the legal rights of patients and the legal and moral obligations of health-care providers to their patients. In addition, seminars on patients' rights concerns should be one focus of in-service education. The seminars should be interdisciplinary and involve staff at various levels of care.

Other in-service education programs must be directed "towards creating a spirit of responsiveness in all hospital personnel."[65] Teaching people to "care" is no small task, but formal and informal mechanisms can help to develop greater sensitivity and responsiveness in hospital personnel. Formal seminars in empathy training might be provided on a hospital-wide basis.[66] Seminars that feature individual patients willing to "educate" health-care providers about the psycho-social effects of their illness and their care can also increase staff responsiveness. Books and other materials are also helpful; a number of books and articles describe the bio-psycho-social aspects of illness from the patient's perspective.[67]

An effective patient's ombudsman can teach hospital staff (by role modelling) the meaning of patient advocacy and of care that enhances the dignity and autonomy of patients and other health professionals. As well, nurses, in their role as "ideology bearers," can show by example a respect for patients and patients' rights in practice. They can demonstrate concern, regard, and respect of one human being toward another, in short, a philosophy of caring.[68]

System-wide Strategies

At least three system-wide strategies are essential for the humanization of health care. First, new service delivery modes must be developed to meet consumer needs for care. Second, there must be greater lay and professional involvement in health-care planning and policy development. And third, all health professionals must understand the legal and moral aspects of patient care, and be taught these matters in their basic educational programs.

New Modes: New Participants Two of the greatest deficits in our present health-care system are

1) the lack of easy and variable ways for the consumer to make initial contact with the system;
2) the lack of a single health professional who is responsible for the consumer's care on a continuous basis.

Nurse practitioners could be relied upon, to a greater extent, as providers of primary care: they could provide both initial contact and continued care. This idea has been alluded to previously in this book, and has been well documented elsewhere.[69]

Consumers need a health professional who can fulfill a sustaining role, who can provide them with support for a multitude of problems.[70] Patients need reassurance; they need someone to listen – someone willing to establish a personal relationship.[71] Our present system is not geared toward these consumer needs. As a result, the consumer either gives up on the health-care system or is forced to use it in a piece-meal and non-therapeutic fashion simply because it is better designed for acute, episodic problems than for long-term supportive functions.

Nurses must advocate for a system that can better meet consumer needs. Nurses have the potential to play a key role in effecting some needed changes; these changes will mean greater and fuller use of all health professionals.

Nurses have a good understanding of the substance of health care – the actual laying on of hands. More than many other health professionals, nurses have the capacity to "maintain and exercise the concept of humanity" in health care[72] and to influence planners and administrators to see, in the statistics and numbers of health care, the human element.

To advocate wisely, nurses will need to become more involved with consumers and other health professionals in health-care planning and policy development. Consumer participation is imperative. As well, health-professional associations can support the consumer and can welcome consumer input to health planning and policy development.

In their professional associations, nurses must find effective ways to involve consumers on their councils and sub-committees, to hear how their deliberations and decisions will affect consumers of care, and to hear consumer ideas on professional accountability. *Ethics, Law, and Nursing Education* Health-care organizations must develop orientation and in-service education programs that focus on patients' rights and humanized care; it is also imperative that law and ethics be considered essential components in the curriculum of students of the health professions. Physicians and nurses, in particular, need greater understanding of the legal and moral concerns of patient care.

Although many medical schools include some attention to medical ethics, the subject is not always given the serious attention it deserves, and is frequently offered only as an elective.

Medical students are bright and ambitious; they have no difficulty ascertaining which subjects are taken seriously by the prestigious, senior members of the faculty. How many take medical ethics seriously? How many are committed to the teaching of ethics in the same way that they are committed to their scientific research?[73]

Nursing educators have begun to focus greater attention on the teaching of law and ethics in patient care, but attention to these subjects is still frequently sporadic and minimal. Many nursing schools have integrated the teaching of law and ethics into other courses. When such an approach is the only one employed, it often means that the teaching of ethics or law becomes a function of the teachers' comfort with the subject and their acceptance of these areas as significant to nursing practice.

If ethics is considered a rigorous discipline in which the students should study schools of thought, learn certain facts, and read and reflect on various problems, then a more specific course with well-prepared teachers and curriculum structure is necessary.[74]

Ethics courses will not necessarily make institutions more ethical; rather, exposure to ethics

...can establish a habit of thought or a technique of approaching patient problems which takes greater consideration of individual rights and needs.[75]

Such attention to rights is enchanced by an understanding of sources of law, principles of law, and the limitations of the law.

Nursing curricula are crowded. There is much that must be learned in a short space of time, and each new subject must be carefully justified.[76] To date, the teaching of ethics and law has often been confined to a presentation of the professional code of ethics and a list of legal principles. But professional nurses must make decisions.[77] Nurses need more than a list of rules to review when choosing between alternative values.

This book is offered as a source that combines principles of law and ethics with the discussion of patients' rights issues. It should be considered only a beginning in the exploration of the problems and issues surrounding legal and moral dilemmas in patient care.

But if it broadens understanding of these issues, for students and for practitioners, the exercise of writing it will have been worthwhile.

REFERENCES FOR CHAPTER 8

[1] Jan Howard, Fred Davis, Clyde Pope, and Sheryl Ruzek, "Humanizing Health Care: The Implications of Technology, Centralization, and Self-Care." *Medical Care* 15 (May 1977): 12.

[2] Robert F. Rushmer, *Humanizing Health Care: Alternative Futures for Medicine* (Cambridge, Mass.: MIT Press, 1975), p. 22.

[3] Rushmer, p. 29.

[4] Eliot Freidson, "Dominant Professions, Bureaucracy, and Client Services," in *Organizations and Clients*, eds. William R. Rosengren and Mark Lefton (Columbus, Ohio: Charles E. Merrill Publishing Co., 1970). See also Carol A. Brown, "The Division of Laborers: Allied Health Professions," *International Journal of Health Services* 3 (Summer 1973): 435.

[5] "Putting 'Health' into Health Care." Submission to Health Services Review '79. (Ottawa: Canadian Nurses Association, 1980), p. ii.

[6] Howard *et al*, p. 19.

[7] Pradip N. Khandwalla, *The Design of Organizations* (New York: Harcourt Brace Jovanovich, Inc., 1977), p. 137.

[8] Shirley M. Stinson, "Professionals in Bureaucracies: Autonomy Vs. Integration." *Nursing Papers* 5:3 (December 1973): 14–17.

[9] Robert Straus, "Hospital Organization from the Viewpoint of Patient-Centered Goals," in *Organization Research on Health Institutions*, ed. Basil S. Georgopoulos (Ann Arbor: Institute for Social Research, University of Michigan, 1972), p. 205.

[10] Basil Georgopoulos and Floyd C. Mann, "The Hospital as an Organization," in *Patients, Physicians, and Illness*, ed. Garthy Jaco (New York: The Free Press, 1972), pp. 299–300.

[11] Georgopoulos and Mann. See also Albert F. Wessen, "Hospital Ideology and Communication Between World Personnel," in *Patients, Physicians, and Illness*, pp. 328–332.

[12] Beatrice J. Kalisch and Philip A. Kalisch, "An Analysis of the Sources of Physician-Nurse Conflict," *Journal of Nursing Administration* 7 (January 1977): 54.

[13] Hans O. Mauksch, "The Organizational Context of Nursing Practice," in *The Nursing Profession*, ed. Fred Davis (New York: John Wiley and Sons, Inc., 1966), p. 113.

[14] Mauksch, pp. 130–131.

[15] Mauksch, p. 123.

[16] Celia Davis, "Experiences of Dependency and Control in Work: The Case of Nurses," *Journal of Advanced Nursing* 1 (July 1976): 279.

[17] For a thorough account of the Mt. Sinai case, see Corinne Sklar, "Sinners or Saints? The Legal Perspective," in *The Canadian Nurse* 75 (November 1979): 14–16 and *Canadian Nurse* 75 (December 1979): 16–21. For a description and analysis of the Vancouver General Hospital controversy see Verna Lovell, *I Care That VGH Nurses Care* (Vancouver: In Touch Publications Ltd. 1981).

[18] See Claire Fagin, "Nurses Rights," in *American Journal of Nursing* 75 (1975): 82; and Bertram Bandman, "The Human Rights of Patients, Nurses, and Other

Health Professionals," in *Bioethics and Human Rights*, eds. Elsie Bandman and Bertram Bandman (Boston: Little Brown and Co., 1978), p. 324.

[19] Jennie Wilting, *People, Patients and Nurses* (Edmonton: University of Alberta, 1980).

[20] M. Patricia Donahue, "The Nurse–A Patient Advocate?" *Nursing Forum* 17 (1978): 147.

[21] Bertram Bandman, "Do Nurses Have Rights?" *American Journal of Nursing* 78 (January 1978): 84–86.

[22] Everett C. Hughes, *Men and Their Work* (Glencoe, Illinois: The Free Press, 1958), p. 135.

[23] Hughes, p. 135.

[24] Harold L. Wilensky, "The Professionalization of Everyone?" *American Journal of Sociology* 70 (September 1964): 144.

[25] Robert K. Merton, "Status-Orientation in Nursing," in *Social Interaction and Patient Care*, eds. James K. Skipper and Robert C. Leonard (Toronto: J.B. Lippincott, 1965), p. 381.

[26] For an overview of changing nursing-staff assignment systems, see Margaret Beswetherick, "Staffing Assignment: A Review of Past and Current Systems of Nursing Care Delivery," in *Canadian Nurse* 75 (May 1979): 18–22.

[27] Beswetherick, pp. 21–22.

[28] Heather Howie, "Getting, and Keeping Your Nurses," *Health Care* 22 (June 1980): 47–48.

[29] Howie, pp. 47–48.

[30] Beswetherick, p. 22.

[31] Marcella Z. Davis, "The Organizational, Interactional and Care-Oriented Conditions for Patient Participation in Continuity of Care: A Framework for Staff Intervention," *Social Science and Medicine* 14A (1980): 39–47.

[32] Leonard Stein, "The Doctor-Nurse Game," *American Journal of Nursing* 68 (January 1968): 101–105.

[33] Florence Nightingale, *Notes on Nursing* (New York: Dover Publications Inc., 1969), p. 105.

[34] Helen Mussallem, "Physician's Associate Also Means Patients' Friend," *The Medical Post* (March 23, 1971), p. 30.

[35] Beatrice Kalisch, "Of Half Gods and Mortals: Aesculapian Authority," in *Humanizing Hospital Care* eds. Gerald P. Turner and Joseph Mapa (Toronto: McGraw-Hill Ryerson, 1979), p. 53.

[36] Martha Weinman Lear, *Heartsounds* (New York: Simon and Schuster, 1980), pp. 141 - 142 and p. 147.

[37] Catherine Moriarty, "Where the Nurse Sometimes Fails," *American Journal of Nursing* 15 (November 1914): 113.

[38] "Nader Group Plans Manual for Hospital Workers," *Modern Hospital* 120 (June 1973): 26.

[39] Norman Cousins, *Anatomy of an Illness (As Perceived by a Patient)* (New York: W.W. Norton and Co., 1979), p. 110.

[40] Rose S. LeRoux, "Sex-Role Stereotyping and Leadership," *Nursing Administration Quarterly* 1 (Fall 1976): 29.

[41] Nightingale, p. 135.

[42] Joan T. Roberts and Thetis M. Group, "The Women's Movement and Nursing," *Nursing Forum* 12 (1973): 303–322.

[43] Carol A. Brown, "Women Workers in the Health Care Industry," *International Journal of Health Services* 5 (1975): 174.

[44] Bonnie Bullough, "Barriers to the Nurse Practitioner Movement: Problems of

Women in a Woman's Field," *International Journal of Health Services* 5 (1975): p. 227. Nightingale refused to allow nurses to give any care to suffering men unless the surgeons ordered them to do so. Bullough suggests that this mechanism gained Nightingale and her thirty-eight nurses the support of the army doctors, but also helped establish the surgeon as superior to the nurse.

[45]Helen K. Mussallem, "The Nurse's Role in Policy-Making and Planning," *International Nursing Review* 20 (1973): 10.

[46]Marjorie Stanton, "Political Action and Nursing," *Nursing Clinics of North America* 9 (September 1974): 579–581.

[47]"Canadian Association's Executive Director Has Advice for Associations," *International Nursing Review* 21:1 (1974): 4. Note that the Executive Director of the CNA is a member of a joint committee of the CHA, the CNA, and the CMA. The joint committee meets periodically to discuss issues of common concern such as bills of rights for patients, ethical aspects of life-saving measures, and so on. See "A Report to the Membership," *Canadian Nurse* 72 (August 1976): 30.

[48]Stanton, p. 584.

[49]Mussallem, p. 11.

[50]Glennis Zilm, "Nursing Associations – Are They Coming or Going?" *Canadian Nurse* 65 (September 1969): 35.

[51]Straus, p. 217.

[52]Straus, p. 221. See also Isabel Schuster, "Patients' Problems Receive Personal Attention," *Dimensions* 57 (September 1980): 12–13.

[53]Information compiled from the American Hospital Association print-outs on the patient representative. See also *Essentials of Patient Representative Programs in Hospitals* (Chicago: American Hospital Association, 1978).

[54]For a more detailed description of the evolution and development of parliamentary ombudsmen, as well as a comparative analysis of the parliamentary ombudsman and the patient ombudsman, see Janet L. Storch, "Consumer Rights and Nursing," unpublished Master's thesis (Edmonton: University of Alberta, Division of Health Services Administration, 1977), Chapter 6.

[55]Donahue, p. 145.

[56]Shelley Van Kempen, "The Nurse as Client Advocate," in *Management in Nursing: A Vital Link in the Health Care System*, eds. Carolyn Chambers Clark and Carole Shea (Toronto: McGraw-Hill Book Co., 1979), p. 195. See also Jean Jenny, "Patient Advocacy: Another Role for Nursing," *International Nursing Review* 26:6 (1979): 176–179. Jenny describes the various facets of patient advocacy, and notes the negative consequences for the nurse in many of these roles.

[57]Natalie Abrams, "A Contrary View of the Nurse as Patient Advocate," *Nursing Forum* 17 (1978): 259–267.

[58]George J. Annas, "The Patient Rights Advocate: Can Nurses Effectively Fill this Role?" *Supervisor Nurse* 5 (July 1974): 20, 23–24.

[59]Leah L. Curtin, "The Nurse as Advocate: A Philosophical Foundation for Nursing," *Advances in Nursing Science* 1 (April 1979): 1–10.

[60]Carol Levine, "Hospital Ethics Committees: A Guarded Prognosis," *The Hastings Center Report* 7 (June 1977): 25–27.

[61]Robert M. Veatch, "Hospital Ethics Committees: Is There a Role?" *The Hastings Center Report* 7 (June 1977): 23–24.

[62]Jay Alexander Gold, "Review of In the Matter of Karen Quinlan: The Complete Legal Briefs, Court Proceedings and Decision in the Superior Court of New Jersey and in the Matter of Karen Quinlan, Vol. II: The Complete Briefs, Oral Arguments, and Opinion in the New Jersy Supreme Court," *American Journal of Law and Medicine* 3 (Spring 1977): 89–94. Karen Quinlan was a twenty-one year-

old patient who, for unknown reasons, ceased breathing and was brought into the emergency department of a hospital in the United States. She was admitted to hospital and placed on a respirator in April of 1975; she remained comatose, but was still alive by medical standards. The family requested that Karen be taken off the respirator, but physicians refused to comply. In September 1975 the family filed a complaint asking that Karen be declared legally incompetent, that her father be appointed guardian, and that her guardian have permission to discontinue life support. The New Jersey superior court ruled against the family's request on grounds that fulfillment of the request would constitute homicide. Later the supreme court reversed the superior court's decision, appointed the father as guardian, and suggested that if the physicians, aided by an ethics committee, concluded there was no hope of recovery, life-support mechanisms could be withdrawn.

[63]Veatch, p. 22.

[64]See, for example, Anne J. Davis, "Ethics Rounds with Intensive Care Nurses," *Nursing Clinics of North America* 14 (March 1979): 45-55; "Caring for a Patient Who Wants to Die: Should You Let Her?" *Nursing 80* 10 (February 1980): 50-53; "Perspectives: Resolving an Ethical Dilemma," *Nursing 80* 10 (May 1980): 39-40, 42, 43.

[65]Lorne Elkin Rozovsky, "A Canadian Patient's Bill of Rights," *Dimensions in Health Services* 51 (December 1974): 10.

[66]See, for example, Elaine L. LaMonica; Donald K. Carew; Alvin E. Winder; Ann Marie Bernazza Haase; and Kenneth H. Blanchard, "Empathy Training as the Major Thrust of a Staff Development Program," *Nursing Research* 25 (November-December 1976): 447-451. See also Sandra Bertram and Melvin J. Krant, "To Know About Suffering and the Teaching of Empathy," *Social Science and Medicine* 11 (September 1977): 639-644.

[67]See, for example, Norman Cousins, *Anatomy of an Illness (As Perceived by a Patient)* (New York: W.W. Norton and Co., 1979); Martha Weinman Lear, *Heartsounds* (New York: Simon and Schuster, 1980); and Robert C. Hardy, *Sick* (Chicago: Teach'em Inc., 1978).

[68]Barbara A. Carper, "The Ethics of Caring," *Advances in Nursing Science* 1 (April 1979): 14-15.

[69]See, for example, "Putting 'Health' Into Health Care," Submission to Health Services Review '79 (Canadian Nurses Assocation, Ottawa, 1980): 6-17.

[70]Helen Nakagawa, "The Social Organization of Health Care and the Myth of Free Choice," in *Health Care Issues*, ed. Madeleine Leininger (Philadelphia, Pa: F.A. Davis Co., 1974), p. 82.

[71]Rushmer, pp. 28-29, 153.

[72]Helen K. Mussallem, "The Nurse's Role in Policy Making and Planning," *International Nursing Review* 20 (1973): 11.

[73]Bernard Barber, "Compassion in Medicine: Toward New Definitions and New Institutions," in *Humanizing Hospital Care*, eds. Gerald P. Turner and Joseph Mapa (Toronto: McGraw-Hill Ryerson, 1979), pp. 169. Reprinted by permission of The New England Journal of Medicine.

[74]Mila Aroskar and Robert M. Veatch, "Ethics Teaching in Nursing Schools," *The Hastings Center Report* 7 (August 1977): 23-26.

[75]Marjorie Jones Stenberg, "Ethics as a Component of Nursing Education," *Advances in Nursing Science* 1 (April 1979): 57.

[76]Stenberg, p. 53.

[77]Paula Sigman, "Ethical Choice in Nursing," *Advances in Nursing Science* 1 (April 1979): 40.

SUGGESTED REFERENCES FOR FURTHER STUDY, CHAPTER 8

Abrams, Natalie. "A Contrary View of the Nurse as Patient Advocate." *Nursing Forum* 17:3 (1978): 258–267.

Abrams develops a rationale for a patient's advocate, discusses the various responsibilities of such an advocate, and examines the suitability of nurses for an advocacy role. She identifies several functions in advocacy: 1) counsellor or lay therapist; 2) advisor in decision-making; 3) information-provider and "watchdog"; 4) representative; 5) quality-control agent.

Implications of these various functions for the nursing role are then examined. Abrams suggests that conflicting demands on the nurse and the nurse's lack of general education background are some impediments to the nurse's effective functioning as patient advocate. She further suggests that patient advocacy should not be the sole responsibility of any one health professional, and that the patient should have a right to as much impartial and extensive advocacy as possible.

Brown, C.A. "Women Workers in the Health Services Industry," *International Journal of Health Services* 5 (1975): 173–184.

Brown maintains that most of the skilled and unskilled workers in the health-service industry are women who have few career alternatives and who are hired because they represent an inexpensive, available, and relatively powerless work force. In spite of the high concentration of women in health care, men control the industry–doctors, hospital administrators, insurance-company directors, and government regulators. She suggests that conflicts between men and women workers in health services are frequently masked as conflicts between occupations. Increasing involvement of governments and insurance companies has caused changes in the patterns of conflict. Brown proposes unionism as a promising source of power for a successful struggle against sexism in health services.

Carper, Barbara A. "The Ethics of Caring." *Advances in Nursing Science* 1:3 (April 1979): 11–19.

Carper emphasizes the centrality of caring as a professional and personal value governing actions and attitudes in patient care. Specialization and the advancement of science and technology are cited as two developments that hinder caring. She offers various definitions of caring, and describes major components of the process of caring as knowledge, patience, honesty, trust, humility, hope, and courage. Three models of health professional-patient relationships–an engineering model, a priestly model, and a contractual model–are then described. Carper suggests that the study of social sciences and the humanities may contribute to understanding of the human condition, but that caring is not readily learned in the classroom. Rather, to be caring one must believe in the worth and dignity of other people and understand one's own value system and "the meaning of values, choices, and priority systems within which values are expressed."

Curtin, Leah L. "The Nurse as Advocate: A Philosophical Foundation for Nursing." *Advances in Nursing Science* 1 (April 1979): 1–10.

In attempting to define the role and function of nursing, Curtin suggests that nursing should be distinguished not by its care functions, but by its philosophy of care. She urges nurses to see nursing as a moral art aimed at seeking good in relationship to other human beings. Advocacy is suggested as the philosophical base of nursing, advocacy based on the shared humanity of nurse and patient. Curtin describes the nurse-patient relationship and the effects of disease on humanity; she describes the loss of independence, loss of freedom of action, interference with ability to make choices, and dependency on health professionals. Responsibilities of human advocacy are then outlined, and the nurse's role in humanizing patient care is emphasized.

Donahue, M. Patricia. "The Nurse: A Patient Advocate?" *Nursing Forum* 17:2 (1978): 143-151.

Using a personal experience in health care as her prime example of unmet need, Donahue develops cogent arguments for the nurse to be the patient's advocate. She refers to early nursing leaders who were advocates for the patient, and questions whether nursing schools are developing nurses who have the motivation, skill, and knowledge to function as advocate. The nurse's own sense of being treated humanely is suggested as essential to effective advocacy. Donahue concludes that "to fully develop the role of nurses as patient advocates – we must develop uncommon nurses!"

Freidson, Eliot. "Dominant Professions, Bureaucracy, and Client Services." In *Organizations and Clients*, pp. 71-92. Edited by William R. Rosengren and Mark Lefton. Columbus, Ohio: Charles E. Merrill Publishing Co., 1970.

Freidson examines the way in which the medical profession, the dominant professional group, influences both health-service delivery and health-services clients. He discusses characteristics of a professional group, focusing on the concept of autonomy, and suggests that the dominance of the medical profession in health services is sustained by its expertise in the division of labor. He contends that this dominance has four implications:

    1) the problems patients experience in health care, such as lack of information, are not problems of the bureaucracy but problems of professional dominance;

    2) the problems of the para-professional, such as low morale, stem from subordination to the authority of the medical profession;

    3) the planning and distribution of health-care resources is weighted in favor of medical influence;

    4) the co-operative exchange and referral of clients is hampered by the posture of the medical profession.

Freidson emphasizes that his intent in this analysis is not to blame but to clarify the sources of problems so that realistic solutions can be found.

Howard, Jan; Davis, Fred; Pope, Clyde; and Ruzek, Cheryl. "Humanizing Health Care: The Implications of Technology, Centralization, and Self-Care." *Medical Care* 15:5 (May 1977): 11-26.

This article is a summary of on-going investigation into humanized care in the light of technological advances and growth of bureaucracies, and of the potentials for self-care to be a humanizing factor. The concept of humanized care is described; the effects of technology on humanized care are discussed. It is suggested that technology may be a scapegoat for explaining dehumanized care, that it might be an indirect or direct cause of dehumanized care, or that it may be a self-fulfilling prophecy to maintain that technology causes dehumanized care. Twelve strategies are suggested to reduce or counteract these dehumanizing effects of technology. The issue of centralization in large-scale organizations is then evaluated in terms of its contribution to dehumanization, with the Kaiser-Permanente HMO plan as an example. Again, a number of specific recommendations are provided to counteract dehumanizing tendencies. The article concludes with a discussion of self-help care, including a description of key features of these groups and some recommendations regarding the improvement of the self-help approach to humanize care.

Levine, Carol. "Hospital Ethics Committees: A Guarded Prognosis." *The Hastings Center Report* 7 (June 1977): 25-27.

In this article, Levine summarizes a two-day conference on the composition and the function of hospital ethics committees. Various types of committees are described. The report sees the essential role of the committees as mediators between conflicting points of view on specific cases and as advisors and counsellors. The matter of committee membership and the problems of access to such committees are reviewed. The conference participants suggest that ethics committees could play a broader role in hospital policy formulation and might serve to educate the staff on legal and ethical issues of care. Further, they suggest that these committees are worthwhile if they "provide a meaningful avenue for the exercise of patients' and families' rights."

Stenberg, Marjorie Jones. "Ethics as a Component of Nursing Education." *Advances in Nursing Science* 1 (April 1979): 53-61.

Although Stenberg acknowledges that nursing curricula are already overcrowded, she develops a case for the inclusion of the study of ethics in nursing education. She describes various theories of moral development and concludes that moral development can take place during both the collegiate and the professional years of nursing. Information on existing programs is provided, and a framework for teaching ethics to nursing students is outlined. Stenberg notes that to teach ethics as a component of other courses is not adequate, and provides some specific direction regarding content areas, suggesting that nursing codes of ethics should be included mainly to demonstrate their limitations in ethical decision-making. Finally, she emphasizes the importance of teaching ethics to all health-care professionals.

Straus, Robert. "Hospital Organization from the Viewpoint of Patient-Centered Goals." In *Organization Research on Health Institutions*, pp. 203-222. Edited by Basil S. Georgopoulos. Ann Arbor: The University of Michigan, 1972.

Among the many goals of hospitals is the goal of patient-centered care. Straus examines this goal in relation to the concept of the patient who is influenced by biological, psychological, environmental, social, cultural, and temporal factors. He discusses the uniqueness of each patient, the variable nature of the patient's illness, and the external and internal circumstances of the hospital (such as the dual or triple lines of authority). He notes the problems of inadequate or inappropriate communication, and the effects of prejudice and routines on patient care. The lack of close relationships between patient and providers amidst imposed dependency are cited as additional problems. Straus identifies a need to study the impact of hospital organization on patient care and suggests the need for the development of the role of patient advocate.

APPENDIX A Bills of Rights

CONSUMERS' ASSOCIATION OF CANADA
CONSUMER RIGHTS IN HEALTH CARE

I   RIGHT TO BE INFORMED

1—about preventive health care including education on nutrition, birth control, drug use, appropriate exercise

2—about the health care system including the extent of government insurance coverage for services, supplementary insurance plans, the referral system to auxiliary health and social facilities and services in the community

3—about the individual's own diagnosis and specific treatment program including prescribed surgery and medication, options, effects and side effects

4—about the specific costs of procedures, services and professional fees undertaken on behalf of the individual consumer

II RIGHT TO BE RESPECTED AS THE INDIVIDUAL WITH THE MAJOR RESPONSIBILITY FOR HIS OWN HEALTH CARE

—right that confidentiality of his health records be maintained

—right to refuse experimentation, undue painful prolongation of his life or participation in teaching programs

—right of adult to refuse treatment, right to die with dignity

III RIGHT TO PARTICIPATE IN DECISION MAKING AFFECTING HIS HEALTH

—through consumer representation at each level of government in planning and evaluating the system of health services, the types and qualities of service and the conditions under which health services are delivered

—with the health professionals and personnel involved in his direct health care

IV RIGHT TO EQUAL ACCESS TO HEALTH CARE (HEALTH EDUCATION, PREVENTION, TREATMENT AND REHABIL- ITATION) REGARDLESS OF THE INDIVIDUAL'S ECONOMIC STATUS, SEX, AGE, CREED, ETHNIC ORIGIN AND LOCATION

—right to access to adequately qualified health personnel

—right to a second medical opinion

—right to prompt response in emergencies

AMERICAN HOSPITAL ASSOCIATION
A PATIENT'S BILL OF RIGHTS

The American Hospital Association Board of Trustees' Committee on Health Care for the Disadvantaged, which has been a consistent advocate on behalf of consumers of health care services, developed the Statement *on a* Patient's Bill of Rights, *which was approved by the AHA House of Delegates February 6, 1973. The statement was published in several forms, one of which was the S74 leaflet in the Association's S series. The S74 leaflet is now superseded by this reprinting of the statement.*

The American Hospital Association presents a Patient's Bill of Rights with the expectation that observance of these rights will contribute to more effective patient care and greater satisfaction for the patient, his physician, and the hospital organization. Further, the Association presents these rights in the expectation that they will be supported by the hospital on behalf of its patients, as an integral part of the healing process. It is recognized that a personal relationship between the physician and the patient is essential for the provision of proper medical care. The traditional physician-patient relationship takes on a new dimension when care is rendered within an organizational structure. Legal precedent has established that the institution itself also has a responsibility to the patient. It is in recognition of these factors that these rights are affirmed.

1. The patient has the right to considerate and respectful care.

2. The patient has the right to obtain from his physician complete current information concerning his diagnosis, treatment, and prognosis in terms the patient can be reasonably expected to understand. When it is not medically advisable to give such information to the patient, the information should be made available to an appropriate person in his behalf. He has the right to know, by name, the physician responsible for coordinating his care.

3. The patient has the right to receive from his physician information necessary to give informed consent prior to the start of any procedure and/or treatment. Except in emergencies, such information for informed consent should include but not necessarily be limited to the specific procedure and/or treatment, the medically significant risks involved, and the probable duration of incapacitation. Where medically significant alternatives for care or treatment exist, or when the patient requests information concerning medical

alternatives, the patient has the right to such information. The patient also has the right to know the name of the person responsible for the procedures and/or treatment.

4. The patient has the right to refuse treatment to the extent permitted by law and to be informed of the medical consequences of his action.

5. The patient has the right to every consideration of his privacy concerning his own medical care program. Case discussion, consultation, examination, and treatment are confidential and should be conducted discreetly. Those not directly involved in his care must have the permission of the patient to be present.

6. The patient has the right to expect that all communications and records pertaining to his care should be treated as confidential.

7. The patient has the right to expect that within its capacity a hospital must make reasonable response to the request of a patient for services. The hospital must provide evaluation, service, and/or referral as indicated by the urgency of the case. When medically permissible, a patient may be transferred to another facility only after he has received complete information and explanation concerning the needs for and alternatives to such a transfer. The institution to which the patient is to be transferred must first have accepted the patient for transfer.

8. The patient has the right to obtain information as to any relationship of his hospital to other health care and educational institutions insofar as his care is concerned. The patient has the right to obtain information as to the existence of any professional relationships among individuals, by name, who are treating him.

9. The patient has the right to be advised if the hospital proposes to engage in or perform human experimentation affecting his care or treatment. The patient has the right to refuse to participate in such research projects.

10. The patient has the right to expect reasonable continuity of care. He has the right to know in advance what appointment times and physicians are available and where. The patient has the right to expect that the hospital will provide a mechanism whereby he is informed by his physician or a delegate of the physician of the patient's continuing health care requirements following discharge.

11. The patient has the right to examine and receive an explanation of his bill regardless of source of payment.

12. The patient has the right to know what hospital rules and regulations apply to his conduct as a patient.

No catalog of rights can guarantee for the patient the kind of treatment he has a right to expect. A hospital has many functions to perform, including the prevention and treatment of disease, the education of both health professionals and patients, and the conduct of clinical research. All these activities must be conducted with an overriding concern for the patient, and, above all, the recognition of his dignity as a human being. Success in achieving this recognition assures success in the defense of the rights of the patient.

APPENDIX B Codes of Ethics

CANADIAN NURSES ASSOCIATION
A STATEMENT ON
AN ETHICAL BASIS FOR NURSING IN CANADA
WITH PROPOSED GUIDELINES

(Note: Section III of this Code has been suspended and the Code is currently under review.)

I. INTRODUCTION

Nursing is a person-oriented health service. It is a service called forth by the experience of human pain and suffering, and directed to the promotion of health, the prevention and alleviation of suffering, and the provision of a caring presence for those for whom cure is not possible. The ethical norms that guide this service evolve from a belief system that perceives the human person to be of incalculable worth, and human life to have a sacred, precious and even mysterious character. Nursing is practised in the context of human relationships, the dominant ethical determinant of which is the principle of respect for persons.

The concept which constitutes the unifying and ethical focus for nursing practice, education, administration, and research is the concept *caring*. Caring, as a characteristic descriptive of all authentic human action is expressed within the discipline of nursing through the following attributes.

1. *compassion* – the human response through which nurses participate in the pain and brokenness of humanity, by entering into the experience of another's suffering, misfortune, or need in such a manner that the needs of that person are the primary basis for the use of the nurse's personal and professional skills.
2. *competence* – the state of having the knowledge, skills, energy, and experience adequate to provide the required service.
3. *conscience* – the sense of what is right or wrong in one's conduct, and the awareness of, and the will to apply relevant ethical principles.
4. *confidence* – the quality which fosters the development and maintenance of trusting relationships.
5. *commitment* – a pledge, based on free choice, to devote oneself to meeting one's professional obligations.

In nursing, the human capacity to care is developed and professionalized through the acquisition of those intellectual, affective and technical skills required to carry out the responsibilities of specific nursing roles. The ethical obligations arising from caring as required by these roles are met at different levels of practice and within varying contexts. This statement considers three categories of obligation, namely, *caring and the profession, caring and the healing community,* and *caring and the individual nurse*.

II. CARING AND THE PROFESSION

The nursing profession as a whole has ethical obligations to society as well as to its own membership. The profession has an obligation to examine its own goals and the service it offers in the light of existing health problems, and to design its programs in collaboration with other professionals which also provide health services within the society. Nursing, in keeping with its mandate as a service profession, is bound to see itself, not as an end to be promoted and served by society, but as a professional body, constituted and legitimized by society's approval, to offer a prescribed service required for the improvement of the health status of people.

In meeting its obligations to society, nursing has responsibility for monitoring the quantity and quality of persons entering the profession, and for identifying and implementing standards that promote the type and quality of nursing service dictated by society's needs. Nursing has a related responsibility to work for those conditions which will enable its members to provide the quantity and quality of service deemed necessary and desirable.

The nursing profession also has responsibilities to the international community. Since health is a basic condition for human development, and as no one nation or country can develop its potential in isolation, the interests of the profession transcend national boundaries. In fact, our credibility as a profession is called into question if we do no collaborate on an international level to promote the health of all peoples, and to work toward the relief of human suffering wherever it is experienced.

These broad obligations constitute the grounds for the ethical responsibilities of nursing's organized professional body, and include the following commitments:

1.   In the context of existing health needs and problems, to identify Canada's need for nursing activities and services.

2.   To establish relevant and realistic goals for the profession of nursing within Canadian society.

3.   To foster collaboration with other health professions, political bodies, and other agencies in responding to the health needs of Canadians.

4.   To collaborate with professional groups, institutions and agencies in promoting the welfare of peoples in other countries of the world.

5.   To provide measures which will ensure that only those with the potential, motivation, and discipline required to function as caring persons are accepted into, and endorsed by the nursing profession.

6.   To work for the realization of working conditions which enable nurses to function as caring persons with the required degree of autonomy.

7.   To promote conditions for nurses which provide for legitimate personal, professional, and economic rewards.

8.   To demonstrate, in its own transactions, accountability for the use of internal and external resources.

III. CARING AND THE HEALING COMMUNITY

The attainment of health, in a holistic sense, requires services from a variety of sources, professional and non-professional. Health disciplines constitute one such source of service, and nursing, as one of these disciplines, is directed by its own unique focus and prescribed boundaries. The achievements of personal and family health goals depends upon a sensitive, deliberate fusion of the knowledge, skills, and resources of all involved in relevant helping services. In health care today, a commitment to the collaboration essential for this process is a fundamental ethical imperative for health professionals. Where such collaboration is visible and operative, it constitutes an authentic sign of a caring, healing community.

With the growing numbers and categories of people providing services in an increasingly complex health care system, the provision of a caring, healing community may be considered a courageous undertaking. Present experience leads some critics to conclude that the present health system is anything but a caring, healing community. Based on the observations of such critics, it would seem that each health professional group is committed to its own various and sundry goals–teaching, practice, administration and research–with token recognition of needs of clients, and, in some cases, operating in adversarial relationships with colleagues in other disciplines.

Many, if not most, of the ethical problems experienced by nurses today have their roots in conflict with other health professionals over what constitutes appropriate care for their clients. Such problems include, for example, confusion and open disagreement about the nature, extent, and timing of information required by patients and families; the initiation and/or prolongation of specific treatment protocols; the use of patients in teaching and research; disclosure of information and intrusions of privacy; threats to clients from known or potential abusers; evidence of incompetency, incapacity, and negligence on the part of health care providers; and limitations on the freedom of nurses themselves to provide services for which they are prepared.

In the face of these issues, it is not sufficient that a nurse maintain 'personal' ethical behavior: responsibility to clients demands a stance which promotes care, and challenges actions which are contrary to acceptable health care goals. When quality of care is jeopardized, merely to 'live by one's own standards' with the attitude that what someone else does is 'none of my business', is to abdicate one's ethical responsibility for promoting the welfare of persons who require health services.

Other conflicts evolve from management relations and working conditions which, from the perspective of the nurse's legitimate needs and rights, may constitute grave violations of justice. In the efforts made to resolve such injustice, there is a serious responsibility to use only those methods which are, in themselves, in accord with ethical principles.

The responsibility to care makes fundamental claims on a person who chooses to enter the profession of nursing. This responsibility is exercised in responding to the needs of others, and the duty to provide needed services remains in the face of conflicting demands which may effect the welfare of the nurse in question. Thus, when a nurse is working under conditions which violate justice, the withdrawal of needed services to patients as a means of resolving such injustices, is unethical. This is not to downplay the gravity or the unethical character of the injustice itself, nor is it to imply that nurses ought to do nothing.

The assurance of working conditions where nurses can fulfill their caring obligations, and through which they can receive just recompense, is a professional obligation which ought not be delegated, and the resolution of conflicts arising out of such working conditions calls for the wisdom and dedication of the whole profession. From an ethical point of view, neither the profession as a whole, nor the individual nurse, may resort to strategies that would compromise the health of clients.

In meeting the collaborative responsibilities inherent in the caring, healing community, the individual nurse does not relinquish the right nor the responsibility to adhere to personal moral principles. The nurse as a moral person has the ethical responsibility to refuse to participate in programs, treatments, or procedures, and to withdraw from situations which are contrary to his or her informed moral conscience.

The design and on-going development of a caring, healing community requires, on the part of all concerned, an ethical sensitivity of the highest order. It presupposes, and is built within, a climate of mutual trust and respect. Nursing does not bear the burden of this responsibility alone, but nursing does have the obligation to contribute its insights and professional resources to bringing about the realization of such a community. In fact, a commitment to work toward the establishment of a truly caring, healing community may be the most critical and fundamental ethical challenge to the nursing profession at this particular time in its history. This ethical challenge is addressed to nursing as a whole through its professional bodies, and to nurses as individuals – educators, practitioners, administrators, and researchers.

No code of ethics can, nor ought it try, to delineate the possible ways in which such a challenge may be met. Such will be accomplished through the efforts of caring nurses – persons who are themselves compassionate, competent, conscionable, confident, and committed – and who have the resourcefulness and creativity to design suitable models and select appropriate measures for implementation.

IV. CARING AND THE INDIVIDUAL NURSE

The final test of the credibility of ethical standards in nursing lies in the behavior of the individual nurse – educator, practitioner, administrator, and researcher. Many of the responsibilities arising out of obligations of the profession as a whole, and the ethical demands of the caring community itself, are fulfilled only in the actions of the individual nurse. While the profession has the obligation to identify, promote, and monitor ethical standards, the execution of such standards is a personal responsibility, the final guarantee of which is in the conscience and commitment of the individual nurse.

V. GUIDELINES

The following guidelines include general principles, with statements of ethical responsibility which flow from these principles. They are intended to provide a guide for reflection and for the articulation of more specific ethical rules and standards applicable to concrete experiences. With the increasing complexity of ethical conflicts in nursing, and the potential for greater ethical concerns in the future, ethical discernment in nursing is an exciting challenge, requiring knowledge, skill, and great moral sensitivity. We have the capacity to meet this challenge – one which could be the greatest in the history of our profession.

A. General Principles
1. The human person, regardless of race, creed, color, social class or health status, is of incalculable worth, and commands reverence and respect.
2. Human life has a sacred and even mysterious character, and its worth is determined not merely by utilitarian concerns.
3. Caring, the central and fundamental focus of nursing, is the basis for nursing ethics. It is expressed in compassion, competence, conscience, confidence, and commitment. It qualifies all the relationships in nursing practice, education, administration, and research including those between nurse-client; nurse-nurse; nurse-other helping professionals; educator-colleague; faculty-student; researcher-subject.

B. Statements of Ethical Responsibility
1. Caring demands the provision of helping services that are appropriate to the needs of the client and significant others.
2. Caring recognizes the client's membership in a family and a community, and provides for the participation of significant others in his or her care.
3. Caring acknowledges the reality of death in the life of every person, and demands that appropriate support be provided for the dying person and family to enable them to prepare for, and to cope with death when it is inevitable.
4. Caring acknowledges that the human person has the capacity to face up to health needs and problems in his or her own unique way, and directs nursing action in a manner that will assist the client to develop, maintain or gain personal autonomy, self-respect, and self-determination.
5. Caring, as a response to a health need, requires the consent and the

participation of the person who is experiencing that need.

6. Caring dictates that the client and significant others have the knowledge and information adequate for free and informed decisions concerning care requirements, alternatives, and preferences.

7. Caring demands that the needs of the client supersede those of the nurse, and that the nurse must not compromise the integrity of the client by personal behavior that is self-serving.

8. Caring acknowledges the vulnerability of a client in certain situations, and dictates restraint in actions which might compromise the client's rights and privileges.

9. Caring, involving a relationship which is, in itself, therapeutic, demands mutual respect and trust.

10. Caring acknowledges that information obtained in the course of the nursing relationship is privileged, and that it requires the full protection of confidentiality unless such information provides evidence of serious impending harm to the client or to a third party, or is legally required by the courts.

11. Caring requires that the nurse represent the needs of the client, and that the nurse take appropriate measures when the fulfillment of these needs is jeopardized by the actions of other persons.

12. Caring acknowledges the dignity of all persons in the practice or educational setting.

13. Caring acknowledges, respects, and draws upon the competencies of others.

14. Caring establishes the conditions for the harmonization of efforts of different helping professionals in providing required services to clients.

15. Caring seeks to establish and maintain a climate of respect for the honest dialogue needed for effective collaboration.

16. Caring establishes the legitimacy of respectful challenge and/or confrontation when the service required by the client is compromised in incompetency, incapacity, or negligence, or when the competencies of the nurse are not acknowledged or appropriately utilized.

17. Caring demands the provision of working conditions which enable nurses to carry out their legitimate responsibilities.

18. Caring demands resourcefulness and restraint – accountability *for* the use of time, resources, equipment, and funds, and requires accountability *to* appropriate individuals and/or bodies.

19. Caring requires that the nurse bring to the work situation in education, practice, administration, or research, the knowledge, affective and technical skills required, and that competency in these areas be maintained and up-dated.

20. Caring commands fidelity to oneself, and guards the right and privilege of the nurse to act in keeping with an informed moral conscience.

Reprinted with the permission of the Canadian Nurses Association.

Code for Nurses

AMERICAN NURSES' ASSOCIATION

PREAMBLE

The *Code for Nurses* is based on belief about the nature of individuals, nursing, health, and society. Recipients and providers of nursing services are viewed as individuals and groups who possess basic rights and responsibilities, and whose values and circumstances command respect at all times. Nursing encompasses the promotion and restoration of health, the prevention of illness, and the alleviation of suffering. The statements of the *Code* and their interpretation provide guidance for conduct and relationships in carrying out nursing responsibilities consistent with the ethical obligations of the profession and quality in nursing care.

CODE FOR NURSES

1 The nurse provides services with respect for human dignity and the uniqueness of the client unrestricted by considerations of social or economic status, personal attributes, or the nature of health problems.

2 The nurse safeguards the client's right to privacy by judiciously protecting information of a confidential nature.

3 The nurse acts to safeguard the client and the public when health care and safety are affected by the incompetent, unethical, or illegal practice of any person.

4 The nurse assumes responsibility and accountability for individual nursing judgments and actions.

5 The nurse maintains competence in nursing.

6 The nurse exercises informed judgment and uses individual competence and qualifications as criteria in seeking consultation, accepting responsibilities, and delegating nursing activities to others.

7 The nurse participates in activities that contribute to the ongoing development of the profession's body of knowledge.

8 The nurse participates in the profession's efforts to implement and improve standards of nursing.

9 The nurse participates in the profession's efforts to establish and maintain conditions of employment conducive to high quality nursing care.

10 The nurse participates in the profession's efforts to protect the public from misinformation and misrepresentation and to maintain the integrity of nursing.

11 The nurse collaborates with members of the health professions and other citizens in promoting community and national efforts to meet the health needs of the public.

Reprinted with the permission of the American Nurses' Association.

INTERNATIONAL CODE OF NURSING ETHICS 1953

Professional nurses minister to the sick, assume responsiblity for creating a physical, social and spiritual environment which will be conducive to recovery, and stress the prevention of illness and promotion of health by teaching and example. They render health-service to the individual, the family, and the community and co-ordinate their services with members of other health professions.

Service to mankind is the primary function of nurses and the reason for the existence of the nursing profession. Need for nursing service is universal. Professional nursing service is therefore unrestricted by consideration of nationality, race, creed, colour, politics or social status.

Inherent in the code is the fundamental concept that the nurse believes in the essential freedoms of mankind and in the preservation of human life.

The profession recognises that an international code cannot cover in detail all the activities and relationships of nurses, some of which are conditioned by personal philosophies and beliefs.

1. The fundamental responsibility of the nurse is threefold: to conserve life, to alleviate suffering and to promote health.
2. The nurse must maintain at all times the highest standards of nursing care and of professional conduct.
3. The nurse must not only be well prepared to practise, but must maintain her knowledge and skill at a consistently high level.

4. The religious beliefs of a patient must be respected.
5. Nurses hold in confidence all personal information entrusted to them.
6. A nurse recognises not only the responsibilities but the limitations of her or his professional functions; recommends or gives medical treatment without medical orders only in emergencies and reports such action to a physician at the earliest possible moment.
7. The nurse is under an obligation to carry out the physician's orders intelligently and loyally and to refuse to participate in unethical procedures.
8. The nurse sustains confidence in the physician and other members of the health team; incompetence or unethical conduct of associates should be exposed but only to the proper authority.
9. A nurse is entitled to just remuneration and accepts only such compensation as the contract, actual or implied, provides.
10. Nurses do not permit their names to be used in connection with the advertisement of products or with any other forms of self-advertisement.
11. The nurse co-operates with and maintains harmonious, relationships with members of other professions and with her or his nursing colleagues.
12. The nurse in private life adheres to standards of personal ethics which reflect credit upon the profession.
13. In personal conduct nurses should not knowingly disregard the accepted patterns of behaviour of the community in which they live and work.
14. A nurse should participate and share responsibility with other citizens and other health professions in promoting efforts to meet the health needs of the public – local, state, national and international.

Adopted by the Grand Council of the International Council of Nurses, Sao Paulo, Brazil, July 10, 1953. Reprinted with the permission of the International Council of Nurses.

INTERNATIONAL COUNCIL OF NURSES
CODE FOR NURSES
Ethical Concepts Applied to Nursing 1973

The fundamental responsibility of the nurse is fourfold: to promote health, to prevent illness, to restore health and to alleviate suffering.

The need for nursing is universal. Inherent in nursing is respect for life, dignity and rights of man. It is unrestricted by considerations of nationality, race, creed, colour, age, sex, politics or social status.

Nurses render health services to the individual, the family and the community and coordinate their services with those of related groups.

Nurses and People

The nurse's primary responsibility is to those people who require nursing care.

The nurse, in providing care, promotes an environment in which the values, customs and spiritual beliefs of the individual are respected.

The nurse holds in confidence personal information and uses judgement in sharing this information.

Nurses and Practice

The nurse carries personal responsibiity for nursing practice and for maintaining competence by continual learning.

The nurse maintains the highest standards of nursing care possible within the reality of a specific situation.

The nurse uses judgement in relation to individual competence when accepting and delegating responsibilities.

The nurse when acting in a professional capacity should at all times maintain standards of personal conduct which reflect credit upon the profession.

Nurses and Society

The nurse shares with other citizens the responsibility for initiating and supporting action to meet the health and social needs of the public.

Nurses and Co-Workers

The nurse sustains a cooperative relationship with co-workers in nursing and other fields.

The nurse takes appropriate action to safeguard the individual when his care is endangered by a co-worker or any other person.

Nurses and the Profession

The nurse plays the major role in determining and implementing desirable standards of nursing practice and nursing education.

The nurse is active in developing a core of professional knowledge.

The nurse, acting through the professional organization, participates in establishing and maintaining equitable social and economic working conditions in nursing.

Adopted by the ICN Council of National Representatives, Mexico City in May 1973. Reprinted with the permission of the International Council of Nurses.

FLORENCE NIGHTINGALE PLEDGE FOR NURSES

I solemnly pledge myself before God and in the presence of this assembly to pass my life in purity and to practise my profession faithfully.

I will abstain from whatever is deleterious and mischievous, and will not take or knowingly administer any harmful drug.

I will do all in my prower to elevate the standard of my profession, and will hold in confidence all personal matters committed to my keeping, and all family affairs coming to my knowledge in the practice of my calling.

With loyalty will I endeavour to aid the physician in his work, and devote myself to the welfare of those committed to my care.

> *"The Florence Nightingale Pledge was prepared by a special committee appointed by the Farrand Training School Committee of Harper Hospital, Detroit, in 1893 ... The name was selected because it represents the highest type of nurse and an ideal."*

quote from: Editorial comment: American Journal of Nursing 11 (10): 777, July, 11, USA.

ETHICS OF NURSING

As a profession committed to the improvement of health services to society, nursing is obligated to develop new knowledge as well as to utilize available knowledge and skills. Such a commitment to the development of nursing theory and to the improvement of nursing practice presupposes a commitment to research. There is, then, an obligation for nurses to undertake studies that produce broad theoretical constructs as well as studies that are directed toward more immediately tangible outcomes.

The ethics of nursing research must be consistent with the ethics of nursing practice. Nurses must not knowingly permit their services to be used for purposes inconsistent with the ethical standards of their profession.

Since nursing research necessarily involves human subjects directly or indirectly, its activities must be guided by certain ethical considerations. The following statements are intended to identify some basic ethical principles that serve as guides for the nurse researcher.

The subject
Respect for the value of human life, for the worth and dignity of human beings, and their rights to knowledge, privacy, and self-determination must underlie research practices in nursing as in other health disciplines. The legitimacy of involving human subjects in nursing research must be assessed within the context of these values. The right of the subject to informed consent, confidentiality, positive risk value, and competence of the investigator must be assured.

Free and Informed Consent
When individuals are involved as subjects of research, the researcher must obtain free and informed consent. Informed consent implies that every effort be made to have the subject understand the purpose and nature of the research and the use or uses to which the findings will be put, in such a way that he can appreciate the implications of participation or non-participation. He must also be informed that if any significant change in purpose, nature, or use of findings is contemplated, he will also be informed and have the right to consent or refuse to participate further.

Free consent means that the relationship between the researcher and the subject, and persons or institutions involved in his care will not place him under any obligation to agree or take part in the project against his own personal inclinations. It also means that his refusal to take part or his withdrawal after having once consented, should not lead to any repercussions or recriminations. Free consent implies informing the subject that he has the right to withdraw at any point during the research.

If the nature of the research is such that fully informing subjects before the study would invalidate results, then this fact must be stated to the subject, together with whatever explanations can be given. There must be provision for appropriate explanation to the subject on completion of the study.

If the subject for any reason is unable to appreciate the implications of participation, informed consent must be obtained from the legal guardian or an impartial committee acting on behalf of the subject. If the research should impinge on the privacy or other rights of any third party, such as the spouse of the subject, this person's consent must also be obtained.

Confidentiality

Subjects must be assured that confidentiality will be respected. Where anonymity is promised, it must be provided. Hidden coding to enable the researcher to identify individuals must not be resorted to. Every effort must be made to ensure that individuals and institutions cannot be identified.

Injury, Risk, and Priorities

Research subjects must be assured protection against physical, mental, or emotional injury. Should the research involve risk of injury, such risk must be weighed against the good to be achieved. Should the risk outweigh the positive value of the research, the project must not be pursued.

Where there is conflict between the rights of the subject and the needs of the researcher for freedom of inquiry, the conflict must be resolved with priority given to the concerns and rights of the subject.

The researcher

In order to maintain high ethical standards, the nurse researcher must possess knowledge and skills compatible with the demands of the investigation to be undertaken. The researcher has responsibility to acknowledge personal limitations and to correct misrepresentations made by others. The researcher is obligated to develop the design and procedures appropriate to the study.

The researcher is accountable in varying ways to those participating in the investigation. The purpose of the research must be honestly represented, and any uses to which the findings may be put, made known to persons or institutions involved. In order to justify the investigation, the researcher must ensure that the purposes and anticipated outcomes are compatible with the financial investment and the people and resources used.

In order to ensure the integrity of the investigation, the researcher must present the project for review to a group of professional peers. With certain studies, ongoing reviews by a peer group may be mandatory.

The setting
The milieu in which an investigation is to be conducted must be assessed in terms of the potential for a nurse researcher to conduct a study that is consistent with these guidelines. While the board and/or administrators of an institution or agency may require approval by its research committee of a nursing study as well as of any other proposal, any such approval body should include nursing representation. There should be ongoing provisions for coping with setting-related ethical problems during the course of the investigation.

The following questions are reflective of the principles inherent in the above guidelines.

Subject
1. How is informed consent of subjects obtained?
2. Is the subject free at any time to withdraw from participation in the research without fear of reprisal?
3. Can the privacy of individuals be assured?
4. Is there a deliberate review to determine that potential benefits outweigh the risks?

The researcher
1. What are the indications that the researchers are competent to conduct this study?
2. Are there ethical conflicts inherent in the purposes, problem and/or methodology?
3. Is participation in the research project compatible with the ethics of nursing practice?
4. Is the project so designed that the highest level of objectivity in collecting, analyzing, and reporting data is assured?
5. Is provision made for accountability
   (a) to the research subjects?
   (b) to the supportive agencies?
6. To whom will outcomes be accessible?

7. Can misuse of outcomes be avoided?
8. Where indicated, is provision made for an ongoing review of the project by a group of professional peers?
9. Is provision made for resolution of ethical conflicts that may arise in the course of the research?

Setting
1. In the light of people and resources, is the project justifiable?
2. Will the rights of the subjects, the researchers, and service personnel be protected?
3. Are appropriate persons fully informed of potential ethical implications?

Nurse researchers ought to be the principal investigators in the study of nursing problems and must be collaborators with other researchers in the study of interprofessional problems of health care. This interprofessional involvement indicates that a common code of ethics for health research should be developed to facilitate research in nursing and its related professions.

Reprinted with the permission of the Canadian Nurses Association.

THE WORLD MEDICAL ASSOCIATION DECLARATION OF HELSINKI

Introduction
It is the mission of the medical doctor to safeguard the health of the people. His or her knowledge and conscience are dedicated to the fulfillment of this mission.

The Declaration of Geneva of the World Medical Association binds the doctor with the words, "The health of my patient will be my first consideration," and the International Code of Medical Ethics declares that, "Any act or advice which could weaken physical or mental resistance of a human being may be used only in his interest."

The purpose of biomedical research involving human subjects must be to improve diagnostic, therapeutic and prophylactic procedures and the understanding of the aetiology and pathogenesis of disease.

In current medical practice most diagnostic, therapeutic or prophylactic procedures involve hazards. This applies *a fortiori* to biomedical research.

Medical progress is based on research which ultimately must rest in part on experimentation involving human subjects.

In the field of biomedical research a fundamental distinction must be recognized between medical research in which the aim is essentially diagnostic or therapeutic for a patient, and medical research, the essential object of which is purely scientific and without direct diagnostic or therapeutic value to the person subjected to the research.

Special caution must be exercised in the conduct of research which may affect the environment, and the welfare of animals used for research must be respected.

Because it is essential that the results of laboratory experiments be applied to human beings to further scientific knowledge and to help suffering humanity, The World Medical Association has prepared the following recommendations as a guide to every doctor in biomedical research involving human subjects. They should be kept under review in the future. It must be stressed that the standards as drafted are only a guide to physicians all over the world. Doctors are not relieved from criminal, civil and ethical responsibilities under the laws of their own countries.

I. BASIC PRINCIPLES

1. Biomedical research involving human subjects must conform to generally accepted scientific principles and should be based on adequately performed laboratory and animal experimentation and on a thorough knowledge of the scientific literature.

2. The design and performance of each experimental procedure involving human subjects should be clearly formulated in an experimental protocol which should be transmitted to a specially appointed independent committee for consideration, comment and guidance.

3. Biomedical research involving human subjects should be conducted only by scientifically qualified persons and under the supervision of a clinically competent medical person. The responsibility for the human subject must always rest with a medically qualified person and never rest on the subject of the research, even though the subject has given his or her consent.

4. Biomedical research involving human subjects cannot legitimately be carried out unless the importance of the objective is in proportion to the inherent risk to the subject.

5. Every biomedical research project involving human subjects should be preceded by careful assessment of predictable risks in comparison with foreseeable benefits to the subject or to others. Concern for the interests of the subject must always prevail over the interests of science and society.

6. The right of the research subject to safeguard his or her integrity must always be respected. Every precaution should be taken to respect the privacy of the subject and to minimize the impact of the study on the subject's physical and mental integrity and on the personality of the subject.

7. Doctors should abstain from engaging in research projects involving human subjects unless they are satisfied that the hazards involved are believed to be predictable. Doctors should cease any investigation if the hazards are found to outweigh the potential benefits.

8. In publication of the results of his or her research, the doctor is obliged to preserve the accuracy of the results. Reports of experimentation not in accordance with the principles laid down in this Declaration should not be accepted for publication.

9. In any research on human beings, each potential subject must be adequately informed of the aims, methods, anticipated benefits and potential hazards of the study and the discomfort it may entail. He or she should be informed that he or she is at liberty to abstain from participation in the study and that he or she is free to withdraw his or her consent to participation at any time. The doctor should then obtain the subject's freely-given informed consent, preferably in writing.

10. When obtaining informed consent for the research project the doctor should be particularly cautious if the subject is in a dependent relationship to him or her or may consent under duress. In that case the informed consent should be obtained by a doctor who is not engaged in the investigation and who is completely independent of this official relationship.

11. In case of legal incompetence, informed consent should be obtained from the legal guardian in accordance with national legislation. Where physical or mental incapacity makes it impossible to obtain informed consent, or when the subject is a minor, permission from the responsible relative replaces that of the subject in accordance with national legislation.

12. The research protocol should always contain a statement of the ethical considerations involved and should indicate that the principles enunciated in the present Declaration are complied with.

II. MEDICAL RESEARCH COMBINED WITH PROFESSIONAL CARE (CLINICAL RESEARCH)

1. In the treatment of the sick person, the doctor must be free to use a new diagnostic and therapeutic measure, if in his or her judgment it offers hope of saving life, reestablishing health or alleviating suffering.

2. The potential benefits, hazards and discomfort of a new method

should be weighed against the advantages of the best current diagnostic and therapeutic methods.

3. In any medical study, every patient—including those of a control group, if any—should be assured of the best proven diagnostic and therapeutic method.

4. The refusal of the patient to participate in a study must never interfere with the doctor-patient relationship.

5. If the doctor considers it essential not to obtain informed consent, the specific reasons for this proposal should be stated in the experimental protocol for transmission to the independent committee (1, 2).

6. The doctor can combine medical research with professional care, the objective being the acquisition of new medical knowledge, only to the extent that medical research is justified by its potential diagnostic or therapeutic value for the patient.

III. NON-THERAPEUTIC BIOMEDICAL RESEARCH INVOLVING HUMAN SUBJECTS (NON-CLINICAL BIOMEDICAL RESEARCH)

1. In the purely scientific application of medical research carried out on a human being, it is the duty of the doctor to remain the protector of the life and health of that person on whom biomedical research is being carried out.

2. The subjects should be volunteers—either healthy persons or patients for whom the experimental design is not related to the patient's illness.

3. The investigator or the investigating team should discontinue the research if in his/her or their judgment it may, if continued, be harmful to the individual.

4. In research on man, the interest of science and society should never take precedence over considerations related to the wellbeing of the subject.

[Adopted by the 18th World Medical Assembly, Helsinki, Finland, 1964, and as revised by the 29th World Medical Assembly, Tokyo, Japan, 1975. Reprinted by permission.]

THE NUREMBERG CODE

The great weight of the evidence before us is to the effect that certain types of medical experiments on human beings, when kept within reasonably well-defined bounds, conform to the ethics of the medical profession generally. The protagonists of the practice of human experimentation justify their views on the basis that such experiments yield results for the good of society that are unprocurable by other methods or means of study. All agree, however, that certain basic principles must be observed in order to satisfy moral, ethical and legal concepts:

1. The voluntary consent of the human subject is absolutely essential.

This means that the person involved should have legal capacity to give consent; should be so situated as to be able to exercise free power of choice, without the intervention of any element of force, fraud, deceit, duress, over-reaching, or other ulterior form of constraint or coercion; and should have sufficient knowledge and comprehension of the elements of the subject matter involved as to enable him to make an understanding and enlightened decision. This latter element requires that before the acceptance of an affirmative decision by the experimental subject there should be made known to him the nature, duration, and purpose of the experiment; the method and means by which it is to be conducted; all inconveniences and hazards reasonably to be expected; and the effects upon his health or person which may possibly come from his participation in the experiment.

The duty and responsibility for ascertaining the quality of the consent rests upon each individual who initiates, directs or engages in the experiment. It is a personal duty and responsibility which may not be delegated to another with impunity.

2. The experiment should be such as to yield fruitful results for the good of society, unprocurable by other methods or means of study, and not random and unnecessary in nature.

3. The experiment should be so designed and based on the results of animal experimentation and a knowledge of the natural history of the disease or other problem under study that the anticipated results will justify the performance of the experiment.

4. The experiment should be so conducted as to avoid all unnecessary physical and mental suffering and injury.

5. No experiment should be conducted where there is an *a priori* reason to believe that death or disabling injury will occur; except, perhaps, in those experiments where the experimental physicians also serve as subjects.

6. The degree of risk to be taken should never exceed that determined

by the humanitarian importance of the problem to be solved by the experiment.

7. Proper preparations should be made and adequate facilities provided to protect the experimental subject against even remote possibilities of injury, disability, or death.

8. The experiment should be conducted only by scientifically qualified persons. The highest degree of skill and care should be required through all stages of the experiment of those who conduct or engage in the experiment.

9. During the course of the experiment the human subject should be at liberty to bring the experiment to an end if he has reached the physical or mental state where continuation of the experiment seems to him to be impossible.

10. During the course of the experiment the scientist in charge must be prepared to terminate the experiment at any stage, if he has probable cause to believe, in the exercise of the good faith, superior skill and careful judgment required of him that a continuation of the experiment is likely to result in injury, disability, or death to the experimental subject.

[Reprinted from *Trials of War Criminals before the Nuremburg Military Tribunals under Control Council Law No. 10*. vol. 2 (Washington, D.C.: U.S. Government Printing Office, 1949), pp. 181-82.]

APPENDIX C # Position Statements and Policies of Professional Nursing Associations

CANADIAN NURSES ASSOCIATION
Statement on Consumer Rights in Health Care

All individuals, sick or well, have the right to be informed, the right to privacy, the right to be respected as individuals and the right to participate in decisions affecting their health.

The Canadian Nurses Association believes health professionals must commit themselves to respect and protect the health care rights of consumers. Nurses must speak out, both as individuals and as a group, to identify and correct violations of these rights.

1 April 1981

Reprinted with permission of the Canadian Nurses' Association.

REGISTERED NURSES ASSOCIATION OF BRITISH COLUMBIA

POLICY STATEMENT ON
INFORMED CONSENT

Definition

'Informed consent' requires that a patient be provided with sufficient information on which to make a reasoned decision whether or not to accept a proposed treatment.

Purpose

The Registered Nurses Association of British Columbia recognizes the publicly expressed concern directed at the need to specify the requirements of informed consent. There is also an increasing demand to outline the responsibilities of those health care professionals who should provide the necessary information to patients. Furthermore, the legal rights which determine the relationship between the health care provider and the patient have become increasingly important.

The purpose of this statement is to provide Registered Nurses with an understanding of their responsibilities regarding informed consent.

Background

The Registered Nurses Association of British Columbia has, for sometime, endorsed the concept of patient's rights.

At the RNABC's 64th Annual Meeting in 1976, Association members endorsed, and urged the Board of Directors to adopt, a comprehensive statement of Consumer Rights on Health Care. Part of that statement gave emphasis to the patient's right to be respected as the individual with the major responsibility for his own health. It also stressed the right of patients to participate in decisions affecting their health.

An integral part of such a position requires the adoption of a policy on 'Informed Consent'.

Subsequently, the Professional Affairs section of the RNABC was assigned the task of collecting information which would assist the Board of Directors to formulate such policy. In March 1979 a comprehensive report on the subject was submitted to the Board for consideration. The report included a review of available literature and a summary of information from other professional associations. A special committee of the Board, consisting of Directors and the Association's legal advisor, was then charged with drafting a position statement on the responsibility of nurses in relation to informed consent. The Board gave responsibility for adoption of such a policy to the Association's Executive Committee.

On April 10, 1980, the Executive Committee of the Registered Nurses Association of British Columbia adopted the following policy.

POLICY

★ The Registered Nurses Association of British Columbia recognizes that the most basic of a patient's legal rights is the *right to consent to treatment*, and that the exercise of that right is in the best interest of patients, health professionals and institutions.

★ Valid consent requires the patients to be of such an age and mental capacity that he is able to reach a reasoned decision on whether or not to accept the proposed treatment. To reach that decision, the patient must be given sufficient information in language he understands about the treatment, its alternatives and inherent risks.

★ It is the responsibility of nurses to explain the care and treatment they give and, except in cases of emergency, to obtain consent before giving treatment. Consent is required for all nursing activities that involve physical touching of the patient.

★ When sufficient information has been given, consent may be expressed in words or writing (consent form), or implied by the patient's actions (holding out a bare arm for an injection). When providing care, nurses can generally rely on the patient's implied consent.

★ The RNABC acknowledges the physician's direct responsibility to inform patients of impending medical or surgical treatment. However, the nurse is often responsible for obtaining a patient's signature on the consent form. At law, witnessing a patient's signature on a consent form does *not* require the nurse to determine if the patient has received sufficient information to give an informed consent. The nurse's signature as a witness only verifies the identity of the patient who signed the form. If any doubt exists about whether a nurse's role as a witness is properly understood by others, the words 'witness as to signature only' should be added after the nurse's signature.

★ The legal implications for the nurse witnessing a signature, however, are different from the moral and ethical implications. For this reason, nurses responsible for obtaining a patient's signature on a consent form have the additional responsibility to:

— assess and document the patient's understanding of the nature, purpose, inherent risks and alternatives of his/her treatment;
— inform the physician and/or the appropriate agency representative if there is reason to believe the patient has any misunderstanding regarding the nature, purpose, inherent risks, or alternatives of his/her treatment;
— inform the physician and/or the appropriate agency representative if there is reason to believe the patient signed the consent while under age, or under sedation or other medication that might affect his/her mental ability and judgement.

Reprinted with permission of the Registered Nurses Association of British Columbia.

STATEMENT ON PATIENT ADVOCACY
REGISTERED NURSES' ASSOCIATION OF ONTARIO

RNAO believes that PATIENT ADVOCACY is an integral part of the role of the registered nurse.

The nurse's prime responsibility as a patient advocate is to educate consumers with regard to their rights and alternatives in health care. The nurse speaks for and assists the client in the attainment of these rights.

The nurse recognizes that consumers hold the major responsibility for their own health and have the right to be informed of all aspects of their health care (both preventive and curative), the right to participate in decision making effecting their health, and the right to equal access to health care regardless of their socio-economic status. The nurse accepts the responsibility to promote an environment in which the values, customs and spiritual beliefs of the individual are respected, and to initiate and support action to meet the health and social needs of consumers.

The nurse is one of many health professionals who has close contact with consumers in many settings: in hospitals, homes, physicians' offices, clinics, schools, industry and through involvement in community activities. Such contact allows the nurse the opportunity to:

1) identify and define health needs with consumers,
2) interpret alternatives and advances in health care,
3) inform consumers of their rights in relation to incompetent, unethical or illegal health services,
4) interpret consumers' health needs to other professionals and policy makers.

Many health problems, personal and environmental, can be prevented through health promotion and interpretation of available services. The nurse is in a position to create greater public awareness of the many facets of health care delivery.

APPENDIX D Government Documents

II. UNIVERSAL DECLARATION OF HUMAN RIGHTS

The references to human rights in the Charter of the United Nations (see preamble, Articles, 1, 55, 56, 62, 68, and 76) have provided the basis for elaboration of the content of standards and of the machinery for implementing protection of human rights. On 10 December 1948 the General Assembly of the United Nations adopted a Universal Declaration of Human Rights (U.N. Doc. A/811). The voting was forty-eight for and none against. The following eight states abstained: Byelorussian S.S.R., Czechoslovakia, Poland, Saudi Arabia, Ukrainian S.S.R., U.S.S.R., Union of South Africa, and Yugoslavia. (The reasons for the abstentions are referred to in Ganji, *ubi infra*, p. 149.) The Declaration is not a legally binding instrument as such, and some of its provisions depart from existing and generally accepted rules. Nevertheless some of its provisions either constitute general principles of law (see the Statute of the International Court of Justice, art. 38 (I) (c)), or represent elementary considerations of humanity. More important is its status as an authoritative guide, produced by the General Assembly, to the interpretation of the Charter. In this capacity the Declaration has considerable indirect legal effect, and it is regarded by the Assembly and by some jurists as a part of the 'law of the United Nations'. On the Declaration, see Oppenheim, *International Law*, 8th ed., i, pp. 744-6; Waldock, 106 *Recueil des cours de l'académie de droit international* (1962, II), pp. 198-9; Verdoodt, *Naissance et signification de la Déclaration Universelle des Droits de l'Homme*, 1964. Generally on human rights see Lauterpacht, *International Law and Human Rights*, 1950; Ganji, *International Protection of Human Rights*, 1962; Ezejiofor, *Protection of Human Rights under the Law*, 1964; Robinson, *The Universal Declaration of Human Rights*, 1958; McDougal and Bebr, 58 *American Journal of International Law* (1964), pp. 603-41; and II *Howard Law Journal*, Spring 1965.

The Declaration has an importance of its own, and, until the status of the Covenants (below) is better known, the Declaration cannot be regarded as having merely an historical significance.

TEXT PREAMBLE

Whereas recognition of the inherent dignity and of the equal and inalienable rights of all members of the human family is the foundation of freedom, justice and peace in the world,

Whereas disregard and contempt for human rights have resulted in barbarous acts which have outraged the conscience of mankind, and the advent of a world in which human beings shall enjoy freedom of speech and belief and freedom from fear and want has been proclaimed as the highest aspiration of the common people,

Whereas it is essential, if man is not to be compelled to have recourse, as a last resort, to rebellion against tyranny and oppression, that human rights should be protected by the rule of law,

Whereas it is essential to promote the development of friendly relations between nations,

Whereas the peoples of the United Nations have in the Charter reaffirmed their faith in fundamental human rights, in the dignity and worth of the human person and in the equal rights of men and women and have determined to promote social progress and better standards of life in larger freedom,

Whereas Member States have pledged themselves to achieve, in co-operation with the United Nations, the promotion of universal respect for and observance of human rights and fundamental freedoms.

Whereas a common understanding of these rights and freedoms is of the greatest importance for the full realization of this pledge.

Now, Therefore,

THE GENERAL ASSEMBLY PROCLAIMS

This universal declaration of human rights as a common standard of achievement for all peoples and all nations, to the end that every individual and every organ of society, keeping this Declaration constantly in mind, shall strive by teaching and education to promote respect for these rights and freedoms and by progressive measures, national and international, to secure their universal and effective recognition and observance, both among the peoples of Member States themselves and among the peoples of territories under their jurisdiction.

Article 1
All human beings are born free and equal in dignity and rights. They are endowed with reason and conscience and should act towards one another in a spirit of brotherhood.

Article 2
Everyone is entitled to all the rights and freedoms set forth in this Declaration, without distinction of any kind, such as race, colour, sex, language, religion, political or other opinion, national or social origin, property, birth or other status.

Furthermore, no distinction shall be made on the basis of the political, jurisdictional or international status of the country or territory to which a person belongs, whether it be independent, trust, non-self-governing or under any other limitation of sovereignty.

Article 3
Everyone has the right to life, liberty and security of person.

Article 4
No one shall be held in slavery or servitude; slavery and the slave trade shall be prohibited in all their forms.

Article 5
No one shall be subjected to torture or to cruel, inhuman or degrading treatment or punishment.

Article 6
Everyone has the right to recognition everywhere as a person before the law.

Article 7
All are equal before the law and are entitled without any discrimination to equal protection of the law. All are entitled to equal protection against any discrimination in violation of this Declaration and against any incitement to such discrimination.

Article 8
Everyone has the right to an effective remedy by the competent national tribunals for acts violating the fundamental rights granted him by the constitution or by law.

Article 9
No one shall be subjected to arbitrary arrest, detention or exile.

Article 10
Everyone is entilted in full equality to a fair and public hearing by an independent and impartial tribunal, in the determination of his rights and obligations and of any criminal charge against him.

Article 11
1. Everyone charged with a penal offence has the right to be presumed innocent until proved guilty according to law in a public trial at which he has had all the guarantees necessary for his defence.

2. No one shall be held guilty of any penal offence on account of any act or omission which did not constitute a penal offence, under national or international law, at the time when it was committed. Nor shall a heavier penalty be imposed than the one that was applicable at the time the penal offence was committed.

Article 12
No one shall be subjected to arbitrary interference with his privacy, family, home or correspondence, nor to attacks upon his honour and reputation. Everyone has the right to the protection of the law against such interference or attacks.

Article 13

1. Everyone has the right to freedom of movement and residence within the borders of each state.

2. Everyone has the right to leave any country, including his own, and to return to his country.

Article 14

1. Everyone has the right to seek and to enjoy in other countries asylum from persecution.

2. This right may not be invoked in the case of prosecutions genuinely arising from non-political crimes or from acts contrary to the purposes and principles of the United Nations.

Article 15

1. Everyone has the right to a nationality.

2. No one shall be arbitrarily deprived of his nationality nor denied the right to change his nationality.

Article 16

1. Men and women of full age, without any limitation due to race, nationality or religion, have the right to marry and to found a family. They are entitled to equal rights as to marriage, during marriage and at its dissolution.

2. Marriage shall be entered into only with the free and full consent of the intending spouses.

3. The family is the natural and fundamental group unit of society and is entitled to protection by society and the State.

Article 17

1. Everyone has the right to own property alone as well as in association with others.

2. No one shall be arbitrarily deprived of his property.

Article 18

Everyone has the right to freedom of thought, conscience and religion; this right includes freedom to change his religion or belief, and freedom, either alone or in community with others and in public or private, to manifest his religion or belief in teaching, practice, worship and observance.

Article 19

Everyone has the right to freedom of opinion and expression; this right includes freedom to hold opinions without interference and to seek, receive and impart information and ideas through any media and regardless of frontiers.

Article 20

1. Everyone has the right to freedom of peaceful assembly and association.

2. No one may be compelled to belong to an association.

Article 21

1. Everyone has the right to take part in the government of his country, directly or through freely chosen representatives.

2. Everyone has the right of equal access to public service in his country.

3. The will of the people shall be the basis of the authority of government; this will shall be expressed in periodic and genuine elections which shall be by universal and equal suffrage and shall be held by secret vote or by equivalent free voting procedures.

Article 22

Everyone, as a member of society, has the right to social security and is entitled to realization, through national effort and international co-operation and in accordance with the organization and resources of each State, of the economic, social and cultural rights indispensable for his dignity and the free development of his personality.

Article 23

1. Everyone has the right to work, to free choice of employment, to just and favourable conditions of work and to protection against unemployment.

2. Everyone, without any discrimination, has the right to equal pay for equal work.

3. Everyone who works has the right to just and favourable remuneration ensuring for himself and his family an existence worthy of human dignity, and supplemented, if necessary, by other means of social protection.

4. Everyone has the right to form and to join trade unions for the protection of his interests.

Article 24

Everyone has the right to rest and leisure, including reasonable limitation of working hours and periodic holidays with pay.

Article 25

1. Everyone has the right to a standard of living adequate for the health and well-being of himself and of his family, including food, clothing, housing and medical care and necessary social services, and the right to security in the event of unemployment, sickness, disability, widowhood, old age or other lack of livelihood in circumstances beyond his control.

2. Motherhood and childhood are entitled to special care and assistance. All children, whether born in or out of wedlock, shall enjoy the same social protection.

Article 26

1. Everyone has the right to education. Education shall be free, at least in the elementary and fundamental stages. Elementary education shall be compulsory. Technical and professional education shall be made generally available and higher education shall be equally accessible to all on the basis of merit.

2. Education shall be directed to the full development of the human personality and to the strengthening of respect for human rights and fundamental freedoms. It shall promote understanding, tolerance and friendship among all nations, racial or religious groups, and shall further the activities of the United Nations for the maintenance of peace.

3. Parents have a prior right to choose the kind of education that shall be given to their children.

Article 27

1. Everyone has the right freely to participate in the cultural life of the community, to enjoy the arts and to share in scientific advancement and its benefits.

2. Everyone has the right to the protection of the moral and material interests resulting from any scientific, literary or artistic production of which he is the author.

Article 28

Everyone is entitled to a social and international order in which the rights and freedoms set forth in this Declaration can be fully realized.

Article 29

1. Everyone has duties to the community in which alone the free and full development of his personality is possible.

2. In the exercise of his rights and freedoms, everyone shall be subject only to such limitations as are determined by law solely for the purpose of securing due recognition and respect for the rights and freedoms of others and of meeting the just requirements of morality, public order and the general welfare in a democratic society.

3. These rights and freedoms may in no case be exercised contrary to the purposes and principles of the United Nations.

Article 30

Nothing in this Declaration may be interpreted as implying for any State, group or person any right to engage in any activity or to perform any act aimed at the destruction of any of the rights and freedoms set forth herein.

Reprinted with the permission of the United Nations, Department of Public Information.

THE BRITISH NORTH AMERICA ACT

(NOTE: In April 1982, this Act was re-named The Constitution Act, 1867, under The Constitution Act of 1982 which incorporates existing provisions of the B.N.A. Act, adds to the former B.N.A. Act a Canadian Charter of Rights and Freedoms, and provides for a means by which Canadians can amend the Constitution in Canada without having to go to the Parliament of Great Britain.)

VI. DISTRIBUTION OF LEGISLATIVE POWERS

Powers of the Parliament

91. It shall be lawful for the Queen, by and with the Advice and Consent of the Senate and House of Commons, to make Laws for the Peace, Order, and good Government of Canada, in relation to all Matters not coming within the Classes of Subjects by this Act assigned exclusively to the Legislatures of the Provinces; and for greater Certainty, but not so as to restrict the Generality of the foregoing Terms of this Section, it is hereby declared that (notwithstanding anything in this Act) the exclusive Legislative Authority of the Parliament of Canada extends to all Matters coming within the Classes of Subjects next herein-after enumerated; that is to say,—

1. The amendment from time to time of the Constitution of Canada, except as regards matters coming within the classes of subjects by this Act assigned exclusively to the Legislatures of the provinces, or as regards rights or privileges by this or any other Constitutional Act granted or secured to the Legislature or the Government of a province, or to any class of persons with respect to schools or as regards the use of the English or the French language or as regards the requirements that there shall be a session of the Parliament of Canada at least once each year, and that no House of Commons shall continue for more than five years from the day of the return of the Writs for choosing the House: provided, however, that a House of Commons may in time of real or apprehended war, invasion or insurrection be continued by the Parliament of Canada if such continuation is not opposed by the votes of more than one-third of the members of such House. (39)

1A. The Public Debt and Property. (40)

---

(39) Added by the *British North America (No. 2) Act, 1949*, 13 Geo. VI, c. 81 (U.K.).
(40) Re-numbered by the *British North America (No. 2) Act, 1949*.

2. The Regulation of Trade and Commerce.

2A. Unemployment insurance. (41)

3. The raising of Money by any Mode or System of Taxation.

4. The borrowing of Money on the Public Credit.

5. Postal Service.

6. The Census and Statistics.

7. Militia, Military and Naval Service, and Defence.

8. The fixing of and providing for the Salaries and Allowances of Civil and other Officers of the Government of Canada.

9. Beacons, Buoys, Lighthouses, and Sable Island.

10. Navigation and Shipping.

11. Quarantine and the Establishment and Maintenance of Marine Hospitals.

12. Sea Coast and Inland Fisheries.

13. Ferries between a Province and any British or Foreign Country or between Two Provinces.

14. Currency and Coinage.

15. Banking, Incorporation of Banks, and the Issue of Paper Money.

16. Savings Banks.

17. Weights and Measures.

18. Bills of Exchange and Promissory Notes.

19. Interest.

20. Legal Tender.

21. Bankruptcy and Insolvency.

22. Patents of Invention and Discovery.

23. Copyrights.

24. Indians, and Lands reserved for the Indians.

25. Naturalization and Aliens.

26. Marriage and Divorce.

27. The Criminal Law, except the Constitution of Courts of Criminal Jurisdiction, but including the Procedure in Criminal matters.

28. The Establishment, Maintenance, and Management of Penitentiaries.

29. Such Classes of Subjects as are expressly excepted in the Enumeration of the Classes of Subjects by this Act assigned exclusively to the Legislatures of the Provinces.

And any Matter coming within any of the Classes of Subjects enumerated in this Section shall not be deemed to come within the Class of Matters of a local or private Nature comprised in the Enumeration of

---

(41) Added by the *British North America Act, 1940*, 3-4 Geo. VI, c. 36 (U.K.).

the Classes of Subjects by this Act assigned exclusively to the Legislatures
of the Provinces. (42)

---

(42) Legislative authority has been conferred on Parliament by other Acts as
follows:

1. The *British North America Act, 1871,* 34-35 Vict., c. 28 (U.K.).

Parliament of
Canada may
establish new
Provinces and
provide for the
constitution etc.,
thereof.

2. The Parliament of Canada may from time to time
establish new Provinces in any territories forming for the
time being part of the Dominion of Canada, but not included
in any Province thereof, and may, at the time of such establishment, make provision for the constitution and administration of any such Province, and for the passing of laws for
the peace, order, and good government of such Province,
and for its representation in the said Parliament.

Alteration of lim-
its of Provinces.

Parliament of
Canada may leg-
islate for any ter-
ritory not
included in a
Province.

3. The Parliament of Canada may from time to time, with
the consent of the Legislature of any Province of the said
Dominion, increase, diminish, or otherwise alter the limits of
such Province, upon such terms and conditions as may be
agreed to by the said Legislature, and may, with the like
consent, make provision respecting the effect and operation
of any such increase or diminution or alteration of territory
in relation to any Province affected thereby.

4. The Parliament of Canada may from time to time make
provision for the administration, peace, order, and good
government of any territory not for the time being included
in any Province.

Confirmation of
Acts of Parlia-
ment of Canada,
32 & 33 Vict.
(Canadian) cap.
3. 33 Vict., (Cana-
dian) cap. 3.

5. The following Acts passed by the said Parliament of
Canada, and intituled respectively — "An Act for the tempo-
rary government of Rupert's Land and the North Western
Territory when united with Canada"; and "An Act to amend
and continue the Act thirty-two and thirty-three Victoria,
chapter three, and to establish and provide for the government of "the Province of Manitoba," shall be and be deemed
to have been valid and effectual for all purposes whatsoever
from the date at which they respectively received the assent,
in the Queen's name, of the Governor General of the said
Dominion of Canada."

Limitation of
powers of Parlia-
ment of Canada
to legislate for an
established Prov-
ince.

6. Except as provided by the third section of this Act, it
shall not be competent for the Parliament of Canada to alter
the provisions of the last-mentioned Act of the said Parliament in so far as it relates to the Province of Manitoba, or of
any other Act hereafter establishing new Provinces in the
said Dominion, subject always to the right of the Legislature
of the Province of Manitoba to alter from time to time the
provisions of any law respecting the qualification of electors
and members of the Legislative Assembly, and to make laws
respecting elections in the said Province.

The *Rupert's Land Act, 1868,* 31-32 Vict., c. 105 (U.K.) (repealed by the *Statute Law Revision Act, 1898,* 56-57 Vict., c. 14 (U.K.)) had previously conferred similar authority in relation to Rupert's Land and the North-Western Territory upon admission of those areas.

Exclusive Powers of Provincial Legislatures.

92. In each Province the Legislature may exclusively make Laws in relation to Matters coming within the Classes of Subject next herein-after enumerated; that is to say, —

1. The Amendment from Time to Time, notwithstanding anything in this Act, of the Constitution of the Province, except as regards the Office of Lieutenant Governor.
2. Direct Taxation within the Province in order to the raising of a Revenue for Provincial Purposes.
3. The borrowing of Money on the sole Credit of the Province.
4. The Establishment and Tenure of Provincial Offices and the Appointment and Payment of Provincial Officers.
5. The Management and Sale of the Public Lands belonging to the Province and of the Timber and Wood thereon.
6. The Establishment, Maintenance, and Management of Public and Reformatory Prisons in and for the Province.
7. The Establishment, Maintenance, and Management of Hospitals, Asylums, Charities, and Eleemosynary Institutions in and for the Province, other than Marine Hospitals.
8. Municipal Institutions in the Province.

2. The *British North America Act, 1886,* 49-50 Vict., c. 35 (U.K.).

Provision by Parliament of Canada for representation of territories. 1. The Parliament of Canada may from time to time make provision for the representation in the Senate and House of Commons of Canada, or in either of them, of any territories which for the time being form part of the Dominion of Canada, but are not included in any province thereof.

3. The *Statute of Westminster, 1931,* 22 Geo. V. c. 4, (U.K.).

Power of Parliament of a Dominion to legislate extra-territorially. 3. It is hereby declared and enacted that the Parliament of a Dominion has full power to make laws having extra-territorial operation.

9. Shop, Saloon, Tavern, Auctioneer, and other Licences in order to the raising of a Revenue for Provincial, Local, or Municipal Purposes.

10. Local Works and Undertakings other than such as are of the following Classes: —

   (a) Lines of Steam or other Ships, Railways, Canals, Telegraphs, and other Works and Undertakings connecting the Province with any other or others of the Provinces, or extending beyond the Limits of the Province;

   (b) Lines of Steam Ships between the Province and any British or Foreign Country;

   (c) Such Works as, although wholly situate within the Province, are before or after their Execution declared by the Parliament of Canada to be for the general Advantage of Canada or for the Advantage of Two or more of the Provinces.

11. The Incorporation of Companies with Provincial Objects.

12. The Solemnization of Marriage in the Province.

13. Property and Civil Rights in the Province.

14. The Administration of Justice in the Province, including the Constitution, Maintenance, and Organization of Provincial Courts, both of Civil and of Criminal Jurisdiction, and including Procedure in Civil Matters in those Courts.

15. The Imposition of Punishment by Fine, Penalty, or Imprisonment for enforcing any Law of the Province made in relation to any Matter coming within any of the Classes of Subjects enumerated in this Section.

16. Generally all Matters of a merely local or private Nature in the Province.

Reprinted with the permission of Supply and Services, Government of Canada.

CONSTITUTION ACT, 1981

PART I   **SCHEDULE B**

CANADIAN CHARTER OF RIGHTS AND FREEDOMS

Whereas Canada is founded upon principles that recognize the supremacy of God and the rule of law:

Guarantee of Rights and Freedoms

Rights and freedoms in Canada

1. The *Canadian Charter of Rights and Freedoms* guarantees the rights and freedoms set out in it subject only to such reasonable limits prescribed by law as can be demonstrably justified in a free and democratic society.

Fundamental Freedoms

Fundamental freedoms

2. Everyone has the following fundamental freedoms:
   (*a*) freedom of conscience and religion;
   (*b*) freedom of thought, belief, opinion and expression, including freedom of the press and other media of communication;
   (*c*) freedom of peaceful assembly; and
   (*d*) freedom of association.

Democratic Rights

Democratic rights of citizens

3. Every citizen of Canada has the right to vote in an election of members of the House of Commons or of a legislative assembly and to be qualified for membership therein.

Maximum duration of legislative bodies

4. (1) No House of Commons and no legislative assembly shall continue for longer than five years from the date fixed for the return of the writs at a general election of its members.

Continuation in special circumstances

(2) In time of real or apprehended war, invasion or insurrection, a House of Commons may be continued by Parliament and a legislative assembly may be continued by the legislature beyond five years if such

continuation is not opposed by the votes of more than one-third of the members of the House of Commons or the legislative assembly, as the case may be.

Annual sitting of legislative bodies

5. There shall be a sitting of Parliament and of each legislature at least once every twelve months.

Mobility Rights

Mobility of citizens

6. (1) Every citizen of Canada has the right to enter, remain in and leave Canada.

Rights to move and gain livelihood

(2) Every citizen of Canada and every person who has the status of a permanent resident of Canada has the right
(a) to move to and take up residence in any province; and
(b) to pursue the gaining of a livelihood in any province.

Limitation

(3) The rights specified in subsection (2) are subject to
(a) any laws or practices of general application in force in a province other than those that discriminate among persons primarily on the basis of province of present or previous residence; and
(b) any laws providing for reasonable residency requirements as a qualification for the receipt of publicly provided social services.

Affirmative action programs

(4) Subsections (2) and (3) do not preclude any law, program or activity that has as its object the amelioration in a province of conditions of individuals in that province who are socially or economically disadvantaged if the rate of employment in that province is below the rate of employment in Canada.

Legal Rights

Life, liberty and security of person

7. Everyone has the right to life, liberty and security of the person and the right not to be deprived thereof except in accordance with the principles of fundamental justice.

Search or
seizure

8. Everyone has the right to be secure against unreasonable search or seizure.

Detention or
imprisonment

9. Everyone has the right not to be arbitrarily detained or imprisoned.

Arrest or
detention

10. Everyone has the right on arrest or detention
(*a*) to be informed promptly of the reasons therefor;
(*b*) to retain and instruct counsel without delay and to be informed of that right; and
(*c*) to have the validity of the detention determined by way of *habeas corpus* and to be released if the detention is not lawful.

Proceedings in
criminal and
penal matters

11. Any person charged with an offence has the right
(*a*) to be informed without unreasonable delay of the specific offence;
(*b*) to be tried within a reasonable time;
(*c*) not to be compelled to be a witness in proceedings against that person in respect of the offence;
(*d*) to be presumed innocent until proven guilty according to law in a fair and public hearing by an independent and impartial tribunal;
(*e*) not to be denied reasonable bail without just cause;
(*f*) except in the case of an offence under military law tried before a military tribunal, to the benefit of trial by jury where the maximum punishment for the offence is imprisonment for five years or a more severe punishment;
(*g*) not to be found guilty on account of any act or omission unless, at the time of the act or omission, it constituted an offence under Canadian or international law or was criminal according to the general principles of law recognized by the community of nations;
(*h*) if finally acquitted of the offence, not to be tried for it again and, if finally found guilty and punished for the offence, not to be tried or punished for it again; and
(*i*) if found guilty of the offence and if the punishment for the offence has been varied between the time of commission and the time of sentencing, to the benefit of the lesser punishment.

Treatment or
punishment

12. Everyone has the right not to be subjected to any cruel and unusual treatment or punishment.

Self-crimination

13. A witness who testifies in any proceedings has the right not to have any incriminating evidence so given used to incriminate that witness in any other proceedings, except in a prosecution for perjury or for the giving of contradictory evidence.

Interpreter

14. A party or witness in any proceedings who does not understand or speak the language in which the proceedings are conducted or who is deaf has the right to the assistance of an interpreter.

Equality Rights

Equality before and under law and equal protection and benefit of law

15. (1) Every individual is equal before and under the law and has the right to the equal protection and equal benefit of the law without discrimination and, in particular, without discrimination based on race, national or ethnic origin, colour, religion, sex, age or mental or physical disability.

Affirmative action programs

(2) Subsection (1) does not preclude any law, program or activity that has as its object the amelioration of conditions of disadvantaged individuals or groups including those that are disadvantaged because of race, national or ethnic origin, colour, religion, sex, age or mental or physical disability.

Official Languages of Canada

Official languages of Canada

16. (1) English and French are the official languages of Canada and have equality of status and equal rights and privileges as to their use in all institutions of the Parliament and government of Canada.

Official languages of New Brunswick

(2) English and French are the official languages of New Brunswick and have equality of status and equal rights and privileges as to their use in all institutions of the legislature and government of New Brunswick.

Advancement of status and use

(3) Nothing in this Charter limits the authority of Parliament or a legislature to advance the equality of status or use of English and French.

Proceedings of Parliament

17. (1) Everyone has the right to use English or French in any debates and other proceedings of Parliament.

Proceedings of New Brunswick legislature

(2) Everyone has the right to use English or French in any debates and other proceedings of the legislature of New Brunswick.

Parliamentary statutes and records

18. (1) The statutes, records and journals of Parliament shall be printed and published in English and French and both language versions are equally authoritative.

New Brunswick statutes and records

(2) The statutes, records and journals of the legislature of New Brunswick shall be printed and published in English and French and both language versions are equally authoritative.

Proceedings in courts established by Parliament

19. (1) Either English or French may be used by any person in, or in any pleading in or process issuing from, any court established by Parliament.

Proceedings in New Brunswick courts

(2) Either English or French may be used by any person in, or in any pleading in or process issuing from, any court of New Brunswick.

Communications by public with federal institutions

20. (1) Any member of the public in Canada has the right to communicate with, and to receive available services from, any head or central office of an institution of the Parliament or government of Canada in English or French, and has the same right with respect to any other office of any such institution where
(*a*) there is a significant demand for communications with and services from that office in such language; or
(*b*) due to the nature of the office, it is reasonable that communications with and services from that office be available in both English and French.

Communications by public with New Brunswick institutions

(2) Any member of the public in New Brunswick has the right to communicate with, and to receive available services from, any office of an institution of the legislature or government of New Brunswick in English or French.

Continuation of existing constitutional provisions

21. Nothing in sections 16 to 20 abrogates or derogates from any right, privilege or obligation with respect to the English and French languages, or either of them, that exists or is continued by virtue of any other provision of the Constitution of Canada.

Rights and privileges preserved

22. Nothing in sections 16 to 20 abrogates or derogates from any legal or customary right or privilege acquired or enjoyed either before or after the coming into force of this Charter with respect to any language that is not English or French.

Minority Language Educational Rights

23. (1) Citizens of Canada

(*a*) whose first language learned and still understood is that of the English or French linguistic minority population of the province in which they reside, or

(*b*) who have received their primary school instruction in Canada in English or French and reside in a province where the language in which they received that instruction is the language of the English or French linguistic minority population of the province,

have the right to have their children receive primary and secondary school instruction in that language in that province.

(2) Citizens of Canada of whom any child has received or is receiving primary or secondary school instruction in English or French in Canada, have the right to have all their children receive primary and secondary school instruction in the same language.

(3) The right of citizens of Canada under subsections (1) and (2) to have their children receive primary and secondary school instruction in the language of the English or French linguistic minority population of a province

(*a*) applies wherever in the province the number of children of citizens who have such a right is sufficient to warrant the provision to them out of public funds of minority language instruction; and

(*b*) includes, where the number of those children so warrants, the right to have them receive that instruction in minority language educational facilities provided out of public funds.

Enforcement

24. (1) Anyone whose rights or freedoms, as guaranteed by this Charter, have been infringed or denied may apply to a court of competent jurisdiction to obtain such remedy as the court considers appropriate and just in the circumstances.

Exclusion of
evidence
bringing
administration
of justice into
disrepute

(2) Where, in proceedings under subsection (1), a court concludes that evidence was obtained in a manner that infringed or denied any rights or freedoms guaranteed by this Charter, the evidence shall be excluded if it is established that, having regard to all

the circumstances, the admission of it in the proceedings would bring the administration of justice into disrepute.

General

Aboriginal rights and freedoms not affected by Charter

25. The guarantee in this Charter of certain rights and freedoms shall not be construed so as to abrogate or derogate from any aboriginal, treaty or other rights or freedoms that pertain to the aboriginal peoples of Canada including
(a) any rights or freedoms that have been recognized by the Royal Proclamation of October 7, 1763; and
(b) any rights or freedoms that may be acquired by the aboriginal peoples of Canada by way of land claims settlement.

Other rights and freedoms not affected by Charter

26. The guarantee in this Charter of certain rights and freedoms shall not be construed as denying the existence of any other rights or freedoms that exist in Canada.

Multicultural heritage

27. This Charter shall be interpreted in a manner consistent with the preservation and enhancement of the multicultural heritage of Canadians.

Rights guaranteed equally to both sexes

28. Notwithstanding anything in this Charter, the rights and freedoms referred to in it are guaranteed equally to male and female persons.

Rights respecting certain schools preserved

29. Nothing in this Charter abrogates or derogates from any rights or privileges guaranteed by or under the Constitution of Canada in respect of denominational, separate or dissentient schools.

Application to territories and territorial authorities

30. A reference in this Charter to a province or to the legislative assembly or legislature of a province shall be deemed to include a reference to the Yukon Territory and the Northwest Territories, or to the appropriate legislative authority thereof, as the case may be.

Legislative powers not extended

31. Nothing in this Charter extends the legislative powers of any body or authority.

Application of Charter

Application of Charter

32. (1) This Charter applies
(a) to the Parliament and government of Canada in respect of all matters within the authority of Parlia-

ment including all matters relating to the Yukon Territory and Northwest Territories; and

(*b*) to the legislature and government of each province in respect of all matters within the authority of the legislature of each province.

Exception

(2) Notwithstanding subsection (1), section 15 shall not have effect until three years after this section comes into force.

Exception where express declaration

33. (1) Parliament or the legislature of a province may expressly declare in an Act of Parliament or of the legislature, as the case may be, that the Act or a provision thereof shall operate notwithstanding a provision included in section 2 or sections 7 to 15 of this Charter.

Operation of exception

(2) An Act or a provision of an Act in respect of which a declaration made under this section is in effect shall have such operation as it would have but for the provision of this Charter referred to in the declaration.

Five year limitation

(3) A declaration made under subsection (1) shall cease to have effect five years after it comes into force or on such earlier date as may be specified in the declaration.

Re-enactment

(4) Parliament or a legislature of a province may re-enact a declaration made under subsection (1).

Five year limitation

(5) Subsection (3) applies in respect of a re-enactment made under subsection (4).

Citation

Citation

34. This Part may be cited as the *Canadian Charter of Rights and Freedoms*.

AUTHOR INDEX

Abrams, Natalie, 182
Agich, George J., 95
Alinsky, Saul, 104
Allentuck, A., 15
Allon, Richard, 145, 157
Annas, George, 15, 85, 155
Antonovsky, Aaron, 48, 68–69
Armitage, Andrew, 127
Aroskar, Mila A., 43

Badgely, Robin, 132
Bandman, Bertram, 95
Bandman, Elsie L., 95
Beauchamp, Tom, 43
Beck, Cornelia, 155
Benjamin, Martin, 43
Bloch, Doris, 95
Bok, Sissela, 69
Brody, David S., 112
Brown, Carol A., 182
Brown, Esther Lucille, 73

Caldwell, Janice M., 156
Callahan, Daniel, 127
Carper, Barbara A., 182
Childress, James F., 43
Christensen, Dale B., 112
Corcoran, Sheila, 96
Crawshaw, Patrick, 69
Crichton, Anne, 127
Cousins, Norman, 99, 113
Coyne, Brian, 155
Curtin, Leah, 43, 173, 182
Curtis, Joy, 43

Davis, Anne J., 28
Davis, Fred, 183
Donahue, M. Patricia, 183
Douglas, Tommy, 118
Dunt, David, 113
Dworkin, Gerald, 145, 156

Elkins, Valmai Howe, 136, 156

Feinberg, Joel, 157
Fenner, Kathleen, 44
Flaherty, M. Josephine, 43
Fletcher, Joseph, 22
Fried, Charles, 127, 140
Freidson, Eliot, 183
Fuchs, Victor, 52

Gall, Gerald, 17, 33, 44

Godbout, Jacques, 113
Good, Shirley R., 44
Gorovitz, Samuel, 44
Gortner, Susan, 95

Hanlan, Archie, 3
Hayter, Jean, 96
Holst, Erik, 69
Howard, Jan, 183

Illich, Ivan, 51, 84
Ingelfinger, Franz, 24

James, Erica L., 145, 157
Jametin, Andrew L., 44
Jenner, Edward, 78
Johnson, Freddie Louise Power, 157

Kant, Immanuel, 26, 27
Kapp, Marshall B., 156
Katz, Alfred H., 69
Kerr, Janet C., 44
King, Carol, 69
Krever, Justice Horace, 60, 76, 97
Kubler-Ross, Elizabeth, 84

Lalonde, Marc, 120
Laskin, Chief Justice Bora, 63
Lear, Martha Weinman, 2, 3n, 73, 168
Levin, Lowell, 69
Levine, Carol, 184
Locker, David, 113

Mackenzie, Cameron, 17
Macklin, Ruth, 44
Mapa, Joseph, 16
Mechanic, David, 121
Meilicke, Carl A., 128
Mill, John Stuart, 23, 26, 27
Mussallem, Helen, 168, 170

Narrow, Barbara, 70
Nightingale, Florence, 19, 168, 169–170

O'Connor, John, H., 44
Orem, Dorothea, 53

Paap, W.R., 113
Patterson, E. Palmer, 158
Perrin, Eugene V., 44
Phillips, Thomas P., 95
Picard, Ellen I., 45
Pope, Clyde, 183

SUBJECT INDEX

Haven of Rest
Box 6800
Vancouver
V6B 4C9